WOMEN AND AGING:

AN ANNOTATED BIBLIOGRAPHY, 1986-1991

D1543611

Monica Mori

and

Janet McNern

Gerontology Research Centre

Simon Fraser University

August 1991

i

WOMEN AND AGING

An Annotated Bibliography, 1986 - 1991

Monica Mori and Janet McNern

Gerontology Research Centre
Simon Fraser University

Established in 1982, the objectives of the Gerontology Research Centre at Simon Fraser University are to conduct research on topics related to aging and the aged, foster and facilitate research by providing consultation and technical assistance, serve as a central source of information about aging and the aged and promote the utilization of existing knowledge.

The research focus of the Centre is on applied gerontology with concentration in: Aging and the Built Environment, Health and Aging, Population Aging and Changing Lifestyles, and Victimization and Exploitation of the Elderly.

Funds to establish the Centre was provided by the Social Sciences and Humanities Council of Canada. Current financial support comes from an endowment fund, research grants and contracts.

The Director of the Gerontology Research Centre is Dr. Gloria Gutman.

Address:

Gerontology Research Centre
Simon Fraser University
515 West Hastings Street
Vancouver, British Columbia
Canada   V6B 5K3
Phone: (604) 291-5062

Cover photo: *Search* by J. Steward Johnson Jr. Statue located in Vancouver, British Columbia.

ISBN 0-86491-112-2

Printed in Canada

Dedication

To my mother, Mary Mitsue Mori -- this is not about you, this is because of you.
And to my grandmothers, Asano Lily Nagami and Mitsuye Mary Mori.

                                                                        M.M.

To my grandmother, Marie Smith.

                                                                        J.M.

Preface

The purpose of this bibliography is to provide a resource and reference tool for those working with elderly women. It is intended for researchers, service providers, policy makers and students who are in the position to enhance the lives of elderly women.

This bibliography follows the Gerontology Research Centre's 1985 publication *Women and Aging: A Comprehensive Bibliography* by Donna Lea Hawley. This earlier bibliography includes some 950 references up to 1985, and this bibliography continues from 1985 up to July 1991.

This bibliography was compiled from the results of several on-line database searches. As a reflection of the multidisciplinary literature on elderly women, among the databases were: Ageline, CancerLit, Economic Literature Index, Family Resources, Health Periodicals, Index Medicus, Nursing and Allied Health, PsychInfo, Sociological Abstracts.

From these searches, 378 references to journal articles between 1985 through to July 1991 were selected for this bibliography. References are evenly distributed during these years with 35 (or 9.2%) references from 1985, 47 (or 12.4%) from 1986, 43 (or 11.4%) from 1987, 68 (or 18%) from 1988, 78 or (20.6%) from 1989, 83 (or 22%) from 1990, and 24 (or 6.3%) from 1991. Most of these references are American in content (291 or 77%), although many entries are Canadian (33 or 8.7%) or foreign (54 or 14.3%).

All of these references are held at the Gerontology Research Centre at Simon Fraser University where the public is welcomed to access them.

References are arranged into 15 chapters according to main topics. And each entry is presented in the style set by the American Psychological Association. In other words, each entry indicates author, year of publication, title of article, journal title, volume, issue and page numbers.

Each entry also provides an abstract. Of the 378 references, 336 (or 88.9%) abstracts were provided by the source. This is indicated by the term "Journal abstract." The remaining 42 (or 11.1%) abstracts were composed by M.M. and are indicated by the term "Author abstract."

And finally, each entry presents keywords which are found in italics following the abstract. Keywords are assigned when significant portions of the work address topics other than its main heading (i.e., topic covered in its assigned chapter). As well, keywords include countries in order to identify information on elderly women in different countries. Indices of keywords and authors appear at the end of this publication: author index, keyword index, and related-keyword index.

Two bibliographies are noteworthy. The first is *Women and Aging: A Selected, Annotated Bibliography* by Jean M. Coyle (1989, New York: Greenwood Press, ISBN: 0-313-26021-4). This annotated bibliography includes over 600 references to books, articles, films, government documents, and dissertations between 1980 to early 1988 on all areas concerning elderly and middle-aged women. A second is *Women and Aging in Canada: Multidisciplinary Annotated Bibliography 1975-1989* by Denise Belisle Gouault (1989, Ottawa: University of Ottawa, Carleton University, ISBN: 0-9694670-0-1). This annotated bibliography includes some 300 articles in English and French, and this publication appears with an inverted French translation.

We are most grateful to the Simon Fraser University libraries, with special thanks to the inter-library loans department. Also, we would like to express our appreciation to Gloria Gutman, Gerontology Research Centre, Simon Fraser University, for her comments on the introduction.

Monica Mori
Janet McNern

Introduction

Aging is a woman's concern. The elderly population has been increasingly dominated by women. Statistics Canada data shows that the proportion of women aged 65 and over has increased steadily from 46% in 1851 to 58% in 1990. As well, closer examination of the data reveals that the proportion of women increases with age. For example, in 1990, women accounted for 57% of the 70 to 74 age group with an increase to 75% in the 90 and over age group. Statistics Canada predicts that these patterns will continue well into the next century.

Unfortunately, while women live longer, they do not always enjoy their later years. The literature reports at least four main, although not mutually exclusive, areas of concern: attitudes toward elderly women, health care, economic status and living arrangements.

A popular area of research is attitudes toward elderly women, with particular attention given to social roles. In earlier societies, the elderly were valued for their wisdom; elderly persons' life experiences were important to the survival and prosperity of the younger generation. However, modern society places less value on one's life experiences; wisdom is considered to be knowledge that is growing out of date. Instead, modern society assigns status based on economic wealth. This shift, from status based on accumulated knowledge to status based on accumulated wealth, has lead to a downward slide in the position of the elderly (de Beauvoir, 1970). The elderly may lose status either by distributing or withholding wealth. Although distribution of wealth leads to an obvious decline in status, withholding wealth does not necessarily preserve status. Wealth wanted by offspring can lead to elder abuse (de Beauvoir, 1970).

Status is especially difficult to attain for elderly women. Elderly women are among the poorest in North America. Hence, they do not gain status through economic wealth. Alternatively, women have gained status through their nurturing role (i.e., raising children, providing for their husbands). However, these roles fade in their later years. For example, children grow independent and leave home; mothers experience what is known in the literature as *empty nest*. Also, most women are widowed in their later years. In 1986, Statistics Canada reported that 60.8% of women between 75 and 84 years of age are widowed and 80.7% of women aged 85 and older are widowed. Hence, while they may have been valued in their younger years, their value diminishes as their relationship changes from a caregiving role into one of care receiving.

Women have also attained status through attractiveness or physical appearance, but quickly lose this status with age. Gee and Kimball (1987) explain that women's attractiveness is closely related to sexuality and reproduction. Hence, in a society that judges according to male standards of continued reproductive function, post-menopausal women are considered to age sooner and to be less attractive than men at older ages - in short, post-menopausal women become invisible.

Hence elderly women have little value in modern society. In fact, they encounter a *double jeopardy*, where they face the combined effects of discrimination against the elderly and discrimination against women. And discrimination is even more profound for elderly minority women, who face racism in addition to sexism and ageism.

It is clear that our attitudes toward elderly women need to change, although it is less obvious how to implement these changes. Given the power of media, perhaps a more favorable portrayal of elderly women would be an effective method of changing attitudes. Currently, elderly women are under-represented and unfavorably represented in television programs (Vernon, Williams, Phillips, & Wilson, 1990) and commercials (Moore & Cadeau, 1985).

A second area of research is how elderly women are cared for. Whereas most elderly men are cared for by their wives, elderly women depend on both formal and informal support networks. Typically, elderly women receive support from daughters and daughter-in-laws. However, many of these women face the insurmountable task of caring for the elderly in addition to participating in the workforce and fulfilling traditional duties, such as raising children and attending to home responsibilities. (Fittingly, these women are known as the *sandwiched generation*.) Given the demands on younger women, elderly women often receive some support from a variety of home care services.

Formal and informal care of elderly women raises global concerns; the availability of services is not only a concern for elderly women, but for women in general. Typically, women are on both sides of the caregiving equation. It is usually younger women who provide care for elderly women, either in the form of familial care or health care and social services. In both cases, caregivers are not adequately financially compensated; at best, women receive nominal income for providing care. As well, caregiver burden, or the physical and emotion cost of providing care, is well documented in the literature. Hence, caregiving has become a double-bind where the provision of adequate care compromises younger women's physical, mental and economic status, and the preservation of younger women's emotional, physical and economic well-being ignores elderly women's needs (Kaden & McDaniel, 1990). Some solutions have been proposed, including financial compensation, home health care services, training and counseling programs, and support groups for caregivers (Abel, 1989).

A third area of concern is elderly women's economic status. Elderly women's economic status largely depends on marital status. A national study of widows in the United States revealed that widowhood resulted in an 18% decrease in living standards which placed 10% of widows in poverty (Bound, Duncan, Laren, & Oleinick, 1991).

Further evidence of elderly women's economic dependency on husbands' incomes comes from Statistics Canada data. In 1988, the incidence of low income for families headed by males 65 and over was 7.3%, (for families headed by females 65 and over was 14.2%, and for unattached males aged 65 and over was 23.3%) whereas the incidence of low income among unattached females aged 65 and over was 43.9%! As pointed out by Gee and Kimball (1987), Statistics Canada employs conservative estimates of poverty when compared to the Canadian Council on Social Development and the Senate Committee. Hence, it is quite likely that their report of the incidence of low income among unattached elderly women is an underestimate.

There are several explanations for elderly women's poverty. Many elderly widows do not benefit from their husbands pensions; often, husbands' pensions are not transferable. As well, elderly women have few sources of income. For example, while the majority of elderly women collected CPP/QPP, only a fifth to a quarter of these women received private retirement incomes. According to Statistics Canada, in 1988, 59.8% of women between the ages of 65 and 69, 60.4% between 70 and 74, and 47.8% aged 75 and over, collected CPP/QPP. However, only 26.7% of women between the ages of 65 and 69, 28.1% between 70 and 74, and 21.5% over 75, collected private retirement income. Hence, in their old age, women pay a high price for economic dependency on a husband, and for a lifetime of traditionally unfair treatment in the workforce.

Elderly women and single women are the poorest in North America; this phenomena is known as the *feminization of poverty*. This identification has lead to some improvements in elderly women's economic status. For example, between 1983 and 1988, Statistics Canada reports a 17.7% drop in the incidence of low income among unattached elderly women (from 61.6% in 1983 to 43.8% in 1988). However, the fact that 43.8% of unattached elderly women remain in the low income bracket is worrisome and warrants continued attention.

A fourth area of research is elderly women's living arrangements. Although the majority of women in their late sixties and early seventies live with family members, the majority of women beyond their seventies do not live with family members and a large group lives alone. According to Statistics Canada, in 1986, 60.4% of women between the ages of 65 and 74 lived in family households whereas only 34.2% of women aged 75 and beyond lived in family households. The majority of these women lived in non-family private households (45.7%) and a large proportion (20.2%) lived in collective dwellings. It is not surprising that women aged 75 and over constitute the largest group of residents in institutions (i.e., hospitals, special care homes, religious institutions). The large proportion of women living alone is distressing. In 1986, 17% of women between the ages of 65 and 74 and 38.4% of women aged 75 and beyond lived alone.

Elderly women's living arrangements poses a variety of emotional and physical concerns. Elderly women tend to relocate either to affordable accommodations or to institutions. Relocation often entails coping with changes in one's social network and losing possessions, while becoming familiar with new surroundings. In addition to relocation stress, a large body of literature is concerned with elderly women who live alone. These women are particularly vulnerable to social isolation and unmet health care needs.

Social roles, health care, economic status and living arrangements are among some of the issues regarding elderly women. There has been some effort towards addressing these concerns as well as discussion on how to address these issues. The literature suggests that a centralized effort is necessary for improving the lives of elderly women. For example, some professionals have suggested that a selective political organization to address elderly women's issues would ensure that their concerns are not ignored (Hudson & Gonyea, 1990). Alternatively, perhaps a more concerted effort among researchers and policymakers is necessary. Although some needs have been recognized, it is clear that much more needs to be done to enhance the quality of life for elderly women.

References

Abel, E. K. (1989). Family care of the frail elderly: framing an agenda for change. Women's Studies Quarterly, 1/2, 75-86.

Bound, J., Duncan, G. J., Laren, D. S., & Oleinick, L. (1991). Poverty dynamics in widowhood. Journals of Gerontology, 46(3), S115-S124.

de Beauvoir, S. (1970). Old Age. Harmondsworth, England: Penguin.

Gee, E. M. & Kimball, M. M. (1987). Women and Aging. Toronto: Butterworths.

Hudson, R. B. & Gonyea, J. G. (1990). A perspective on women in politics: political mobilization and older women. Generations, Summer, 67-71.

Kaden, J. & McDaniel, S. A. (1990). Caregiving and care-receiving: a double bind for women in Canada's aging society. Journal of Women and Aging, 2(3), 3-26.

Leacy, F. H.. (1983). Historical Statistics of Canada (2nd Ed.). Ottawa: Canada Government Publishing Centre.

Moore, T. E. & Cadeau, L. (1985). The representation of women, the elderly and minorities in Canadian television commercials. Canadian Journal of Behavioral Sciences, 17(3), 215-225.

Statistics Canada. (1990). A Portrait of Seniors in Canada. Ottawa: Minister of Supply and Services. (Cat. No. 89-519, ISBN 0-660-54851-8)

Table of Contents

Statistics Canada. (1990). Post censal annual estimates of population by marital status, age, sex, and components of growth for Canada, provinces and territories. Ottawa: Minister of Supply and Services. (Cat. No. 91-210)

Vernon, J. A., Williams, J. A., Phillips, T., & Wilson, J. (1990). Media stereotyping: a comparison of the way elderly women and men are portrayed on prime-time television. Journal of Women and Aging, 2(4), 55-68.

Chapter 1

Attitudes toward Elderly Women

1.1   Portrayal in Literature

1. Kehl, D. G. (1988). The distaff and the staff: stereotypes and archetypes of the older woman in representative modern literature. International Journal of Aging and Human Development, 26(1), 1-12.

Belles-lettres, dealing with what it means to be human, serve to expose stereotypes, strip them away, and reveal the truth behind the misconceptions, often in terms of archetypes. An all-too-common subject of stereotyping is the aging of women. Much modern fiction and poetry cogently exposes such demeaning stereotypes. References to twenty-five representative poems and nine works of fiction by thirty-five modern authors (American, British, Australian, French) demonstrate that the elderly woman often survives with dignity, even nobility, in a society often insensitive to her plight, that she often ages with grace, retaining her independence, fortitude, and passion for life. (Journal abstract).

Australia, England, France, United States.

2. Macdonald, B. (1989). Outside the sisterhood: ageism in women's studies. Women's Studies Quarterly, 17(1/2), 6-11.

This article originated as a keynote address to the June, 1985 annual conference of the National Women's Studies Association. (Journal abstract).

ageism, social roles, United States.

3. Sokoloff, J. M. (1986). Character and aging in Moll Flanders. Gerontologist, 26(6), 681-685.

Daniel Defoe, writing in 1721, offers a portrait of female aging, timely for today's readers in gerontology. While maintaining a fidelity to eighteenth-century values, Defoe shows a remarkable understanding for twentieth-century concerns in regard to age-grading and the life cycle. (Journal abstract).

England.

4. Wyatt-Brown, A. M. (1986). The loathly lady and the edwardian statue: life in pensioner hotels. <u>Gerontologist</u>, <u>26</u>(2), 207-210.

Two contemporary British novelists provide insight into the difficulties faced by aging women pensioners. Keith Colquhoun and Elizabeth Taylor create vigorous heroines, both of whom refuse to succumb passively to their fates. Since the success of Colquhoun's protagonist results from her uncommon talents, her example has limited usefulness. In contrast, Mrs. Palfrey's way of meeting death embodies the kind of heroic fortitude that affirms the strength of the human personality and can be emulated by more ordinary folk. Both novels deepen our empathy and increase our admiration for the elderly. (Journal abstract).

England, living arrangements.

1.2 Portrayal on Television

---

1. Moore, T. E., & Cadeau, L. (1985). The representative of women, the elderly and minorities in Canadian television commercials. <u>Canadian Journal of Behavioural Sciences</u>, <u>17</u>(3), 215-225.

A content analysis was performed on 1733 television commercials shown on three Canadian TV networks during an 8-week period in the spring of 1983. The analysis revealed that: (1) Men accounted for over 88% of voice-overs. (2) For those commercials having an identifiable central character, 35% were female. Of these, 54% were supported by a male voice-over. (3) Fewer than 2% of all commercials included elderly people as central characters. Elderly males outnumbered elderly females by a ratio of 2:1. (4) Visible minorities were shown in fewer than 4% of all commercials. When present, they were usually males playing secondary roles. A comparison of the present findings with previous research suggests that little has changed in the representation of women in the last ten years. These data are discussed in the context of television's potential role as an influencer of behaviours and attitudes. (Journal abstract).

Canada, gender differences.

2. Vernon, J. A., Williams, J. A., Phillips, T., & Wilson, J. (1990). Media stereotyping: a comparison of the way elderly women and men are portrayed on prime-time television. <u>Journal of Women and Aging</u>, 2(4), 55-68.

This content analysis of 139 programs and 2,211 characters updates and extends previous research on the way elderly people, and especially elderly women, are presented on prime-time television. Findings indicate that females and the elderly continue to be significantly underrepresented. Comparisons of elderly men and women showed patterns of traditional stereotypes, with men more likely to be depicted positively on 7 of 9 desirable traits and women more likely to be depicted negatively on 6 of 7 undesirable traits which showed a gender difference. However, the proportional differences for specific characteristics typically were neither large nor statistically significant, suggesting that there has been some change in television's portrayal of the elderly during the 1980s. It also was noted that television appears to be more accepting and open to the portrayal of older middle-aged men than women in the same age category. (Journal abstract).

gender differences, United States.

3. Walsh, A. (1989). "Life isn't yet over": older heroines in American popular cinema of the 1930's and 1970/80's. <u>Qualitative Sociology</u>, <u>12</u>(1), 72-95.

This article analyzes the evolution of a significant undercurrent within American culture challenging the dominance of the cult of youth and masculinity, through the interpretation of selected American popular films of the 1930's and 1970's/80's featuring heroines over 60 years of age. These two eras, which witnessed the impact of elder advocacy on national legislation and social policy, generated films such as If I Had A Million (1932), Make Way for Tomorrow (1937), Harold and Maude (1971) and The Trip to Bountiful (1985). Through analyzing these films as well as related media trends, psychoanalytic approaches often stress the cultural dominance of an ahistorical patriarchy, a sociological model conceptualizes culture as a process constituted by communication and negotiation, resistance and rebellion as well as oppression and domination. (Journal abstract).

gender differences, movies, United States.

1.3 Self-Concept

1. Coleman, L. M., Antonucci, T. C., Adelmann, P. K., & Crohan, S. E. (1987). Social roles in the lives of middle-aged and older black women. <u>Journal of Marriage and the Family</u>, <u>49</u>(4), 761-771.

Participation in and the impact of social roles on the psychological and physical health of middle-aged and older black women participate in the three roles of parent, spouse, and employee simultaneously. Of these three roles, only employment had a significant relationship to well-being; among the middle-aged group, employed women had higher self-esteem and better health, and in the older group, employed women had higher self-esteem and better health. Sociodemographic characteristics also contributed to well-being in the midlife group. It appears that particular roles (i.e. employment) or clusters of roles (employment and marriage) rather than the sheer number of roles benefit well-being; a greater number of roles was related only to better health in the middle-aged group. The importance of employment role and other sociodemographic factors in understanding the well-being of middle-aged and older black women is discussed. (Journal abstract).

Blacks, self-esteem, social roles, well-being, United States.

2. De Rango, R. (1987). My elderly sisters of Italy. <u>Canadian Woman Studies</u>, 8(2), 47-49.

A geriatric social worker describes the lives of three Italian immigrant women to Canada. (Author abstract).

Canada, Italian, life review.

3. Friedan, B. (1987). The mystique of age. <u>Journal of Geriatric Psychiatry</u>, <u>20</u>(2), 115-124.

The author describes her experiences and observations of the aging process. Of particular interest is the impact of the women's movement (feminine mystique) on aging (aging mystique). (Author abstract).

social change, United States.

---

4. Furstenberg, A. L. (1989). Older people's age self-concept. <u>Social Casework</u>, <u>70</u>(5), 268-275.

Many people consider themselves middle-aged at a time when society defines them as old. The author examines how people come to view themselves as old or avoid such definitions. Social workers can apply this information to help older people maintain functional capacities and self-esteem. (Journal abstract).

age identification, self-esteem, United States.

5. Gee, E. M. (1990). Preferred timing of women's life events: a Canadian study. <u>International Journal of Aging and Human Development</u>, <u>31</u>(4), 279-294.

Since Neugarten, Moore, and Lowe, in a 1965 article, reported finding widespread consensus regarding the timing of major life events, the concept of normative social timetables has become incorporated into the life course perspective and into the general stock of gerontological knowledge. However, subsequent research has been rare. This study examines the degree of adherence to age norms and mean preferred ages for five life course events among a random sample of 1,583 women (cohorts born between 1905 and 1949) surveyed in two British Columbia cities. It is found that, using a non-forced choice format, proportionally more women provide "right ages" for family events than for non-family events. Preferred timing varies by level of education and by birth cohort; place of birth has no effect. Results are discussed in terms of their implications for the salience of age norms in the Canadian context and in terms of future research directions. (Journal abstract).

age differences, age identification, Canada.

6. Hale, N. (1990). Being old: seven women, seven lives. <u>Journal of Women and Aging</u>, 2(2), 7-17.

Part of a larger study to ascertain learning needs elderly women experienced over their lifetimes, this essay describes firsthand what it is like to grow old in America today. Selected excerpts from the life histories of seven women communicate this perspective. (Journal abstract).

life review, United States.

7. Mac Rae, H. (1990). Older women and identity maintenance in later life. <u>Canadian Journal on Aging</u>, 9(3), 248-267.

This research examines the nature and basis of self-identity in later life and the way in which it is maintained. In contrast to an identity crisis view, which emphasizes role as the link between individual and society and roles as the primary components of identity, this study assumes self to be the important connecting link and self-identity is conceptualized as complex and multi-dimensional. Based on the underlying assumption that identity emerges and is sustained through social interaction, the research focuses on older women's social network involvements. Data obtained through participant observation and 142 personal interviews with elderly women reveal that most of the women studied here do not view themselves as "elderly" or "old". Age identity is found to be more relevant to some interactions than others. Moreover, the majority have managed to retain a positive identity which is deeply embedded within their formal role involvements and social network ties. (Journal abstract).

age-identification, Canada, social interaction.

8. Rehm, J., Lillie, W., & van Eimeren, B. (1988). Reduced intergroup differentiation as a result of self-categorization in overlapping categories. A quasi-experiment. <u>European Journal of Social Psychology</u>, 18(4), 375-379.

A quasi-experiment was conducted to examine the effects of self-categorization in overlapping categories on intergroup differentiation. `Old aged women' was used as the first, `sports' as the additional category. It could be shown that intergroup differentiation was significantly reduced under crossed categorization conditions. Implications for social compensation strategies are discussed. (Journal abstract).

age differences, Germany.

9. Roscoe, B., & Peterson, K. L. (1989). Age appropriate behaviours: A comparison of three generations of females. <u>Adolescence</u>, 24(93), 167-178.

The purpose of this study was to examine differences in older adolescent and adult females' perceptions of age-appropriate behavior in adults. Subjects were three generations of maternally related females (95 older adolescents, 78 mothers, 83 grandmothers) who were administered a questionnaire designed to assess age-appropriate behaviors in three broad categories; recreation, occupation/career, and family. Major findings were that older adolescents were most tolerant of behaviors performed by individuals at varying ages while older women most closely ascribed to age constraints concerned family relationships while least agreement concerned recreational activities. Results support the view that adolescents' values on family issues are consistent with those of their parents, and suggest that adherence to age norms increases throughout the life span or are the result of generational differences in socialization. (Journal abstract).

age differences, age identification, United States.

10. **Seltzer, M. M. (1989). Random and not so random thoughts on becoming and being a statistic: professional and personal musings. International Journal of Aging and Human Development, 28(1), 1-7.**

This article contains personal and professional musings on becoming and being an old woman. Becoming and being an old woman (I had no choice) and being a "gerontologist" (I had a choice), results in experiencing at least two realities, that of subject and that of researcher (an interesting word in itself). We daily face the leap across the chasm between science and personal experiences; between swimming in the subject pool and being a life guard or researcher into the life of guarded subjects. How permeable are the boundaries between subject and objectivity? Do gerontological data inform our experiences of becoming old? Are they providing us with norms for aging? Dear Virginia, there are age and sex norms and Enforcers enforce them. And, dear Virginia, there is more to life than research. (Journal abstract).

age identification, United States.

11. **Stone, S. D. (1986). Emelia's story: a Ukrainian grandmother. Canadian Woman Studies, 7(4), 10-12.**

This article describes the life history of an elderly Canadian woman who was raised in an Ukrainian community. (Author abstract).

Canada, life review, Ukrainian.

12. **Tien-Hyatt, J. L. (1986/87). Self-perceptions of aging across cultures: myth or reality? International Journal of Aging and Human Development, 24(2), 129-148.**

This study attempted to correct the methodological shortcomings of previous studies by using semi-structured interviews to explore the differences and similarities of self-perceptions of aging and associated factors among Anglo Americans, Chinese Americans, and Chinese in Taiwan. Each of the three subgroups consisted of twenty middle- or lower class female community residents who were sixty to seventy-five years of age. The results of both quantitative and qualitative analyses reveal that all three subgroups had positive self-perceptions of aging, with Anglo Americans being most positive; Chinese Americans, the next; Chinese in Taiwan, the least. Correlates of self-perceptions of aging for each subgroup are presented . Implications for practice, policy, program development, and service delivery are also discussed. (Journal abstract).

Chinese, Taiwan, United States.

1.4 Social Change

1. Datan, N. (1989). Aging women: the silent majority. Women's Studies Quarterly, 17(1/2), 12-19.

This article addresses how elderly women have been ignored in research, graduate education (in psychology) and public policy.(Author abstract).

education, policy, research, United States.

2. Gibson, M. J. (1985/1986). Older women: an overlooked resource in development. Ageing International, 12(4), 12-15.

This article will provide an overview of the contributions made by older women to social and economic development in the Third World, as well as how the forces of modernization are affecting their roles and status in society. (Journal abstract).

economic status, employment, family relationships, Third World.

3. Oxedine, J. B. (1987). Alliance attitudes regarding human rights. Journal of Physical Education, Recreation and Dance, 58(2), 80-83.

This article reports on a survey of 438 members of the American Alliance for Health, Physical Education, Recreation and Dance. The questionnaire was designed to assess the Alliance's efforts towards human rights and equity. Of particular concern were the rights of minorities, women, disabled ad aged. Results indicate that equity and equal opportunity have not been fully achieved within the Alliance. (Author abstract).

ageism, racism, sexism, United States.

4. Roebuck, J. (1983). Grandma as revolutionary: elderly women and some modern patterns of social change. International Journal of Aging and Human Development, 17(4), 249-266.

Despite the disadvantages they face, women in western nations have coped very successfully with the problems of aging during the past century and, with limited material resources, have responded positively to great social and personal changes. Although women make up the majority of the elderly population, these achievements have received little attention. As we face the continued aging of the population and its attendant massive social changes in a setting of increasingly scarce resources, it is essential that all aspects of female aging be studied more closely. They may well provide us with the insights necessary to clarify our vision of the past and future and provide us with appropriate models for survival in a less-than-ideal world. (Journal abstract).

New Mexico.

5. Sternheimer, S. (1985). The vanishing babushka: A roleless role for older Soviet women? Current Perspectives of Aging and the Life Cycle, 1, 315-333.

The demographic changes associated with modernization in the USSR have left large numbers of Soviet women of pension age (55 years or more) facing many of the same dilemmas as older women in other societies. The "feminization" of the older Soviet population and the large numbers of single older women mean that Soviet female old age pensioners bear a disproportionate share of the burdens of old age, even as satisfactory roles have yet to be institutionalized or diffused. Work roles, as a rule, are not eagerly embraced by women beyond pension age and then only to a lesser extent than by their male counterparts. When such roles are adopted, material need rather than intrinsic gratification from the work itself is the motivating factor. Meanwhile, the traditional role of babushka (grandmother, child minder, housekeeper) holds little appeal for many contemporary Soviet female pensioners even as changing family structures and patterns of residence make such a role inaccessible for large numbers of older Soviet women. What will eventually fill the vacuum of a "roleless role" that aging currently presents to older Soviet women still remains unclear. There is no indication that older women themselves will play an active part in framing the policies that shape such roles. (Journal abstract).

employment status, family relationships, Russia.

1.5 Social Roles

---

1. Campbell, R., & Brody, E. K. (1985). Women's changing roles and help to the elderly: attitudes of women in the United States and Japan. <u>Gerontologist</u>, <u>25</u>(6), 584-592.

A three-generation study of women's attitudes toward gender-appropriate roles and filial responsibility was conducted by the Philadelphia Geriatric Center and replicated by the Tokyo Metropolitan Institute of Gerontology. U.S. gender-role attitudes were more egalitarian than those of the Japanese. In both countries, all three generations agreed that care of the elderly is a family responsibility, but attitudes toward filial responsibility were more positive among the Americans than among the Japanese. (Journal abstract).

age differences, family relationships, Japan, United States.

2. Davis, D. L. (1985). Belligerent legends: bickering and feuding among outport octogenarians. <u>Ageing and Society</u>, 5(4), 431-448.

In a southwest coast Newfoundland fishing village elderly outporters are accorded special licence to behave in ways considered inappropriate for younger generations. Capitalising on their status as folk heroes and heroines of traditional outport culture, older people challenge each other to redress old wrongs or actively create new issues for dispute. The entire family many reluctantly become involved in these imbroglios. This case study of a land feud between an elderly woman and man demonstrates how aggression is mediated by the structural confines of local sex roles and outport egalitarianism, which severely limit the potential of octogenarians' altercations of disrupt village life. (Journal abstract).

age differences, Canada, social interaction.

3. DeLorey, C. (1989). Women at midlife: women's perceptions, physicians' perceptions. <u>Journal of Women and Aging</u>, 1(4), 57-69.

Research and assessment of the well-being of women at midlife, for the most part, focuses on assumptions based on stereotypes and myths that hinder our ability to realistically appraise women's experiences. Women's reproductive role, manifested in the centrality of menopause, predominates in the health literature. This paper looks at how physicians and midlife women view the experiences of midlife women. Attribution theory is used to offer explanations for different perceptions that may hinder appropriate health care. Suggestions to mitigate these differences in the future are offered. (Journal abstract).

physicians, United States, well-being.

4. Foner, N. (1988). Older women in nonindustrial cultures: consequences of power and privilege. <u>Women and Health</u>, <u>14</u>(3/4), 227-237.

In old age, women in many non-Western cultures gain influence, prestige, and freedom. Tensions, however, often develop with disadvantaged younger women who are subject to old women's authority and resent the privileges of their elders. After outlining the benefits of aging for women in nonindustrial cultures, this article examines the particular relations between old and young women that are subject to strain. It is argued that older women have a strong interest in maintaining young women's subordinate position. In a concluding section, the question of how social change affects the position of old women is considered. (Journal abstract).

age differences, family relationships, international.

5. Gottlieb, N. (1989). Families, work, and the lives of older women. <u>Journal of Women and Aging</u>, 1(1/2/3), 217-244.

This article addresses three areas of understanding about older women. First, the later consequences of lifetime messages are discussed; how societal expectations form women's roles and what the economic and political consequences are for women who play these roles. Second, this article discusses how the family and the workplace impact on women in their later years. And finally, this article addresses the potential of older women and the future. (Author abstract).

employment status, family relationships, United States.

6. Kite, M. E., Deaux, K., & Miele, M. (1991). Stereotypes of young and old: does age outweigh gender? Psychology and Aging, **6(1), 19-27.**

Stereotypes of age and gender are examined with 35-year-old and 65-year-old men and women as target persons. Age stereotypes were more pronounced than gender stereotypes; respondents offered more elaborate free-response descriptions of older targets than of younger targets and described same-age targets more similarly than same-sex targets. On the rating scales, older people were judged less likely to possess masculine characteristics, but ratings of feminine characteristics were largely unaffected by age. Older people were uniformly devalued on the age-stereotypic characteristics, but when negative evaluations occurred they were of the older targets. These results attest to the importance of a multidimensional conception of age and gender stereotypes. (Journal abstract).

age differences, ageism, gender differences, sexism, United States.

7. Nelson, M. C. (1988). Reliability, validity, and cross- cultural comparisons for the simplified attitudes toward women scale. Sex Roles, 18(5/6), 289-296.

This article investigates the use of the simplified version of the Attitudes Toward Women Scale with 278 American adults taken from the general population. Normative data and estimates of internal consistency reliability are reported, both for the overall sample and for selected subgroups. Females are found to have more liberal sex role attitudes than males, younger people to have more liberal attitudes than older people, and those of higher social status to have more liberal attitudes than those of lower status, supporting the contrast validity of the scale. A cross-cultural comparison is also made between the scores of
British and American women. (Journal abstract).

age differences, England, measurement tools, United States.

8. O'Bryant, S. L. (1991). Older widows and independent lifestyles. International Journal of Aging and Human Development, 32(1), 41-51.

Societies differ over the importance of individualistic/independent behavior. In the United States, such behaviors are highly valued. Thus, subtle pressures exist in older widowed Americans to develop and maintain independent lifestyles. Respondents (N=300) were older widows, aged 60+, who were individually interviewed in their own homes. Various measures of self-sufficiency were derived from a list of fifteen life-maintenance tasks. The ability of widows to accomplish traditionally females tasks is significantly related to health, education, age and work history, whereas their ability to accomplish traditionally male tasks is significantly related to income, living alone and work history. Results did not support the hypotheses in that neither high levels of overall self-sufficiency or male-task sufficiency are related to widows' psychological well-being or life satisfaction. (Journal abstract).

life satisfaction, psychological well-being, United States, widows.

9. Sanchez-Ayendez, M. (1988). Puerto Rican elderly women: the cultural dimension of social support networks. <u>Women and Health,</u> <u>14</u>(3/4), 239-252.

The ethnographic study of elderly Puerto Rican women living in Boston explored the influence of cultural meanings on patterns of social interaction and support. Women's roles and social relations were found to reflect the importance of motherhood and domestic responsibilities. With aging, women expect and value respect from their children and younger persons and regard this as even more important than affection. These cultural factors affect friendship selection, family interdependence and exchanges as well as relations with the formal health care system. (Journal abstract).

intergenerational relationships, peer relationships, Puerto Ricans, social interaction, social support networks, United States.

10. Sennott-Miller, L. (1989). The central role of midlife and older women in Latin America and the Caribbean. <u>Ageing International,</u> <u>16</u>(1), 25-32.

This article addresses the role of women who are 40 years and older in urban and rural areas of Latin America and the Caribbean. Topics include: population distribution, marital status, employment, work, family structure and function. (Author abstract).

Caribbean, employment, family relationships, Latin America, marital status.

11. Siegal, D. L. (1990). Women's reproductive changes: a marker, not a turning point. <u>Generations,</u> <u>summer,</u> 31-32.

This article discusses the physical, psychological and social meanings of menopause. (Author abstract).

menopause, United States.

12. Siegel, R. J. (1990). We are not your mothers: report on two groups for women over sixty. Journal of Women and Aging, 2(2), 81-89.

A therapist reflects on the isolating effect of ageist stereotyping on women over sixty. She identifies our need to be seen and be heard. She reports on a support group and a therapy group for women over sixty, focusing on group formation, dynamics, communication patterns, and content of discussion. (Journal abstract).

ageism, support groups, United States.

13. Van Buren, J. B., Daines, J. R., & Burtner, J. B. (1990). Gender equity: an issue throughout the life span. Journal of Home Economics, 82(1), 3-9.

This article addresses gender differences throughout the life span. Topics include academic expectations in the early years, work expectations in adolescence, occupational segregation in the working years, and poverty, health care and institutionalization in the retirement years. (Author abstract).

economic status, education, employment, gender differences, health care, lifespan, United States.

14. Yee, B. W. K. (1990). Gender and family issues in minority groups. Generations, Summer, 39-42.

The following remarks will highlight some of the critical gender and family issues that impinge upon adaptation of elderly minority in today's society, and will focus on the sources of strength in minority families. (Journal abstract).

Asians, Blacks, ethnicity, family relationships, gender differences, Hispanics, Native Indians, United States.

Chapter 2

Crime and Victimization

2.0   Crime and Victimization

1. Bristowe, E., & Collins, J. B. (1989). Family mediated abuse of noninstitutionalized frail elderly men and women living in British Columbia. <u>Journal of Elder Abuse and Neglect</u>, 1(1), 45-64.

Characteristics of 66 frail elderly men and women and their family caregivers living in British Columbia are examined in this descriptive study to determine factors which differentiate between appropriate and abusive care situations. Data sources are Homemakers, an in-home support service, and media-initiated community reports. Contrary to earlier Canadian research, caregiver rather than victim characteristics are important. The typical victim is an old woman who exhibits fewer mental and physical health problems than a recipient of appropriate care. It is alcohol use by a male caregiver that is significantly related to abuse. (Journal abstract).

Canada, elder abuse, gender differences.

2. Duenas, M. T. (1986). Impact of long term sexual abuse. <u>Clinical Gerontologist</u>, 4(4), 47-50.

This article describes a case study of an elderly women who has endured long term sexual abuse. Feelings of isolation, depression, low self-esteem, guilt, anger and aloneness are described. (Author abstract).

sexual abuse, United States.

3. Kaneko, Y., & Yamada, Y. (1990). Wives and mothers-in-law: potential for family conflict in post-war Japan. <u>Journal of Elder Abuse and Neglect</u>, 1(1/2), 87-99.

Elder abuse exists in Japan. Not only is social recognition of the problem inadequate, but there are few systematic efforts to deal with it. This paper describes a small-scale survey that explored the conflictual relationship between wives and mother-in-laws. Since the end of World War II, the positions of the wife and that of the mother-in-law have been reversed, resulting in a weaker position for the latter. This change from the traditional relationship may be a source of elder abuse. (Journal abstract).

elder abuse, Japan.

4. Steffenmeier, D. J. (1987). The invention of the "new" senior citizen criminal: an analysis of crime trends of elderly males and elderly females, 1964-1984. <u>Research on Aging</u>, 9(2), 281-311.

Using arrest statistics of the Uniform Crime Reports for the years of 1964 and 1984, this report examines the claim of some commentators of rising levels of and more serious criminality on the part of elderly persons. The first year when arrest figures are broken out by age 65 and over is 1964. There have been sharp rises in elderly arrest rates for three offenses: larceny-theft, driving under influence, and other but traffic. But the rates have fallen sharply for four offenses: public drunkenness, disorderly conduct, gambling, and vagrancy. Both today and 20 years ago, elderly arrests are overwhelmingly for alcohol-related crimes (but the type of "alcohol" crime has changed somewhat). There has been, however, somewhat of a crime-profile shift toward comparatively more arrests for larceny-theft (shoplifting), especially on the part of the elderly female offender. The most important finding is that the proportionate criminal involvement of the elderly is about the same now as two decades ago, in spite of dramatic fluctuations in arrest rates for some offenses. Actually, when considering only the directionality of change, the trend is a small decline in the relative criminality of the elderly across the majority of UCR offenses, including the "serious" crimes. This trend pattern was held for both elderly males and elderly females. (Journal abstract).

criminals, gender differences, longitudinal study, national study, United States.

Chapter 3

Demographic Characteristics

> ## 3.0   Demographic Characteristics

1. Anzola-Perez, E. (1990). Finances and health key concerns of Latin American and Caribbean elderly. <u>Ageing International</u>, 17(2), 42-44.

This article presents preliminary results of the ongoing Pan American Health Organization survey of the needs and status of elderly men and women in Latin America and the Caribbean. Topics that are addressed include health, income and living arrangements. (Author abstract).

Caribbean, economic status, health status, Latin America, living arrangements.

2. Coopmans, M., Harrop, A., & Hermans-Huiskes, M. (1990). How do older women fare in the European community? <u>Ageing International</u>, 17(2), 38-42.

This article describes older women in twelve European states: Belgium, Denmark, France, Germany, Greece, Ireland, Italy, Luxemburg, Netherlands, Portugal, Spain, and United Kingdom. The European community is described in terms of demographics, education, employment, and income security, health and health care, and housing. (Author abstract).

economic status, education, employment, health care, health status, housing, international.

3. Gee, E. M. (1986). The life course of Canadian women: an historical and demographic analysis. <u>Social Indicators Research</u>, 18, 263-283.

The life course of Canadian women over the last 100-150 years is examined, using data extracted from census and vital statistics publications. Cohort analysis and synthetic cohort analysis are employed as means to focus upon changes in the occurrence and timing of age-related life course transitions related to the family. Three substantive themes emerge: the increased predictability, standardization, and compression in age-related family life course transitions. Major changes and continuities are outlined, as well as implications related to the atypical life course experience of the cohorts of women who produced the "baby boom," and to the emergence of temporally-related mechanisms of social control. (Journal abstract).

Canada, lifespan, longitudinal study, marital status, mortality, national study.

4. Gould, K. H. (1989). A minority-feminist perspective on women and aging. <u>Journal of Women and Aging</u>, 1(1/2/3), 195-216.

Although the population of minorities aging in the U.S. is growing faster than the white population, this group has gone relatively unrecognized by gerontologists. As well, elderly minority women are ignored by women's groups who are primarily concerned with issues relating to young and middle-aged women. This article attempts to understand the social reality facing older nonwhite women. A minority-feminist approach is presented which recognizes the impact of racism, sexism, ageism and the interactions between these forms of victimization. More specifically, this article describes elderly minority women in terms of: demographics, population, educational and economic levels, marital status, living arrangements, health status, use and delivery of services. And finally, this paper concludes with some recommendations and futuristic visions. (Author abstract).

economic status, education, ethnicity, health status, living arrangements, marital status, service utilization, United States.

5. Heisel, M. A. (1988). Older women in developing countries. <u>Women and Health</u>, <u>14</u>(3/4), 253-272.

Women's issues are markedly underrepresented in international policy and research discussions. This paper addresses these deficits by delineating the particular conditions of aging women in developing countries. While these women experience many of the age-related problems as their counterparts in developing countries, cultural and economic influences place them at greater disadvantage. (Journal abstract).

health status, informal support networks, international, longevity.

6. Hess, B. B. (1990). The demographic parameters. <u>Generations</u>, <u>Summer</u>, 12-15.

The underlying argument of this essay on gender and aging is that the position of older men and women in the various status hierarchies of our society is a reflection of the importance of gender in past and present systems of work and family and a reflection of a value system based on an essentially masculine work ethic in which peoples' moral worth is measured by their market value. Thus we find that with the exception of life expectancy, women are relatively disadvantaged along most of the demographic parameters reviewed here. Inequalities between the sexes in old age are not unique to that life stage but are continuous, with patterned inequalities throughout the life course. By placing the demographic data already familiar to most of us within the emergent gender/structure paradigm, perhaps we can find fresh insights into the interaction of social systems and the life chances of older Americans. (Journal abstract).

economic status, health care, living arrangements, United States.

7. Mercer, S. O., & Garner, J. D. (1989). An international overview of women. <u>Journal of Women and Aging</u>, 1(1/2/3), 13-45.

The purpose of this discussion is to summarize international demographics, socioeconomic statistics, and trends on older women. Older women are viewed in diverse ways around the world, but they remain vulnerable to some universal problems. This big picture of older women on our planet will reveal their marvelous diversity, special needs, myriad roles, living arrangements, education, employment and income status, and health care needs. International demographics trends are presented first in each section, followed by statistics from the United States. This disaggregation of the data shows important gender differences that must be reckoned with at all levels of policy making and planning. (Journal abstract).

economic status, education, employment, gender differences, health status, institutionalization, international, living arrangements, longevity, marital status.

8. Olson, L. K. (1988). Aging is a woman's problem: issues faced by the female elderly population. <u>Journal of Aging Studies</u>, 2(2), 97-108.

Demographic trends indicate that the number and percentage of single, older females have been increasing dramatically each year, particularly in the upper age groups. Consequently, there is a growing economically and socially deprived older population. Women, who have greater health problems, face government cost containment measures that have both undermined access to quality medical care and engendered greater home care needs. At the same time, the paucity of appropriate home health services, along with public programs that encourage institutional care, force many single, elderly women into nursing homes. While costs and profits of such institutions have increased significantly, fraud and patient abuse continue unabated. It is evident that aging is a women's problem and that its sources are the social systemic problems of deprived, or soon to be deprived, younger women. (Journal abstract).

economic status, health care, home health care, institutionalization, isolation, United States.

9. Serow, W. J., & Sly, D. F. (1988). Trends in the characteristics of the oldest-old: 1940-2020. <u>Journal of Aging Studies</u>, 2(2), 145-156.

This article analyzes observed and projected changes in the economic, social and demographic characteristics of that segment of the American population which is now growing at the fastest rate, namely those persons aged 85 and over, the so-called oldest-old. In addition to the rapid increase in numbers, this population will also be quite different in the future in terms of variables such as marital status, educational attainment, and probable level of income. Compared with both current and previous cohorts, the oldest-old of the future will have greater levels of education and, in all probability, greater access to pension income. This will be particularly the case among the female segment of the oldest-old, who will continue to comprise the majority of the population. (Journal abstract).

economic status, education, future projections, living arrangements, marital status, United States.

10. Wheeler, H. R. (1990). A multidisciplinary facts on women's aging quiz to enhance awareness. <u>Journal of Women and Aging</u>, 2(4), 91-107.

The Facts on Aging Quiz (FAQ) was introduced by Professor Erdman Palmore in 1976 in connection with his Social Aspects of Aging course. The feminist Awareness Inventory was introduced in a 1972 book and has relevance for learning and knowing about aging of females. A Facts on Women's Aging Quiz (FWAQ) is introduced. (Journal abstract).

measurement tools, United States.

Chapter 4

Drug Use, Misuse and Abuse

4.0   Drug Use, Misuse and Abuse

---

1. Bissell, L., & Skorina, J. K. (1987). One hundred alcoholic women in medicine: An interview study. <u>Journal of the American Medical Association</u>, <u>257</u>(21), 2939-2944.

To examine the patterns of diagnosis, referral, and help-seeking behaviors of alcoholic women physicians, 95 women physicians and five women medical students were interviewed. Both groups were self-described alcoholics and members of Alcoholics Anonymous and were abstinent from alcohol for at least one year. Subjects participated in one-hour interviews with a recovered alcoholic professional woman. Addictions to drugs other than alcohol were common, with only 40% reporting addiction to alcohol alone. Seventy-three reported serious suicidal ideation prior to sobriety, 26 after the drinking ended. Thirty-eight had made overt suicide attempts, 15 more than once. The presence of alcoholics in the nuclear family and marital instability were common. Treatment experiences varied from none other than Alcoholics Anonymous (21%) to long-term residential treatment of 15 weeks or more per episode (23%). Most had reached treatment through circumstances other than referral by therapists or intervention by impaired-physician committees. Their current procedures should be evaluated with the particular needs of women in mind. (Journal abstract).

crime, drug abuse, family relationships, gender differences, suicide, United States.

2. Garrity, T. F., & Lawson, E. J. (1989). Patient-physician communication as a determinant of medication misuse in older, minority women. <u>Journal of Drug Issues</u>, <u>19</u>(2), 245-259.

This paper focuses on factors in the doctor-patient relationship that affect misuse of prescription drugs and other medically recommended regimens. The review first examines the patient compliance literature as regards the general population and then narrows the focus to the situations of older, minority females. In both sections, the reviews are organized around four aspects of the clinician-patient encounter: teaching efforts, sharing of expectations, activity vs. passivity of the two participants, and emotional tone. In general, there is limited research available on either the general or the older, minority, female patient populations in this area. To the extent that there are data available, both patient groups appear similarly affected by the factors identified. In the latter population (older, minority, female patients) there appear to be several ways in which risk of misuse is heightened. (Journal abstract).

communication, ethnicity, United States.

3. Glantz, M. D., & Backenheimer, M. S. (1988). Substance abuse among elderly women. Clinical Gerontologist, 8(1), 3-26.

Many elderly are likely to be involved in inappropriate drug and/or alcohol use. The probable forms of the inappropriate use are more varied than with other age populations, the elderly themselves may not be the perpetrators, and identification and differential diagnosis will often be difficult. As sparse as the data on elderly drug use, misuse and abuse are, the data related to elderly women are even less complete. Nevertheless, research support is available for the following conclusions: (1) alcohol abuse and the abuse of illegal drugs are not now widespread problems for elderly women but are likely to increasingly become problems as younger women drinkers and illicit drug users age, (2) elderly women are at risk for self- and other-prepetrated drug misuse including drug-drug and drug-alcohol interactions, and may also be at some risk for self-perpetrated abuse involving legal psychotropics, and lastly, (3) elderly women appear to be at greater risk for physician-perpetrated drug abuse involving prescription psychoactive drugs than any other age by gender group. (Journal abstract).

drug abuse, drug interaction, drug use, drug misuse, United States.

4. Iliffe, S., Haines, A., Booroff, A., Goldenberg, E., Morgan, P., & Gallivan, S. (1991). Alcohol consumption by elderly people: a general practice study. Age and Ageing, 20, 120-123.

A random sample of 241 patients from General Practice registers in London were interviewed to assess alcohol consumption, cognitive impairment, depression and other factors. Fifty-one percent of men and 22% of women reported use of alcohol in the previous 3 months. No significant association was found between reported drinking status and age, score on a depression scale, falls in the previous 3 months, attendance at outpatient clinics or inpatient care in the previous year. In the men abstainers were significantly more likely to show cognitive impairment than were drinkers. Amongst those respondents who admitted to drinking within the previous 3 months, total stated weekly alcohol consumption was not associated with age, cognitive impairment scores on the depression scale, and there was no association with falls, or with outpatient care. Only three men (3.6%) and five women (3.2%) admitted consuming more than 21 and 14 units of alcohol per week, respectively. (Journal abstract).

alcohol consumption, England.

5. Kail, B. L. (1989). Drugs, gender and ethnicity: is the older minority woman at risk? Introduction to drug use and minority older women. Journal of Drug Issues, 19(2), 171-189.

Our knowledge of drug misuse by older women of color is very limited. This introductory article attempts to provide some background for the following chapters and an integrated overview of the issue as a whole. The reader is provided with a discussion of ethnicity and some data describing the experiences of the ethnic women of color. Then the scope of the problem of drug misuse in considered. Finally the role the professionals and non-professionals in prevention and treatment is explored, followed by policy considerations. (Journal abstract).

ethnicity, gender differences, United States.

6. Kurfees, J. F., & Dotson, R. L. (1987). Drug interactions in the elderly. Journal of Family Practice, 25(5), 477-488.

Polypharmacy and its dangers in the elderly are of increasing concern. The purpose of this study was to determine the incidence of drug with drug, drug with food, and drug with alcohol interactions in a population aged 60 years or greater. Four hundred patients were randomly selected from a university family medicine outpatient clinic population of 4,483 in this age group. A total of 292 drugs were involved for a total of 1,052 potential interactions: 310 drug-food, 316 drug-alcohol, and 426 drug-drug . Interactions were analyzed using the Drug Master computer program and rated as to their clinic significance. Chart review revealed no serious actual interaction for any patient even though potential interactions could be categorized as highly significant for 27 percent of the drug-drug, 11 percent of the drug-alcohol, and 3 percent of the drug-food. Third-two percent of the total population were taking five or more drugs concurrently. The mean number of drugs for men was 3.75 and for women 4.22 (P<.05). Age and race differences were also noted in the number of drugs taken. The most common drugs and their interactions with drug, food, and alcohol are reviewed. (Journal abstract).

age differences, drug interactions, drug use, racial differences, United States.

7. Landahl, S. (1987). Drug treatment in 70-82-year-old persons. A longitudinal study. Acta Medica Scandinavica, 221(2), 179-184.

The drug consumption has been studied in two 70-year-old cohorts within the frames of the longitudinal population study "70-year-old people in Goteborg, Sweden". The first cohort has been followed for 12 years and the second, which was born 5 years later, for 5 years. In the first cohort the proportion of men and women on drug treatment increased from 61 and 77% at age 70 to 90 and 97% at age 82. The average number of drugs among those on treatment increased from 3.1 (men) 3.4 (women) to 3.9 and 5.4 respectively. The most common drugs at age 70 were anxiolytics (20 and 29%), diuretics (15 and 29%), analgesics (12 and 20%), and digitalis (13 and 14%) and at 82 years of age analgesics (39 and 56%), anxiolytics (27 and 49%), diuretics (26 and 42%), and laxatives (19 and 28%). The second examined cohort used more drugs mainly at age 75 than the first cohort. The longitudinal follow-up of the first cohort indicated an overmortality mainly among men on drug treatments at ages 70 and 75. The patients' knowledge of the indications for the treatment was often weak and at age 82, 25% of the patients were unaware of the indications for one or more of the drugs. (Journal abstract).

drug use, gender differences, longitudinal study, Sweden.

8. Magaziner, J., Cadigan, D. A., Fedder, D. O., & Hebel, J. R. (1989). Medication use and functional decline among community-dwelling older women. Journal of Aging and Health, 1(4), 470-484.

This prospective study evaluates the relationship between the number of prescription and over-the-counter medications used in community-dwelling aged women and changes in mental, physical, and instrumental functioning. Data are derived from two in-home interviews (one year apart) of 609 women 65 years or older identified through a random sample of households in a 20-contiguous census tract area of Baltimore, Maryland. After controlling for age, education, physical health, number of chronic conditions, and baseline functional status, prescription medications use is associated with declines in ability to perform PADL and IADL tasks and increases in symptoms of depression. No associations are observed between prescription drug use and changes in cognitive functioning over one year. The use of over-the-counter drugs is associated with declines in PADL tasks only. Several explanations for results are discussed. Suggestions for future study and prescribing to the significant minority of persons taking multiple medications are given. (Journal abstract).

drug use, functional assessment, United States.

9. Mayers, R. S. (1989). Use of folk medicine by elderly Mexican-American women. Journal of Drug Issues, 19(2), 283-295.

There is a vast anthropological/sociological literature on the use of folk healers in Hispanic (Mexican-American) communities. While the use of folk healers has decreased with urbanization, acculturation, and increased education, recent studies done in Dallas, Texas, show that elderly Hispanic women are familiar with, and use a variety of informal healing methods and substances for a variety of illnesses, both physical and mental. The folk-healing system is used to supplement the formal scientific one, rather than replace it. Informants seemed to have a clear idea about the point at which one or the other should be consulted. There are a variety of herbs readily available for use and sold in boticas or botanicas. (Journal abstract).

drug use, folk medicine, Mexicans, United States.

10. Ruben, D. H. (1987). Improving communication between the elderly and pharmacies: a self-initiative training program. <u>Journal of Alcohol and Drug Education</u>, <u>32</u>(2), 7-12.

Twenty residential elderly women receiving antidepressant medication (Elavil) participated in a three-phase training program on types of questions to ask pharmacists. PreBaseline and Baseline phases established the current level at which participants knew or asked about aspects of their medication regimen. Training phases 1 and 2 introduced a simple recording from which listed specific questions and statements that participants read verbatim in role-play (analogue) situations. Telephone analogues using confederate pharmacists help to develop a basic communicative repertoire for Training phase 3, wherein participants actually called local area pharmacists. Efforts toward skill generalization involved the same procedure when calling area physicians. Training results strongly indicated that seniors who can follow and incorporate instructions reliably and accurately can broaden their access to information about medical health. (Journal abstract).

communication, drug use, training program, United States.

11. Weedle, P. B., & Poston, J.W., & Parish, P.A. (1990). Drug prescribing in residential homes for elderly people in the United Kingdom. <u>DICP, The Annals of Pharmacotherapy</u>, <u>24</u>(5), 533-536.

Data relating to the use of medicines from a prescriptive epidemiologic study of drug use in 55 residential homes for elderly people in Britain were analyzed. Of the 1888 residents included in the study, 1617 (85.6 percent) received a total of 5535 medicines. The median number of medicines received per day was three and the per-day range varied from one to thirteen medicines. Significantly more women than men received medicines and women also received more medicines each. The most frequently prescribed groups of medicines were those acting on the central nervous (34.0 percent), the cardiovascular (27.2 percent), and the gastrointestinal (8.9 percent) systems. Deficiencies were identified in doses, duration, and selection of drugs in certain therapeutic groups. (Journal abstract).

drug use, gender differences, United Kingdom.

Chapter 5

Economic Status

5.1 Income

---

1. Axinn, J. (1989). Women and aging: issues of adequacy and equity. <u>Journal of Women</u> <u>and Aging</u>, 1(1/2/3), 339-362.

This article will undertake the following two tasks: (1) it will probe the basis of the improved economic condition of the aging in general and examine the reasons why so many women have been left out and (2) it will explore the issue of "affordability". Are we really engaged in intergenerational conflict? Have the number of aged grown so rapidly that we need be concerned about our ability to support all of the dependent populations in society? Can we support older women with minimal adequacy only at risk of neglect of other groups, or is it possible to be more sanguine about our fiscal future? (Journal abstract).

age differences, gender differences, poverty, social security, United States.

2. Even, W. E., & Macpherson, D. A. (1990). The gender gap in pensions and wages. <u>Review</u> <u>of Economics and Statistics,</u> <u>72</u>(2), 259-265.

This study provides rationale for the underrepresentation of women in the pension sector, and examines the consequences of the gender wage gap. For a given set of observed characteristics, a women is 11%-19% less likely than a man to have a pension. Of the unexplained portion of the gender wage gap, 10%-38% is due to unexplained differences in pension coverage. Finally, consistent with a screening effect of pensions, women are paid more equally in the pension sector. (Journal abstract).

gender differences, pensions, United States.

3. Glasse, L. (1990). Growing old: it's different for men and women. <u>Generation</u>, <u>Summer</u>, 73-75.

This article addresses the financial difficulties facing many older women. Low income in old age is often a result of work and family issues. Hence the author proposes equity in the workforce. Recognition of women's role in the home and workplace will help to prevent economic distress in the next generation of retiring women. (Author abstract).

employment, gender differences, United States.

4. Lingg, B. A. (1990). Women beneficiaries aged 62 or older, 1960-88. <u>Social Security Bulletin</u>, <u>53</u>(7), 2-12.

This article briefly describes the effects of increased labor force participation and of changes in the Social Security program on the types of benefits received by women aged 62 or older. Benefit data have been derived from the Social Security Administration's principal administrative beneficiary data file, the Master Beneficiary Record. (Journal abstract).

employment, social security, United States.

5. Morgan, L. A. (1986). The financial experience of widowed women: evidence from the LRHS. <u>Gerontologist</u>, <u>26</u>(6), 663-668.

Older widowed women are believed to be vulnerable due to income loss at widowhood and inexperience with money. Examined were reports of 606 white widows from the Longitudinal Retirement History Survey. Results suggest that many widows had experience in managing money, some had discussed financial survival with their spouses, but less than one-third received financial counseling as widows. A majority of the widows were poor, and experience with handling money did not decrease risk of poverty. (Journal abstract).

longitudinal study, poverty, United States, widowhood.

6. Nusberg, C. (1986). Pension and long-term care policies for mid-life and older women: a perspective from the U.S. and Canada. <u>Ageing International</u>, <u>13</u>(5), 9-17.

This article reports on a meeting hosted by the Women's Initiative of the American Association of Retired Persons in Washington, DC on October 9-10, 1986. Thirty experts from government, advocacy organizations and research discussed policies concerning midlife and older women. The goals were to address Canadian and American income security and long term care, and to discuss recent reforms and proposals for change that would result in better protection for women. (Author abstract).

Canada, health care, pensions, policy, United States.

7. O'Bryant, S., & Morgan, L. A. (1989). Financial experience and well-being among mature widowed women. <u>Gerontologist</u>, <u>29</u>(2), 245-251.

Widowhood for women may be complicated by a lack of financial experience or knowledge, further diminishing well-being. Analyzed were data from 300 widowed women aged 60 and older regarding financial experience prior to widowhood, planning undertaken before death of spouse, and their effects on well-being in early widowhood. Shown by the finding was that preparation was associated with somewhat better well-being among widows, but financial experience prior to widowhood had no effect. (Journal abstract).

United States, widowhood.

8. Tibaudin, R. J. (1987). The problem of women's pensions. <u>International Social Security Review</u>, <u>40</u>(3), 290-297.

This article addresses women's pensions in Latin American countries. Topics include old age and retirement pensions (age of retirement, levels of contribution), invalidity pension (survivors' pension), women as self-employed workers, women at home, plurality of benefits. (Author abstract).

international, pensions.

9. Tracy, M. B. (1987). Credit splitting and private pension awards in divorce: a case study of British Columbia, Canada. <u>Research on Aging</u>, 9(1), 148-159.

This study examines the experience of earnings-splitting under the Canada Pension Plan and private pension assignments in British Columbia. The findings indicate that the low take-up rate of shared public pensions is primarily a result of the voluntary nature of the program. A comparably low incidence of future private pension awards to women as part of the property settlement is related to prevailing judicial attitudes, length of marriage, and the preference of women for immediate payment of cash or in-kind benefits. (Journal abstract).

Canada, divorce, pensions.

10. Tracy, M. B. (1987). Women's old-age pension replacement rates in ten industrial countries. Journal of International and Comparative Social Welfare, 2(1-2), 37-43.

One indicator of older women's economic status among industrial nations is the value of old-age pensions relative to prior income. This study examines the impact of program changes and wage levels on old-age pension replacement rates (benefit amount divided by previous year's wage) for women in ten industrial countries from 1960 to 1980. The findings suggest that greater attention needs to be given to how women pension beneficiaries are affected by policy decisions and that a replacement rate index is a viable means of measuring such change. (Journal abstract).

international, longitudinal study, physicians.

11. Tracy, M. B., & Ward, R. L. (1986). Trends in old-age pensions for women: benefit levels in ten nations, 1960-1980. Gerontologist, 26(3), 286-291.

This study analyzes how the development of women's pensions compare to the progress of men's benefits from 1960 to 1980 in industrial countries. Comparisons are based on benefit amounts of average male and female wage earners in manufacturing. The findings are that women's benefits did not keep pace with men's pensions in 5 of the nations studied. The implications are that greater attention should be given to the impact of program revisions and benefit computation methods on the relative position of women's pensions. (Journal abstract).

gender differences, international, longitudinal study, pensions.

12. Uhlenberg, P., & Salmon, M. A. P. (1986). Change in relative income of older women, 1960-1980. Gerontologist, 26(2), 164-170.

Using income data from the 1960, 1970, and 1980 U.S. Censuses of Population, the relative change in income of older women was examined from several perspectives. As expected, the income distribution of cohorts entering old age more recently is well above that of the preceding cohorts, and there is some decline in inequality among older women over the past 20 years. The position of older women relative to middle-aged women, however, has not improved, and cohorts continue to experience large drops in income as they enter old age. (Journal abstract).

age differences, longitudinal study, United States.

_____

13. Wolff, N. (1988). Women and the equity of the social security program. Journal of
Aging Studies, **2(4), 357-377.**

Over the past decade there has been a keen interest in the relative treatment of women
and men under Social Security. There is generally consensus that the program contains de
facto discrimination against certain identifiable groups, such as market working women,
two-earner married couples, and single persons. To clarify the equity issues surrounding
the Social Security program, this article begins with a brief historical review of the
program, emphasizing statutory provisions affecting the equitable treatment of men and
women, followed by a descriptive analysis of the distributional impact of the Social Security
program. Equity implications are examined under two within-household property
ownership: one is the individually owned benefit rule, where benefit ownership rights
within the family unit are exclusively assigned to the individual who incurred the old age
insurance (OAI) tax liability; the other is the community-owned benefit rule, where benefit
ownership rights are assumed to be equally owned by the husband and wife, independent of
who incurred the OAI tax liability. The analysis of 3,141 Social Security beneficiaries who
retired between 1962 and 1972 uses an annuity-welfare model of the Social Security
program. It reveals that conclusions regarding the differential treatment of women and
men depend on the within-household property rights assumptions underpinning the
distribution of earned retirement benefits within a married household. (Journal abstract).

gender differences, social security, United States.

**14. Woods, J. R. (1988). Retirement-age women and pensions: findings from the beneficiary
survey.** Social Security Bulletin, **51(12), 5-16.**

This article examines the extent of employer-sponsored pension receipt and the amounts of
pension benefits among a cohort of retirement-age women interviewed in the New
Beneficiary Survey. These women reported relatively low levels of pension protection.
Only 27 percent were receiving a pension in late 1982, either from their own employment
or as survivors. This was one-half the rate of current pension receipt among a comparable
cohort of men. An additional 17 percent of the women are expecting pensions of their own
or had potential survivor protection through their husbands' pensions. Among those
receiving a pension, women reported median monthly benefits of $250, compared with
$460 among men. Pension benefits were a fairly important source of income or these
women, particularly those who were unmarried. Almost one-half of the unmarried
recipients depended on their pensions for one-third or more of their total incomes, and
without their pension income 11 percent would have been below poverty income levels.
(Journal abstract).

gender differences, pensions, United States.

5.2   Poverty

1. Bound, J., Duncan, G. J., Laren, D. S., & Oleinick, L. (1991). Poverty dynamics in widowhood. Journals of Gerontology, 46(3), S115-S124.

Data from a national sample of widows of all ages were used to examine links between poverty and widowhood. We found that widowhood drops living standards by 18 percent, on average, and pushes 10 percent of women whose incomes were above the poverty line prior to widowhood into poverty after it. Not surprisingly, economic status prior to widowhood is the strongest predictor of status during widowhood. Striking in the data is the instability of family income during widowhood, producing substantial numbers of exits from poverty. (Journal abstract).

gender differences, United States, widowhood.

2. Coe, R. D. (1988). A longitudinal examination of poverty in the elderly years. Gerontologist, 28(4), 540-544.

Utilizing data from the Panel Study of Income Dynamics, a dichotomy was found in the experience of poverty in the elderly years. In the first three years of such poverty, exit probabilities were relatively high, comparable to those in the non-elderly years. After spending three elderly years in poverty, however, the probability of escaping poverty was extremely low. Elderly women had considerably less probability of escaping poverty than men. No racial differences were found. (Journal abstract).

gender differences, longitudinal study, racial differences, United States.

3. Davis, K., Grant, P., & Rowland, D. (1990). Alone and poor: the plight of elderly women. Generations, Summer, 43-47.

This article reviews the current and future demographic profile of elderly women, their economic status and the reasons for the gender gap among elderly poor, and the financial burdens associated with chronic illness and out-of-pocket medical expenses. The article also proposes policies aimed at improving the lives of elderly people and analyzes the potential impact on those most vulnerable. (Journal abstract).

living arrangements, policy, United States.

4. Dressel, P. L. (1988). Gender, race, and class: beyond the feminization of poverty in later life. Gerontologist, 28(2), 177-180.

As appealing as the feminization of poverty argument may be to age-based and feminist advocacy organizations, it has the potential for distorting and simplifying the issue of old age poverty and for being politically divisive. It is necessary to discuss how race, as well as gender, is interlocked with social class and to demonstrate how a singular emphasis on gender misrepresents the phenomenon of poverty in later life. (Journal abstract).

Blacks, gender differences, United States.

5. Glasse, L., & Leonard, F. (1988). Policy from the older woman's perspective. Generations, 12(3), 57-59.

The astonishing projection of poverty among older women in the twenty-first century need not be overly discouraging. Income related inequities respond most quickly to realistic, appropriate policy changes. More difficult are biological and quality-of-life problems, ethical issues surrounding death and dying, and the pressures of demographics. Policy makers wield powerful tools, which, when accurately focused, yield such encouraging results as the slowly improving income picture for most retired Americans. It is time to concentrate our attention on the differences in American elders, so that women may also benefit fully from our public policies. (Journal abstract).

policy, United States.

6. Holden, K. C. (1988). Poverty and living arrangements among older women: are changes in economic well-being underestimated? Journals of Gerontology, 43(1), S22-S27.

Poverty rates have fallen more slowly over the last three decades among older women living alone than for other groups of elderly persons. The simultaneous increase in the percentage of elderly women living alone has given rise to speculation that these two phenomena are related. Using 1950 and 1980 Census data this relationship was explored. Over the 30-year period, poverty among elderly women fell by 35.9 percentage points. It would have fallen further if women had not changed the types of households in which they lived, but by only an additional 3 percentage points. The effect of changes in household composition, however, was greatest for the oldest of the elderly individuals. (Journal abstract).

living alone, living arrangements, longitudinal study, United States.

7. **McLaughlin, D. K., & Sachs, C. (1988). Poverty in female-headed households: residential differences. Rural Sociology, 53(3), 287-306.**

Individual and structural explanations for poverty have been applied in studies of the poverty status of particular individuals. In this paper, we examine how individual characteristics and the employment opportunity structure vary for female-headed households in nonmetropolitan areas, central city areas, and metropolitan areas that are not central city areas. Using data from the 1980 Census of Population and Housing, we find that individual household characteristics do differ by residence, but that there is generally no difference by residence in the characteristics that influence poverty status. Employed nonmetro female heads of households are more likely to report poverty incomes, and the relatively low contribution of wages and in raising nonmetro households above the poverty level suggests that the opportunity structure for female-headed households varies by residence and is poorer for nonmetro residents. (Journal abstract).

age differences, national study, rural community, United States, urban community.

8. **Minkler, M., & Stone, R. (1985). The feminization of poverty and older women. Gerontologist, 25(4), 351-357.**

This paper examines the "triple jeopardy" of being old, poor, and female in the United States. The structural roots of the feminization of poverty are explored, with particular attention to the sexual division of labor, the dual labor market economy, and notions of dependency and deservingness in American society. Current and proposed budget cuts of the Reagan administration are seen as further contributing to a "greying" of the feminization of poverty, and implications for research, practice and policy are presented. (Journal abstract).

employment, gender differences, marital status, United States.

---

9. Slesinger, D. P., & Cantley, E. (1988). Determination of poverty among rural women who live alone. <u>Rural Sociology</u>, <u>53</u>(3), 307-320.

We examine the poverty levels of two distinct groups of women who live alone; those under 65 years of age and those 65 and over. On the average, 30 percent of the elderly women who live alone and 21 percent of the younger women are in poverty. Multivariate analyses of poverty rates based on data from the 1980 census indicate that lack of participation in the labor force, lower levels of education, and being under 20 or over 50 years of age explain much of the variance for younger women. For elderly women, the most important variables were whether they had only Social Security income, had less education, and were nonwhite. In both age groups, women in small towns or rural areas were more likely to be in poverty than those in central cities or suburbs when all other variables were controlled. (Journal abstract).

age differences, living arrangements, rural community, United States, urban community.

10. Stone, R. I. (1989). The feminization of poverty among the elderly. <u>Women's Studies Quarterly</u>, <u>17</u>(1/2), 20-34.

This article will demonstrate that poverty among the elderly is concentrated among women. The first section describes the current gender gap in poverty and highlights the importance of marital status and living arrangements in differentiating the economic status of men and women. This is followed by a discussion of key reasons for this gender gap including a history of female dependency reflected in current employment and retirement policies, the gender division of labor in which women assume the primary role of caregiver, and labor market discrimination which limits women's access to financial resources in their pre- and postretirement years. The final section of this article briefly discusses current and proposed policy initiatives designed to eliminate gender inequities which contribute to poverty among elderly females. (Journal abstract).

gender differences, living arrangements, marital status, policy, United States.

11. Warlick, J. L. (1985). Why is poverty after 65 a women's problem? <u>Journals of Gerontology</u>, <u>40</u>(6), 751-757.

This paper compares the composition of family income for families with aged male and female heads to determine why poverty during old age is so heavily concentrated among the families of aged women. Data from the March 1968 and 1979 Current Population Surveys were used. The inferior economic position of women is due to deficient market incomes and dependence upon deceased husbands for private and public pensions.

Policies that encourage work and insure adequate survivor benefits will raise the relative economic status of these families. (Journal abstract).

United States, widowhood.

12. Wilson-Ford, V. (1990). Poverty among black elderly women. Journal of Women and Aging, 2(4), 5-20.

Older Black women, categorically rank at the top with regards to the greatest incidence of poverty. This paper examines the construct of poverty among older Black women. An analysis of the various factors: income, Social Security, private pensions, widowhood, labor force participation and education, all of which contribute to the impoverishment of women in late life, are explored. Implications for policy as well as recommendations to reduce poverty among older Black women are provided. (Journal abstract).

Blacks, education, employment, income, pensions, social security, United States, widowhood.

Chapter 6

Education

6.0 Education	

---

1. Dellman-Jenksins, M. M. (1984-1985). Continuing education in later adulthood: Implications for program development for elderly guest students. International Journal of Aging and Human Development, 20(2), 93-102.

While more and more institutions of higher education are offering cost-free continuing education programs to older men and women, the enrollment of this target population is quite low. This study was conducted to identify factors that would positively influence the decisions of individuals over sixty years of age to participate in such programs. Sixty-five white predominantly upper middle-class, highly educated (X = 16.92 years of schooling) women aged sixty years and over (X = 68.80) were given a questionnaire concerning attitudes toward continuing education. The majority (86%) indicated a high level of interest in taking geology, political science, world and art history, music, literature, and language courses. In addition, 85 percent preferred to participate in learning situations that included younger and older individuals; 58 percent reported interest in having a companion enroll with them; 48 percent preferred no specific learning environments (i.e., lecture, discussion, or workshop); and 75 percent reported that family members did not suggest that they enroll in continuing education classes. It is suggested that the high level of interest in taking courses offered by institutions of higher education displayed by the women surveyed is because of personal experience with university level education in young adulthood. (Journal abstract).

continuing education, United States.

2. Heisel, M. (1985). Assessment of learning activity level in a group of black aged. Adult Education Quarterly, 36(1), 1-14.

A learning activity level (LAL) scale was developed to assess the learning efforts of older persons with minimal formal education. Learning was broadly defined to include all purposeful attempts to acquire knowledge and information. The scale consisted of three components: reading, educational use of television and radio, and formal and informal learning endeavors in the recent past. The alpha reliability coefficient for the scale was .81.

The sample consisted of 132 urban, black men and women, aged 60 to 94, with mean educational attainment of 6 grades. Results of a multiple regression analysis showed that sex, age, educational attainment, having participated in organized adult education, self-perceived reading ability, health and life satisfaction accounted for over forty percent of the variance associated with LAL scores, with sex and self-perceived reading ability emerging as the most significant predictors. (Journal abstract).

Blacks, continuing education, gender differences, United States.

3. Kanter, S. (1989). The value of the college degree for older women graduates. Innovative Higher Education, 13(2), 90-105.

A survey examining the economic benefits of returning to college for older women was conducted in 1986 at the College of Public and Community Services at UMass/Boston, a competency based educational institution for poor and working class adults. The results of the survey show that, while monetary returns are quite limited, the college degree has given older women access to professional and managerial positions. The vast majority of the women believe that the acquisition of the college degree greatly improved their economic opportunities. (Journal abstract).

higher education, United States.

4. Paludi, M. A., Meyers, D., Kindermann, J., Speicher, H., & Haring-Hidore, M. (1990). Mentoring and being mentored: issues of sex, power, and politics for older women. Journal of Women and Aging, 2(3), 81-92.

This paper examines the interface of sexism and ageism when older women are part of a mentoring relationship as either mentors of proteges. Specifically, issues related to transitional phases, chronological age, and causal attributions for success are reviewed. Educational policies more responsive to the needs of women mentors and proteges are suggested. (Journal abstract).

ageism, sexism, United States.

5. Speer, L. J., & Dorfman, L. T. (1986). The outcomes of reentry education: Personal and professional development in middle-aged and older women graduates. Educational Gerontology, 12(3), 253-265.

This study investigated factors related to personal and professional development in mature (age 35 and over) reentry women graduates. Questionnaire data were gathered from 109 graduates of 8 liberal arts colleges in Iowa. The strongest correlates of rated level of personal development were: (a) support from classmates; (b) desire for intellectual stimulation; (c) desire for a career identity; and (d) desire for a meaningful role. The strongest correlates of rated level of professional development were: (a) helpfulness of financial aid; (b) desire for a career identity; (c) desire for job preparation; (d) desire for a meaningful role; and (e) desire for achievement. Multiple regression showed that support from classmates and desire for intellectual stimulation were equally good predictors of perceived personal development, and that desire for a career identity was the only predictor of perceived professional development. Implications of the findings for educators, counselors, and reentry women are discussed. (Journal abstract).

higher education, United States.

6. Sturges, P. J., Bombyk, M. J., & Chernesky, R. H. (1989). Social work education and the older woman student. <u>Journal of Women and Aging</u>, 1(4), 119-131.

This article presents the results of a study of a group of social work graduate women students over 40. The study explored developmental issues, identified major stressors while in school, and indicated the ways that these students coped. The discussion highlights the unique responses of the midlife woman student and suggests ways that schools can work more effectively with them. Directions for future research are identified, and suggestions given for how the experiences of these older students can be used positively in their work with older women clients. (Journal abstract).

higher education, United States.

Chapter 7

Employment Status

7.1   Employment

7.2   Retirement

7.1 Employment

1. Clark, R. L., & Anker, R. (1990). Labour force participation rates of older persons: an international comparison. <u>International Labour Review</u>, <u>129</u>(2), 255-271.

This article reports the findings of an analysis of labour force participation of older persons across nations, as assessed in 1980. The principal focus is on LFPRs for men and women aged 65 and older. Information sources include internationally comparable data published by the ILO for labour force estimates; the World Bank for key economic indicators; the United Nations for demographic information; and the United States Social Security Administration for information on national social security systems.

The next section of the article briefly reviews previous retirement studies and outlines a model of retirement decisions that identifies the primary factors influencing the labour supply of older persons. This discussion forms the framework for the analysis of retirement patterns contained in the remainder of the article. The third section describes the cross-national data used. The fourth presents national LFPRs of older men and women and compares these rates by level of per capita income and geographical region. This relatively simple, descriptive analyses is followed by findings from an economic estimation of LFPR equations for men and women in sections 5 and 6. Section 7 considers how much of the decrease in participation rates with economic development can be attributed to our explanatory variables and the final section presents our general conclusions. (Journal abstract).

economic status, gender differences, international, retirement, United States.

2. Grambs, J. D. (1987). Are older women teachers different? <u>Journal of Education</u>, <u>169</u>(1), 47-64.

Most teachers are women, and most older teachers are women. Does this group of educators comprise a distinctive population in terms of their own growing older and/or in the ways they teach and participate in school affairs? Low status is associated with being older, being female, and being a teacher. When combined, there are some expected stresses and problems not encountered by male counterparts. The double pressure of job and family for a women in midlife often produces personal crises since work situations do not respond to these pressures on women. Unfortunately, research on aging and teaching is almost nonexistent and there is very little on gender and teaching. Despite much negative commentary about women teachers in the educational literature, there are no studies showing women teachers to be less effective than men at any age. More study is needed to determine the impact of age, sex, and work on performance and quality of life. Meanwhile, school systems could be more responsive to the stresses older women face as well as the ways in which women use the workplace. (Journal abstract).

age differences, gender differences, teachers, United States.

3. Kahne, H. (1985-1986). Not yet equals: Employment experience of older women and older men. International Journal of Aging and Human Development, 22(1), 1-13.

Women age forty-five and over are an important component of all working women and of the older labor force. They make up almost 30 percent of the female civilian labor force. Of the older labor force, 40 percent are women. Yet contrary to societal values about equality in the market place, employment-related experience of older women is not only different from that of men but frequently disadvantaged. This article examines the growing importance of the issue of market equality of older working women. It then considers six ways in which their employment-related experience differs from that of men: labor force participation rates; occupational distribution; earnings; unemployment; poverty; and retirement income. The article concludes with suggested policy directions that would improve the status of older women. Some of these would assist, as well, employment needs of older men. (Journal abstract).

economic status, gender differences, policy, United States.

4. Kletke, P. R., Marder, W.D., & Silberger, A.B. (1990). The growing proportion of female physicians: implications for US physician supply. American Journal of Public Health, 80(3), 300-304.

This study analyzes how the growing proportion of women in the United States physician population will affect the amount and type of physician services available to the US population. Female physicians work fewer hours per week, are slightly less likely to be in patient care, and tend to enter different specialties than male physicians. Female physicians also have higher retirement rates than male physicians, but due to their lower mortality rates, have work lives nearly as long as male physicians. We examined how the changing composition of the physician population will affect the availability of physician services by comparing historical and projected trends for the number of active post-residency physicians with comparable trends for a full-time-equivalent measure takes into account the different labor supply behavior of key subpopulations (e.g., women and graduates of US versus foreign medical schools). The results suggest that the changing composition of the physician population will reduce the growth of effective physician supply between 1986 and 2010 but only by four percentage points. (Journal abstract).

age differences, gender differences, physicians, retirement, United States.

5. McCarthy, T. A. (1990). The effect of social security on married women's labor force participation. National Tax Journal, 43(1), 95-110.

The Social Security program potentially affects labor supply decisions by altering the wage rate and by creating non-labor retirement income. As a group, married women's wage rates are reduced by relatively high net payroll tax rates. Using a probit procedure to estimate a labor force participation equation with data from the Retirement History Survey, we find that high net payroll rates are a labor supply disincentive for many married women, particularly those near retirement age. However, Social Security wealth, the present value of claims to future benefits, does not appear to affect women's labor supply decisions. (Journal abstract).

married, Social Security, United States.

6. Nuccio, K. E. (1989). The double standard of aging and older women's employment. Journal of Women and Aging, 1(1/2/3), 317-338.

The status of older women's employment remains a neglected area of interest and research by both the gerontological and women's studies fields (Congressional Quarterly, 1981: Shaw & Shaw, 1987). The preponderance of studies on "older workers" focuses on men, and interest in the employment problems of women centers on the dilemmas of combining work and family life (Fox & Hess-Biber, 1984; Voydanoff, 1984). Yet in a patriarchal society that values youth, older women bear unusual economic penalties that increase with age. This article provides an overview of the special status of the older woman worker, her economic vulnerability, and the effects on her of the double standard of aging, both in employment and in pensions and retirement. It also reviews the available legal remedies and their limitations. (Journal abstract).

ageism, economic status, sexism, United States.

7. Rife, J. C., & Toomey, B. G., & First, R.J. (1989). Older women's adjustment to unemployment. <u>Affilia</u>, 4(3), 65-77.

Few studies of unemployment have examined the impact of joblessness on older women. The exploratory study reported in this article examined the differences in adjustment to unemployment of 72 women and 76 men, aged 50 and over. The results reflect the vulnerability and special challenges that older unemployed women face and the need for social work services that are targeted to this population. (Journal abstract).

gender differences, United States.

8. Rodeheaver, D. (1990). Labor market progeria. <u>Generations</u>, <u>Summer</u>, 53-58.

This paper began with a consideration of social ambivalence toward women's roles, their sexuality, their appearance, and their aging. One of the functions of attractiveness in the work place appears to be reducing the ambivalence men experience when working with women. In an era that equates attractiveness with youth, the older women at work may be particularly vulnerable because she is already the source of so much social ambivalence. (Journal abstract).

social roles, United States.

9. Scott, W. E. (1985). Variables that contribute to leadership among female occupational therapists. <u>American Journal of Occupational Therapy</u>, <u>39</u>(6), 379-385.

This study determined which variables differentiated occupational therapy leaders from nonleaders and identified factors that contributed to leadership. The subjects were 405 occupational therapists 36 to 74 years old. Some (79) were leaders in the field, and others (326) were randomly selected members of The American Occupational Therapy Association who did not occupy leadership roles. Eighty-nine percent of the questionnaires were returned.

Few demographic differences separated the two groups; however, the findings showed that a substantial portion of the leaders shared experiences in childhood, adolescence, and early adulthood that the nonleaders did not share. Leaders viewed themselves as leaders, desired leadership, and saw leadership as an appropriate activity for women. Their view of the female role was less traditional than that of nonleaders. They married much less frequently; those who did marry had fewer children. Most married leaders' husbands highly supported their wives' leadership activities. (Journal abstract).

leadership, lifespan, marital status, social roles, United States.

7.2   Retirement

---

1. Belgrave, L. L. (1988). The effects of race differences in work history, work attitudes, economic resources, and health on women's retirement. <u>Research on Aging</u>, <u>10</u>(3), 383-398.

The effects of work history, work attitudes, economic resources, and health on the retirement of women, particularly Black women, are poorly understood. This report examines racial differences in these factors and in their effects on the decision to retire, using data gathered from 258 Black and white women aged 62 through 66. Results showed that Black women were considerably more likely than whites to have worked steadily most of their adult lives, although Black and white women expressed quite similar attitudes toward work. Reflecting their work histories, Black women were more likely than whites to be eligible for pensions but were less likely to have retired. In multivariate analysis poor health was a predictor of retirement for both Black and white women, while low average income over the last five years of employment was a predictor only for Blacks. Work history and attitude were unrelated to retirement. (Journal abstract).

Blacks, economic status, health status, racial differences, United States, Whites.

2. Campione, W. A. (1987). The married woman's retirement decision: a methodological comparison. <u>Journals of Gerontology</u>, <u>42</u>(4), 381-386.

Data from the University of Michigan's Panel Study of Income Dynamics were used to investigate married women's retirement decisions. Results are presented from a methodological comparison of parameter estimates derived under both single-and multiple-equation frameworks using logit analyses. This study finds that: (a) the married woman's decision is influenced significantly by her own wage wealth, Social Security wealth, pension wealth, and age, and (b) it is significantly influenced by her spouse's wage wealth and his labour force status. (Journal abstract).

economic status, married, United States.

3. Connidis, I. (1986). The relationship of work history to self-definition of employment status among older women. <u>Work and Occupations</u>, <u>13</u>(3), 348-358.

This article examines the relationship of six work history dimensions to the self-definitions of employment status among older women. Women defining themselves as retired are compared to women defining themselves as housewives despite having worked outside the home. Work continuity, type of occupation, and work satisfaction do not vary significantly between the retired and housewives. However, the two employment-status groups do differ significantly in number of years worked, age at generally continue to hold when marital status and age are introduced as control variables. The implications of these findings for the comparative study of women's work and for the study of women and retirement are discussed. (Journal abstract).

Canada.

4. Dorfman, L. T., & Hill, E. A. (1986). Rural housewives and retirement: joint decision-making matters. <u>Family Relations</u>, <u>35</u>(4), 507-514.

This study investigated (1) reactions of rural housewives to their husbands' retirement and (2) factors associated with satisfaction of rural wives during the retirement years. Interviews were conducted with 95 Midwestern housewives whose husbands had been retired for 6 months to 10 years. Positive and negative aspects of retirement and a range of variables associated with life satisfaction and with four specific domains of satisfaction were investigated. The most striking finding was the highly consistent relationship between joint decision-making by husband and wife and satisfaction of the wife in retirement. (Journal abstract).

decision making, life satisfaction, married, rural community, United States.

5. Dorfman, L. T., & Moffett, M. M. (1987). Retirement satisfaction in married and widowed rural women. <u>Gerontologist</u>, <u>27</u>(2), 215-221.

Compared were correlates of retirement satisfaction for married and widowed rural women. Increase in voluntary association memberships and health were predictors of retirement satisfaction for both groups. Financial adequacy and frequency and certainty of aid from friends were predictors of satisfaction for married women, whereas maintenance of preretirement friendships and frequency of visits with friends were predictors of satisfaction for widowed women. (Journal abstract).

informal support networks, life satisfaction, married, rural community, United States, widowed.

6. Erdner, R. A., & Guy, R. F. (1990). Career identification and women's attitudes toward retirement. <u>International Journal of Aging and Human Development</u>, <u>30</u>(2), 129-139.

This study seeks to heighten understanding of the retirement process as experienced by women through an examination of working women's attitudes toward retirement. The subjects for this study were 201 female teachers employed in the public school system in central Oklahoma district. The survey instrument used was a questionnaire consisting of sociodemographic and work-related variables. The findings indicate that overall, females with stronger work identities have significantly more negative attitudes toward retirement than those with weaker work identities; this difference remains significant when controls are introduced for years of teaching experience, expected age of retirement, and attitude toward work. The implications of these findings are discussed. (Journal abstract).

retirement adjustment, teachers, United States.

7. Hayward, M. D., Grady, W. R., & McLaughlin, S. D. (1988). The retirement process among older women in the United States. <u>Research on Aging</u>, <u>10</u>(3), 358-382.

Recent changes in the retirement patterns of older women in the United States are examined and the uniformity of changes across occupations is evaluated. Results indicate that both the volume of retirement and labour force reentry increased; women increasingly experienced their first retirement at younger ages; and women's working life expectancy declined while nonworking life expectancy increased and lower mortality. Many of these changes were fairly uniform across the occupational structure, maintaining the generally higher levels of working life expectancy in primary occupations. These patterns are compared to those previously observed for older men. (Journal abstract).

employment, longevity, United States.

8. Johnson, D. F., Wells, C. M., & Breckenridge, R. (1989). Service as a female naval officer: implications for aging? <u>Journal of Aging Studies</u>, 3(3), 183-209.

An ex-post facto research design was employed comparing 241 female ex-naval officers to a group of 96 women who were their peers at the time they entered the Navy in World War II. Various psychological and sociological dimensions were compared in order to assess the impact of naval office service. Data was gathered on status, goal attainment, family history, social participation, sex role effects, self-esteem, timing of life events, and financial situation. The former naval officers are all over 66 years of age; strategies and coping skills learned in the Navy may enable them to make a better adjustment to the aging process. The research addresses the question of the usefulness of military service as a bridging environment by providing skills leading to enhanced life satisfaction in the later years. (Journal abstract).

life satisfaction, military personnel, retirement adjustment, United States.

9. Matthews, A. M., & Brown, K. H. (1987). Retirement as a critical life event: the differential experiences of women and men. <u>Research on Aging</u>, 9(4), 548-571.

This article examines the experience of adaptation to retirement among a sample of women (n=124) and men (n=176) retired an average of three years and living in an urban area of Ontario, Canada. The impact of retirement as a life event relative to other life experiences was examined, and found to be distinctly less critical than previous research would suggest. (Journal abstract).

Canada, gender differences, retirement adjustment.

10. Pitaud, P. (1988). Observations on social gerontology in France. <u>International Journal of Aging and Human Development</u>, 26(2), 107-115.

In this article, the author attempts to make an assessment of some of the most important French contributions to social gerontology, isolating the main characteristics of the works encountered. We successively review some of the few studies concerning old women as well as studies dealing more generally with the social and economic aspects of aging. These lines show social gerontology in France as a forum for specialists from various disciplines; it is a specialty still in its infancy, but its multi-disciplinary approach will, no doubt contribute to its fruitfulness. (Journal abstract).

France, health status, policy, review.

11. Richardson, V. (1990). Gender differences in retirement planning among educators: implications for practice with older women. <u>Journal of Women and Aging</u>, 2(3), 27-40.

Gender differences in amount of retirement financial planning are examined among 3,064 retirees from a major state retirement system. Significant gender differences were found in amount of personal financial planning, perceived adequacy of planning and attendance at retirement workshops with women planning less than men. Factors most important for retirement planning among women are identified and intervention strategies for

_____

practitioners to help women better prepare for retirement are suggested. (Journal abstract).

gender differences, retirement planning, teachers, United States.

12. Szinovacz, M. (1986/87). Preferred retirement timing and retirement satisfaction in women. International Journal of Aging and Human Development, 24(4), 301-317.

Previous research on retirement relied heavily on samples of male retirees; it also emphasizes objective predictors of retirement adjustment, such as occupational position, income, or age. Some recent studies, however, indicate that retirement signifies a major life event for women. Furthermore, as the literature on role transitions suggests, it is a combination of objective and subjective retirement circumstances that impinge on adaptation to this life event. This study explores retirement conditions affecting women's preferred retirement timing and retirement satisfaction. It is based on the assumption that sex differences in the retirement experience render retirement adjustment processes different from men and women, and it aims at identifying retirement conditions that are of primary importance to women. (Journal abstract).

Blacks, racial differences, retirement adjustment, United States, Whites.

```
┌─────────────────────────────────────────────────────┐
│ ┌─────────────────────────────────────────────────┐ │
│ │                                                 │ │
│ │                                                 │ │
│ │                   Chapter  8                    │ │
│ │                                                 │ │
│ │                                                 │ │
│ │                  Health  Care                   │ │
│ │                                                 │ │
│ │                                                 │ │
│ └─────────────────────────────────────────────────┘ │
└─────────────────────────────────────────────────────┘
```

8.1   General

---

1. Kerson, T. S. (1989). Women and aging: a clinical social work perspective. <u>Journal of Women and Aging</u>, 1(1/2/3), 123-147.

Clinical social work helps aging women to manage the physical and psychological realities of aging. This article describes clinical social work with middle-aged (i.e., widows, displaced homemakers, caregivers) and elderly (i.e., elderly, frail elderly) women. (Author abstract).

employment, home health care, institutionalization, lifespan, United States.

2. Kinderknecht, C. H. (1989). Aging women and long-term care: truth and consequences. <u>Journal of Women and Aging</u>, 1(4), 71-92.

As the primary givers and recipients of care, elderly and middle-aged women comprise the population segment most significantly affected by the long-term care issue. Salient demographic and social factors relating to this phenomenon are explored, and the benefits and shortfalls of the current long-term care payment sources are identified. Despite the recent financial protection afforded by Medicare "Catastrophic Coverage," financing (or directly providing) long-term care still remains the responsibility of the elderly and their families. Privately purchased long-term care insurance provides some protection to those who can afford it, but elderly women continue to constitute a group at high risk for devastation by long-term care needs and costs. (Journal abstract).

long term care, Medicaid, Medicare.

3. Kinderknecht, C. H. (1989). What's out there and how to get it: a practical resource guide for the helpers of older women. <u>Journal of Women and Aging</u>, 1(1/2/3), 363-395.

Elderly women are typically in need of health care and financial resources. This article presents programs, policies, and resources that are currently available in the areas of: Older Americans Act, income programs, health care insurance and services, nutrition and food programs, housing, emergency shelter, utilities, clothing, legal assistance, transportation, home health and hospice care, homemaker chore services, mental health services, socialization and institutionalization. (Author abstract).

home health care, institutionalization, Medicaid, Medicare, United States.

4. McElmurry, B. J., & Zabrocki, E. C. (1989). Ethical concerns in caring for older women in the community. Nursing Clinics of North America, 24(4), 1041-1050.

Given the preceding discussion, what can be summarized at this point about the ethical concerns we face in the care of older women? Overall, we have presented a perspective that combines our understanding of women's health and nursing ethics. The essence of much of our concern about caring for older women is that we have views about their care that reflect our understanding of what it means to be professionals who have a social contract with our clients. We have discussed nursing ethics as a process that occurs within a social context that emphasizes working to maximize self-determination and informed choices for older women. We have emphasized autonomy and a perspective that places the nurse in an advocacy position with the patient in a relationship of partners. Arriving at reasoned positions on the ethical issues in the care of older women leads to agreement with Gloria Steinem that women may be the one group that grows more radically with age. (Journal abstract).

United States.

5. Sorensen, K. H., & Sivertsen, J. (1988). Follow-up three years after intervention to relieve unmet medical and social needs of old people. Comprehensive Gerontology B, 2(2), 85-91.

A follow-up study was conducted 3 years after a socio-medical intervention had been performed as part of an epidemiological study of 75-, 80- and 85-year-old citizens of Copenhagen. The intervention was aimed at relieving unmet medical and social needs of this group of citizens. The main recipients of social services were the oldest, single persons and women. The main preponderance of the oldest had unmet social needs, but the need for health intervention did not vary according to age or sex. Although a fifth of the participants displayed unmet health needs and a third unmet social needs, no difference could be demonstrated at follow-up between participants and controls with regard to mortality, hospitalization, and institutionalization. Nor could any difference be found regarding subjective health and economy, loneliness, quality of life and functional ability. This is in contrast to the findings of another recent Danish intervention study. On the basis of the present study and other Scandinavian intervention studies, the authors conclude that in countries with a well-developed social system, efforts to improve the living conditions of the elderly should be concentrated to those who are at particular risk. Also for ethical reasons individualized intervention is greatly preferable to general intervention. It is conceivable, however, that not all risk factors, perhaps not even the most important, can be eliminated by intervention. (Journal abstract).

Denmark, gender differences, home health care, institutionalization, service need.

8.2 Counseling and Therapy

---

1. Burlingame, V. S. (1988). Counseling an older person. Social Casework, 69(9), 588-592.

Arriving at a diagnosis for older, depressed persons is often a difficult process. The present article addresses the diagnostic and treatment process for such a client. Client contracts included a home visit, three clinic interviews, a psychiatric evaluation, and four group-therapy sessions. The client aptly described her problems and feelings about declining health, depression, and altered self-concepts, many of which are common to the aging process. The following discussion also presents countertransference issues that influenced the therapeutic process. (Journal abstract).

assessment, depression, group therapy, United States.

2. Burnside, I. M. (1989). Group work with older women: a modality to improve the quality of life. Journal of Women and Aging, 1(1/2/3), 265-290.

The purpose of this article is fourfold: (1) to locate and describe articles about group work with older women, (2) to emphasize the need for prevention and health promotion in elderly women, (3) to present perspectives on teaching group work with this select group, and (4) to suggest, in a brainstorming mode, ideas for future group work. (Journal abstract).

group therapy, health promotion, reality orientation, reminiscence therapy, remotivation therapy, United States.

3. Drake, M., & Donsky, A. (1988). Widowed or alone--a supportive network for older women. Aging, 357, 25-26.

This article describes the Supportive Older Women's Network (SOWN). SOWN was designed exclusively for women 60 years and older to help them cope with their concerns about aging. Among the services provided by SOWN are: support groups, leadership training seminars, consultation and outreach services, and a newsletter. (Author abstract).

single, support groups, United States.

4. Giltinan, J. M. (1990). Using life review to facilitate self-actualization in elderly women. Gerontology and Geriatrics Education, 10(4), 75-83.

This article explores the effect of life review discussions on the self-actualization process in a group of elderly women. The information can be used by health care professionals in helping the aged attain their optimum potential. The conceptual framework was developed from Maslow's self-actualization which was measured by Shostrum's Personal Orientation Inventory. Robert Butler's concept of life review provided structure for the reminiscing experiences. Seven life review sessions, conducted in an uncontrolled environment, focused on facilitating continued growth and expansion of the participants' inner selves. The group process also provided socialization opportunities and fostered cohesiveness among group members by developing a sense of belonging through shared experiences. (Journal abstract).

group therapy, life review, reminiscence therapy, self-actualization, United States.

5. Hayslip, B., Schneider, L. J., & Bryant, K. (1989). Older women's perceptions of female counselors: the influence of therapist age and problem intimacy. Gerontologist, 29(2), 239-244.

Elderly women (N=96, Mn age=69.6) who served as pseudoclients in an analogue study were more positive toward all counselors when vignettes dealt with less intimate rather than more intimate problems. Older counselors were preferred when less intimate concerns were discussed whereas younger counselors were preferred for more intimate problems. Perceived differences in helper expertness, attractiveness, and trustworthiness were also influenced by perceptions of the individuality of counselors. These findings have significance for the delivery of mental health services to older persons. (Journal abstract).

age differences, counselors, United States.

6. Hu, T. W., Igou, J. F., Kaltreider, D. L., Yu, L. C., Rohner, T. J., Dennis, P. J., Craighead, W. E., Hadley, E. C., & Ory, M. G. (1989). A clinical trial of a behavioral therapy to reduce urinary incontinence in nursing homes: outcome and implications. Journal of the American Medical Association, 261(18), 2656-2662.

One hundred thirty-three incontinent women in seven nursing homes were assigned randomly to a 13-week behavior therapy program for urinary incontinence or to a control group that received usual incontinence-related care. The therapy became effective after 6 weeks of training. By the final month of training, the treatment women's wet episodes had been reduced by 0.6 episodes per day, a 26% reduction over baseline. This reduction in the number of wet episodes was statistically significant, both with respect to this group's baseline levels of incontinence and in comparison with the performance of the control women. The number of wet episodes in the control group remained about the same throughout training and the 22-week follow-up period. The treatment women improved partly because they learned to request help, a response prompted and reinforced by the program. Trainees with a high frequency of incontinence during baseline, the more cognitively intact residents, and residents with normal bladder capacity responded better to this behavior therapy program. (Journal abstract).

behavior therapy, incontinence, United States.

7. Kaufman, S. (1988). Illness, biography, and the interpretation of self following a stroke. Journal of Aging Studies, 2(3), 217-227.

Drawing on case material from interviews with a 65-year-old woman who had suffered a stroke, this article explores the concept of biography as both knowledge of the self and as an expression of part of the self that needs attention following serious illness. Using a phenomenological approach, the kinds of biographical work that individuals define and face as they recover from major illness are elucidated. The goal is to explore the consequences of a stroke for biographical issues that emerge in later life. (Journal abstract).

life review, stroke, United States.

8. Shulman, S. C. (1985). Psychodynamic group therapy with older women. Social Casework, 66(10), 579-586.

Although therapy groups are often assumed to be unsuitable for older patients, this article reports the effectiveness of one such group. The clinician was able to enhance the members' coping skills, their acceptance of good and bad, and their ability to share within the group. (Journal abstract).

coping, group therapy, United States.

8.3   Health Promotion and Disease Prevention

---

1. Baker, J. (1989). Breast self-examination and the older woman: field testing an educational approach. Gerontologist, 29(3), 405-407.

The effectiveness of theoretically based educational strategy was compared with a standard breast self-examination strategy. It was found that women in the experimental treatment group (n=68) were significantly (p=.029) more likely to perform breast self-examination appropriately 3 months following instruction than women in the standard treatment comparison group (n=66) after controlling for pretest scores and age. (Journal abstract).

breast cancer, United States.

2. Brown, J. T., & Hulka, B. S. (1988). Screening mammography in the elderly: a case-control study. Journal of General Internal Medicine, 3(2), 126-131.

This case-control study tested the hypothesis that elderly women with metastatic breast cancer were previously screened less than controls. Cases included women over 60 years old who had metastatic breast cancer; the tumor registry provided controls. Identical criteria yielded comparable groups (cases=109, controls=211) receiving primary care at this tertiary center. Radiology and medical records were examined for mammograms; these were blindly categorized "diagnostic," "screening," or "indeterminate." The major, unexpected finding was less than 6% of controls had ever had screening mammography. The associations between screening and metastatic cancer (odds ratios) suggest a beneficial effect of screening: OR/0.73 for ever screened and OR/ 0.71 if screened within the year of cancer diagnosis. All confidence intervals include one; however, low screening participation leaves this study with little power. The major implication is that despite the current recommendations, the elderly are not being included in screening mammography programs. (Journal abstract).

breast cancer, United States.

3. Burack R.C., & Liang J. (1989). The acceptance and completion of mammography by older black women. <u>American Journal of Public Health</u>, <u>79</u>(6), 721-726.

We assessed the relation of patient characteristics, knowledge and beliefs to the utilization of mammography in an inner-city setting by 187 Black women over the age of 50. Thirty per cent of those who were offered mammography initially declined the offer and 40 per cent were subsequently unable to complete the procedure. Patient interviews were used to derive 27 potential knowledge and health belief predictor scales. In multiple regression analysis, two health belief scales and two knowledge scales accounted for 15 per cent of the observed variance in the model of acceptance. The strongest predictor of subsequent completion was initial acceptance. The presence of breast symptoms and two health belief scales together with initial acceptance accounted for 26 per cent of variance in the model of completion. These results suggest that the successful accomplishment of mammography requires coordinated efforts at the level of the provider, patient, and setting. Health beliefs may influence the patient's behavior in this process but their effect appears to be modest. (Journal abstract).

Blacks, breast cancer, service utilization, United States.

4. Chao, A., Paganini-Hill, A., Ross, R. K., & Henderson, B. E. (1987). Use of preventive care by the elderly. <u>Preventive Medicine</u>, <u>16</u>(5), 710-722.

Use of five early detection tests were examined in relation to history of specific chronic diseases and other health habits, as part of a cohort study including 11, 888 residents of a retirement community in Southern California. Self-reported utilization rates by residents in the year preceding the study entry were approximately 90, 30, 60 and 10% for blood pressure measurement, fecal occult blood test, Papanicolau test, and mammography, respectively. Breast self-examination was practiced by 37% of the women on a regular basis. With the exception of the Pap test and blood pressure check, the majority of the study population did not use preventive procedures at the recommended frequencies. The most important determinants of use of screening tests in the elderly population were previous diagnosis of chronic disease, especially of disease detected by the test itself, and having a regular physician. These two factors appeared to affect use independently. (Journal abstract).

blood pressure, breast cancer, cervical cancer, service utilization, United States.

5. Dobson, E. (1987). Good health for women. <u>Health Visitor</u>, <u>60</u>(11), 363.

A health education discussion group for women has proved successful in generating interest in a wide range of topics relating to women's health, including pre-menstrual tension, the menopause, breast examination, cervical screening, relaxation, diet, stress management and general health care. (Journal abstract).

breast cancer, cervical cancer, menopause, United States.

6. Gale, B. J., & Clark, H. (1986). Well woman's clinic: a health promotion program. Journal Community Health Nursing, 3(2), 75-85.

In the typical health care setting of our day, true health promotion is often overlooked. Most authors agree that health promotion activities involve healthy people and serve to encourage growth and improvement in well-being. Community health nurses can be very instrumental in planning and implementing primary prevention programs that are of good quality and are cost effective. The nursing process provides a scientific, systematic framework and will be used to discuss a women's health promotion program that is the focus of this article. The program is called "The Well Woman's Clinic" (WWC) and is sponsored by the Temple St. Luke's Hospital, Arizona State University, and Dr. H.C. Watters. (Journal abstract).

cancer, United States.

7. Hamwi, D. A. (1990). Screening mammography: increasing the effort toward breast cancer detection. Nurse Practitioner, 15(12), 27-32.

Mammography is the only modality with the potential for detecting a breast cancer while it is non-palpable and at a stage of high curability. Early detection of breast cancer is important because survival is directly related to tumor size and lymph node status, and prognosis is best for small lesions without axillary node metastasis. Many studies have indicated that screening mammography is tremendously underused. This article focuses on the effectiveness of mammography and the importance of detecting a breast cancer at an early stage. Health care providers have a responsibility to inform their clients about the benefits of mammography. In addition, women need to be taught breast self-examination and undergo regular clinical breast examinations by a health care professional. The American Cancer Society guidelines for screening breast cancer are given. (Journal abstract).

breast cancer, United States.

---

8. Lashley, M. E. (1987). Predictors of breast self-examination practice among elderly women. <u>Advances in Nursing Science</u>, 9(4), 25-34.

The purpose of the study presented in this article was to examine predictors of breast self-examination (BSE) practice among elderly female subjects in selected senior citizen centers. The health belief model served as the theoretical framework for the research study. Both the frequency of BSE performance and the techniques subjects used to examine their breasts were measured by a questionnaire. Subjects who perceived few barriers to BSE had higher BSE technique scores. The findings also indicated that receiving instructions through a class on BSE was related to improved BSE technique. Perceived susceptibility to breast cancer and perceived benefits of BSE were not found to be significantly predictive of BSE practice. (Journal abstract).

breast cancer, United States.

9. Lierman, L. M., Young, H. M., Kasprzyk, D., & Benoliel, J. Q. (1990). Predicting breast self-examination using the theory of reasoned action. <u>Nursing Research</u>, <u>39</u>(2), 97-101.

The personal and normative influences on breast self-examination (BSE) behavior in older women were examined using the Theory of Reasoned Action. The sample consists of 93 volunteers ranging in age from 52 to 90 years. A structured questionnaire was used for data collection. Direct and indirect measures of attitude and social norm were used to predict intention to perform BSE and BSE frequency. Contrary to the model assumptions, indirect measures accounted for more variance in both intention and behavior, and explained actual behaviors better than intention to perform. Both the indirect and direct measures of attitude and social norm explained a significant amount of the variance in intention and BSE frequency. There were significant differences on all the model components (direct and indirect measures of attitude, social norm, and intention) between frequent and infrequent BSE performance groups. Discriminant analysis using the indirect measures of attitude and social norm correctly classified 76% of the women into infrequent performance groups. (Journal abstract).

breast cancer, United States.

10. Mandelblatt, J., Gopaul, I., & Wistreich, M. (1986). Gynecological care of elderly women: Another look at Papanicolaou smear testing. <u>Journal of the American Medical Association</u>, <u>256</u>(3), 367-371.

Mortality from cervical cancer is decreasing in countries where aggressive Papanicolaou smear screening programs are in place. However, elderly women are likely to be lifelong nonusers or underusers of Papanicolaou screening, and mortality has not declined for older women. Many studies have noted that nonparticipants in Papanicolaou screening have a 2.7 to four times greater incidence of cervical cancer when they are screened at least once. Gynecological screening was offered to 1542 elderly women in primary care setting; 75% of the women had not had regular prior screening and 25% had never been screened. Half of these women chose to participate in our screening program. An overall prevalence rate of 13.5 per 1000 abnormal Papanicolaou smears (95% confidence interval, 5.6 to 21.4) was noted in the group. Age, race, prior screening history, and abnormal Papanicolaou smears. Our results suggest that cervical cancer screening should continue beyond 65 years of age if women have not received regular prior screening. (Journal abstract).

cervical cancer, United States.

11. Marks, G. (1987). Health behaviour of elderly Hispanic women: does cultural assimilation make a difference? <u>American Journal of Public Health</u>, <u>77</u>(10), 1315-1319.

The role of cultural assimilation in Hispanic health behavior has received little empirical examination. Prior studies have operationalized assimilation primarily in terms of language preference and have obtained weak or no effects. We interviewed 603 elderly Hispanic women residing in Los Angeles to evaluate the usefulness of cultural factors as predictors of preventive health behavior (e.g., physical examination, screening for breast cancer) more rigorously. Factor analysis of responses yielded four dimensions of cultural assimilation: "language preference", "country of birth", "contact with homeland", and "attitudes about children's friends." After controlling for education and age, no dimension of assimilation associated strongly or consistently with health behavior. Of the four dimensions, use of English language associated most closely with increased screening, although most of the effects for language were small in magnitude. These findings, coupled with those of other studies, strongly suggest that cultural factors may have little impact on the health behavior of Hispanics. Access to and availability of services, affective reactions toward screening, and sociodemographic factors are stronger determinants of Hispanic health practices. (Journal abstract).

Hispanics, service utilization, United States.

12. Moon, T. E. (1991). Estrogens and disease prevention. <u>Archives of Internal Medicine</u>, <u>151</u>(1), 17-18.

This article describes the effects of postmenopausal estrogen. While it is used in the prevention of some diseases, it also increases morbidity of other diseases. (Author abstract).

breast cancer, estrogen, United States.

13. Murray, M. (1990). Well-woman clinics: audit. <u>Practitioner</u>, <u>234</u>(1489), 516-517.

This article describes the service provided by a well-women's clinic in England. An audit of the health problems found among their patients are provided. (Author abstract).

England.

14. Woodman, C. B., & Jordan, J. A. (1989). Colposcopy services in the West Midlands region. <u>British Medical Journal</u>, <u>299</u>(6704), 899-901.

A survey of all 72 consultant gynaecologists in the West Midlands region was carried out to determine their views on colposcopy services. All districts provided a colposcopy service and 47 consultants practised colposcopy. The consultants differed considerably in their views on criteria for referring women for investigation after smears. All but one thought that a positive smear result was an indication for immediate referral but whereas 55 thought that women with one or more inflammatory smear should be referred, 17 did not believe this to be necessary. Sixty seven consultants thought a preoperative colposcopic assessment desirable, but 10 had to ration referrals because of limited resources. Four forms of treatment were used; 17 districts had a carbon dioxide laser, eight used low voltage diathermy loop excision, two had only a cold coagulator, and one used only cold cautery. There was widespread dissatisfaction with resources and about the increasing amount of time spent on the service at the expense of other work. Consultants were also concerned about the relevance of much of what was done to the aim of the screening programme - reducing mortality from cervical cancer. Although additional resources are needed in some districts, referral policies, indications for colposcopic assessment, training, choice of treatment, and the value of follow up need to be reviewed if the service is to be improved. (Journal abstract).

cervical cancer, England, physician services.

8.4   Home Health Care

---

1. Donovan, R. (1989). "We care for the most important people in your life": home care workers in New York City. Women's Studies Quarterly, 17(1/2), 56-65.

Home health care is a women's issue; typically, women are both the recipients and the providers of home care. This article describes the recipients and caregivers of home care and a Personal Care Program in New York. (Author abstract).

United States.

2. Feldblum, C. R. (1985). Home health care for the elderly: programs, problems, and potentials. Harvard Journal on Legislation, 22(1), 193-254.

The current provision of health care for our country's elderly is inadequate for several reasons. First, government health care programs offer inadequate benefits to those elderly who wish to avoid institutionalization and remain at home with their families. Services authorized by such programs are ill-equiped to satisfy the growing needs of an elderly population that is projected to constitute an increasingly significant percentage of our country's total population. Second, current programs fail to provide services to help alleviate the psychological and emotional stress experienced by unpaid family caregivers. Finally, policymakers have often failed to consider the effects of these programs on women in their roles as providers and recipients of home health care.

In this Note, Ms. Feldblum analyzes the federal and federal-state programs that currently provide home health care services for the elderly. After this analysis, she offers her own description of a comprehensive home health care system. She then reviews, in light of this system, the strengths and weaknesses of home health care legislation recently proposed in the Ninety-eighth Congress. Finally, Ms. Feldblum recommends that an expansion of home health care services for the elderly must properly reflect the changing roles of women in our society. (Journal abstract).

informal support networks, Medicaid, Medicare, service need, United States.

8.5   Hospitalization

---

1. Hendriksen, C., Lund, E., & Stromgard, E. (1989). Hospitalization of elderly people a 3-year controlled trial. <u>Journal of the American Geriatrics Society</u>, <u>37</u>(2), 117-122.

In a controlled epidemiologic intervention study, preventive home visits to elderly people aged 75 or older were made every third month over 3 years. Two hundred eighty-five (62% women) elderly participated in the intervention group and 287 (62% women) in the control group. Information about the number of admissions to hospitals, the number of bed days, the main reason for hospitalization, the diagnoses on discharge, and the residence after discharge was collected. Two hundred nineteen admissions (4,884 bed days) were registered for the intervention group compared with 271 (6,442 bed days) for the control group. During the second half of the study, a significant reduction in the number of admissions -especially readmissions - to hospitals was seen in the intervention group. The mean risk per person of being hospitalized was 24%, 20% and 20% in years 1, 2, and 3, respectively, for the intervention group, and 22%, 25%, and 28% for the controls. The mean number of bed days per admission did not differ between the two groups. Using the results to make a general epidemiologic and longitudinal assessment of the admissions of elderly aged 75 or older, the following can be concluded: 4% of the participants used 42% of the bed days, and most of these people awaited alternative residential accommodation; 62% stayed less than 2 weeks in the hospital. The main reason for hospitalization was fall episodes among women (20%) and dyspnea among men (18%). Approximately three-fourths were discharged to their own homes or to the family, while 18% died. Preventive home visits seem to be one of the tools to improve the future lives of the elderly in their own homes. (Journal abstract).

Denmark, longitudinal study.

2. Hodkinson, E., McCafferty, F. G., Scott, J. N., & Stout, R. W. (1988). Disability and dependency in elderly people in residential and hospital care. <u>Age and Ageing</u>, <u>17</u>(3), 147-154.

Physical dependency and mental impairment were assessed in 143 residents of residential accommodation for the elderly and 125 patients in geriatric continuing-care wards in South Belfast. Although dependency, immobility and incontinence were more common in the hospital patients, there was considerable overlap in the disability levels in the two types of care. There was evidence of dementia in 51% of the residents and 71% of the patients, while 29% of residents and 70% of patients were incontinent. Overall, less than 1% of the elderly population was in each of residential or geriatric hospital care but the proportion rose with age and was greater in older women. About 17% of elderly people in South Belfast with dementia were in residential or geriatric hospital care. The projected increase in the number of oldest old people, particularly women, and the increased risk of dementia in this age group, means that the need for residential and continuing hospital care for the elderly will continue to increase. (Journal abstract).

dementia, gender differences, incontinence, Ireland, residential care.

3. Reardon, G. T., Blumenfield, S., Weissman, A. L., & Rosenberg, G. (1988). Findings and implications from preadmission screening of elderly patients waiting for elective surgery. Social Work in Health Care, 13(3), 51-63.

Volunteers trained by a social worker did a telephone screening of 716 elderly persons waiting for elective surgery to determine in advance of admission their need for social services. On the basis of their findings patients were given a risk rating by a social worker. While the survey was experienced positively by patients, volunteers, and social workers, the results do not establish in value in terms of shortened length of stay. Aging females living alone required the greatest amount of social work and had the longest length of stay. This group requires further study, along with the connection between intensity of illness with social problem vulnerability. The study raises other important questions critical to programming for an increasingly older population. (Journal abstract).

gender differences, service need, United States.

8.6 Institutionalization

---

1. Burr, J. A. (1990). Race/sex comparisons of elderly living arrangements: factors influencing the institutionalization of the unmarried. Research on Aging, 12(4), 507-530.

This article describes recent trends in the total institutionalization rates among unmarried Black and White populations, by sex. In addition, an analysis is provided that evaluates the individual attributes associated with the probability of institutionalization for these same groups in 1980. To accomplish these goals, U.S. Census data from the 1960, 1970, and 1980

Public Use Samples are employed. The evidence suggests convergence over time in age-standardized rates across both race and sex groups. Also, there is considerable consistency among the groups in the factors that predict the likelihood of being in a formal long-term care situation. Although the Black population continues to access formal institutions less frequently than does the White population, the findings suggest that forecasters and planners need to take into account the increasing rate of elderly Black institutionalization along with the individual characteristics that influence these rates. (Journal abstract).

Blacks, gender differences, racial differences, single, United States, Whites.

8.7   Service Utilization

1. Doty, P. (1987). Health status and health services use among older women: an international perspective. World Health Statistics Quarterly, 40(3), 279-290.

This article addresses women's health status and health services. Major topics include: a profile of women's health in developing countries, women's health in developed countries, use of health services by older women, older women as caregivers, the future. Note that this article appears alongside a french translation. (Author abstract).

health status, home health care, hospitalization, institutionalization, international.

2. Dvoredsky, A. E., & Cooley, W. (1985). The health care needs of women veterans. Hospital and Community Psychiatry, 36(10), 1098-1102.

Although women veterans accounted for 4.1 percent of all veterans in 1983, they accounted for only 1.5 percent of all discharges from Veterans Administration hospitals in that year. These data suggest that women veterans are not utilizing their health care benefits as often as male veterans do, possibly because they are choosing to receive health care in non-VA facilities. Furthermore, the patterns of utilization for women veterans suggest a selective use of VA hospitals for serious illnesses that require protracted care. The author explores some possible explanations for this phenomenon and emphasizes the need for the VA health care system to incorporate such information in the planning of health care services for women veterans. (Journal abstract).

gender differences, hospitalization, United States, veterans.

3. Eve, S. B. (1988). A longitudinal study of use of health care services among older women. Journals of Gerontology, 43(2), M31-M39.

This research tested the hypothesis that the percent of variance explained in use of health care services by the health care services utilization model could be significantly increased by including measures of past use of health care services and of past health status. Data from older women who participated in the Social Security Administration's Longitudinal Retirement History Survey (N = 1894) were analyzed by means of regression analysis. The results revealed that measures of previous use of health care services were more strongly related to current use of health care services in 1979 than were measures of previous health status. Inclusion of previous use and previous health care services in 1979 than were measures of previous health status. Inclusion of previous use and previous health care services variables almost doubled the amount of variance explained by current predictors in number of physician visits, and more than doubled the explained variance in having to put off health care while the amount of variance explained in number episodes and in number of hospitalized nights was increased by approximately one-third. (Journal abstract).

hospitalization, longitudinal study, physician services, United States.

4. Ishii-Kuntz, M. (1990). Formal activities for elderly women: determinants of participation in voluntary and senior center activities. Journal of Women and Aging, 2(1), 79-97.

In this study, theoretical views previously used to explain health service utilization by the elderly are extended to explain how predisposing (age, race, education, and marital status), enabling (income, employment status, health status, and transportation), and need (loneliness and living arrangement) factors influence elderly women's participation in voluntary organizations and senior centers. Hypotheses are tested using a nationwide probability sample of elderly women who are 65 and above. The major findings indicate that age, race, and health status influence participation in voluntary organizations and senior centers. Elderly widows are also more likely to participate in voluntary organizations than married women. Loneliness has a positive impact on senior center participation of these women. (Journal abstract).

senior centres, United States.

5. Joseph, A. E., & Cloutier, D. S. (1990). A framework for modeling the consumption of health services by the rural elderly. <u>Social Science and Medicine</u>, <u>30</u>(1), 45-52.

This paper reports on an ongoing research program which seeks to assess the implications of population aging for housing, services and transportation in rural communities in the Province of Ontario. Specifically, the focus is on the modeling of health and social service consumption by elderly (over 65) persons. Following a review of the literature on service provision to senior citizens in Ontario, a modeling framework conceptualizing the process of service utilization at both the aggregate (user and nonuser characteristics) and individual (decision-making) levels is introduced. Data on use of community support services drawn from a survey of elderly residents in two communities in Grey County, Ontario (Mealford, population 4380 in 1986, and Markdale, population 1226 in 1986) are used to illustrate the general features of the modeling framework. Particular attention is paid to the ability of the modeling framework to yield insights into the origins of notable variations in service use rates between men and women. Overall, the results are taken to be supportive of the usefulness of the modeling framework as a template for guiding results are taken to be supportive of the usefulness of the modeling framework as a template for guiding empirical analysis of service utilization patterns. At the same time the case study testifies to the complex and dynamic nature of service provision issues in rural communities. The challenge of providing services effectively to an elderly rural population located in scattered villages and small towns will continue to tax the imagination and resources of responsible agencies. (Journal abstract).

Canada, gender differences, home health care, rural community.

6. Keith, P. M., & Wickrama, K. A. S. (1990). Use and evaluation of health services by women in a developing country: is age important? <u>Gerontologist</u>, <u>30</u>(2), 262-268.

Today, the majority of the world's older persons live in less developed countries, where they represent an increasing proportion of the population. Using interviews conducted with 136 female heads of households in rural Sri Lanka, we considered the importance of age relative to other factors (e.g. marital status, education, employment, diet, and health practices) in accounting for use and evaluation of health services. Marital status figured more importantly than age in the use of services. As unmarried heads of households increase in less developed places, their demands for health care at the village level likely will escalate. (Journal abstract).

age differences, health promotion, hospitalization, marital status, physician services, Sri Lanka.

7. Morabia, A., Loew, F., & Takla, H. (1986). Medical care and social support for the elderly in Switzerland: imbalance and mix. Social Science and Medicine, 23(12), **1327-1332.**

Medicalization refers to the current practice of providing medical solutions to broad social problems facing the old. This approach is destined to bring about serious economic and sociocultural dilemmas in the coming decades due to the aging trends in Switzerland.

On the one hand, additional bed requirements will double, really jeopardizing the present federal savings policy on health and welfare. On the other side, ignoring the specific needs of nearly 20% of the population (as the 65 and over group are expected to reach in the year 2010), will provoke unwielding social/political tensions.

Assigning medical answers to social needs is both expensive and inadequate. This proposition is illustrated by two aspects of the Geneva's medical care system for the aged: (a) At the University Geriatric Hospital a large proportion of the patients are admitted for purely social reasons ("home maintenance impossible"). The long term bed stays, medically unjustified, constrains the optimal functioning of this acute care and rehabilitation hospital. The prolonged length of institutionalization reduces the capacity of the elderly out-patients to carry on autonomously. This observation is confirmed by many Swiss medical and sociological surveys which reveal that institutionalization is rarely necessary or desirable in the 10 to 20 first years of post-retirement provided that there is an adequate system of social and primary care services available. (b) The drug prescription to those 65 and over consulting at the out-patient department of the Geneva University Medical Polyclinic typically amounts to excessive prescription for women and especially of psychotropic drugs. In many cases, the prescribed care appears as an unsatisfactory substitute for loneliness and the lack of regular mental or social activity. Medicalization thus often means negation of existing social problems and marginalization in nursing homes and hospitals. Social support to the elderly by a well-balanced system of health and social welfare emphasizing their autonomy and dignity is an alternative to medicalization. Its goals should include reducing inequities, lowering financial burdens, rationalizing medico-social support and creating the conditions indispensable to an active independent life for the aged. (Journal abstract).

drugs, gender differences, home care, hospitalization, Switzerland.

8. Mutran, E., & Ferraro, K. F. (1988). Medical need and use of services among older men and women. Journals of Gerontology, 43(5), **S162-S171.**

This article presents a model of the process by which men and women evaluate their health and utilize the medical care system. It is argued that an analysis of the effects of sex roles on medical care must look at the entire process and not just focus on the outcome variables of physician visits and hospitalization. Gender interactions are emphasized, but race interactions also are examined. Findings show that women differ in the number of illnesses they report, the likelihood of having a life-threatening illness, the degree of disability, and their perception of their health. Indicators of medical need were found to be the strongest measures in predicting the recency of seeing a physician; however, the physician visit had the strongest effect in determining hospitalization. No direct effects of gender or race on physician visits were found, and only one interaction was significant; however, the results were very different when the measure of medical care use was hospitalization. Both additive and interactive effects by gender and race were found predicting hospitalization. (Journal abstract).

gender differences, health status, hospitalization, physician services, racial differences, United States.

9. Peterson, S. A. (1989). Elderly women and program encounters: a rural study. Journal of Women and Aging, 1(4), 41-56.

This study investigates elderly men and women's program awareness and use. A sample of 456 rural elderly men and women were interviewed for their program awareness and use, social resources, personal resources and need. Results indicate that 1) personal and social resources are related to greater program awareness and have mixed relationships with program use, 2) need is related to less awareness but with greater program use, 3) greater social resources are the most important predictors of elevated awareness, 4) greater need and program awareness shape increased program use, 5) personal resources have an indirect impact on program use for males but not for females. Results are discussed in terms of implications for outreach programs. (Author abstract).

gender differences, home health care, rural community, United States.

Chapter 9

Housing

9.1 Housing Types

1. Harris, M., & Bachrach, L. L. (1990). Perspectives on homeless mentally ill women. Hospital and Community Psychiatry, 41(3), 253-254.

This article presents some preliminary observations of 25 homeless mentally ill women. (Author abstract).

homeless, United States.

2. Leavitt, J., & Welch, M. B. (1989). Older women and the suburbs: a literature review. Women's Studies Quarterly, 17(1/2), 35-47.

This article first discusses some of the methodological difficulties of examining women in suburbs. It then surveys both the problems faced by all elderly suburbanites and the particular hardships encountered by elderly women. Finally, it explores several recommendations for change. (Journal abstract).

suburban community, United States.

3. Saegert, S. (1989). Unlikely leaders, extreme circumstances: older black women building community households. American Journal of Community Psychology, 17(3), 295-316.

This study began as a policy assessment of New York City's low-income, limited equity co-ops in landlord-abandoned buildings, with a special concern for the large number of female residents. Research participants' interactions with researchers led to a grounded theory approach to interviews with 88 residents including 54 co-op residents. Focusing on the 37 black co-op residents, the study elucidates the importance of gender, race, and age in determining tenant responses to abandonment, leadership style and co-op organization, place attachment, and empowerment. The availability of community resources and support also varied over time and played a critical part in tenant actions and experiences. The Community Household Model integrates various levels of analysis. Data from a survey of

131 residents is compared and discussed in the light of debates about transactional research. (Journal abstract).

age differences, Blacks, co-operatives, gender differences, leadership, racial differences, United States.

4. Schank, M. J., & Lough, M. A. (1989). Maintaining health and independence of elderly women. Journal of Gerontological Nursing, 15(6), 8-11.

This study investigated the relationship between health and social support. A sample of 100 elderly women were interviewed and asked to respond to a 37 item questionnaire. The questionnaire was designed to measure health status, social support and biographical data. Two major findings were revealed: 1) elderly women with a reported health status of excellent or good indicated that they had a greater degree of social support than respondents reporting a fair or poor health status, 2) women residing in private housing reported having an excellent or good health status and a greater degree of social support more frequently than women in public housing. Implications and limitations of these findings are discussed. (Author abstract).

health status, social interaction, United States.

5. Young, W., & Hasell, D. (1988). 2008: housing the elderly: perceptions of community planners, gerontologists, and women in research. Canadian Home Economics Journal, 38(3), 125-128.

The purpose of this paper is to integrate the discussions and ideas of community planners, professionals working in gerontology, and women involved in research. Each group discussed findings related to the housing of the elderly using the Wagschal Futures Wheel discussion technique. The findings were generated in a study of the housing of elderly and disabled subjects in urban and rural Saskatchewan. Comments from the participants include the effect of the increase in the number of elderly persons on housing; isolation, which was identified as a major problem of the elderly in future; and the impact of increased numbers of the elderly needing rental accommodation. These ideas may assist the planning of housing and communities for the elderly in the future. (Journal abstract).

Canada, future projections, isolation, rural community, United States, urban community.

9.2   Living Arrangements

1. Anson, O. (1988). Evidence that elderly women living alone may be in better health than their counterparts. Sociology and Social Research, 72(2), 114-115.

Past research disagrees about whether elderly persons living alone are less healthy than those living with others. This study is based upon an national sample of 6261 women aged 60-74 and 2384 women aged 75 or older were studied. Non-married women who live alone report better health status and less illness behavior than their peers who live with others. These differences are more pronounced among the older age group. Widows who live alone reported better health status than the married, but more illness behavior. (Journal abstract).

health status, living alone, United States.

2. Carp, F. M., & Christensen, D. L. (1986). Older women living alone: technical environmental assessment of psychological well-being. Research on Aging, 8(3), 407-425.

Relationships of subjective residential satisfaction to psychological well-being have been demonstrated, but it has proved difficult to document relationships between objective environmental variables and well-being. In this study, environmental variables were selected on the basis of a theoretical model for relevance to human needs and were measured with technical assessment items scaled for internal consistency. Outcomes were two factors derived from a battery of instruments in the domain of psychological well-being. Direct effects of objective environment measures on psychological well-being were observed as well as indirect effects through subjective satisfaction with home and neighborhood. (Journal abstract).

living alone, psychological well-being, United States.

3. Carp, F. M., & Christensen, D. L. (1986). Technical environmental assessment predictors of residential satisfaction: a study of elderly women living alone. Research on Aging, 8(2), 269-287.

Residential satisfaction is important in its own right and as an influence on general well-being. Previous research suggests that objective environmental characteristics amenable to societal manipulation affect residential satisfaction. Environmental predictors were selected on the basis of a theoretical model for relevance to human needs and measured with technical-assessment items scaled independently of subjective judgments. For 88 older women living independently and alone in the community, the objective environmental variables accounted for 28% of the variance in satisfaction with housing and 26% of the variance in neighborhood satisfaction additional to that attributable to personal competence and socioeconomic status. (Journal abstract).

living alone, United States, well-being.

4. Cooney, T. M. (1989). Co-residence with adult children: a comparison of divorced and widowed women. Gerontologist, 29(6), 779-784.

This study compares patterns of co-residence with adult offspring for divorcees and widows, aged 40 and over, using 1985 Current Population Survey data. Co-residence with offspring is most likely for recent widows in midlife and recent divorcees in later life. Older recent divorcees are less likely than recent widows to be household heads in these living situations. Finally, daughters appear especially important in the co-resident situations of divorcees. These results are discussed in light of changing patterns of divorce and widowhood in later life. (Journal abstract).

adult children, divorced, United States, widowed.

5. Goldmeir, J. (1986). Pets or people: another research note. Gerontologist, 26(2), 203-206.

Four samples of elderly women were compared who were living alone or with other persons, some with and some without a companion pet. Pets only made a difference for those living alone. At best, pets only attenuate the sense of loneliness that may be felt from the lack of human companionship. In intervention with the elderly, the provision of human supports should remain a priority. (Journal abstract).

living alone, loneliness, pets, United States.

---

6. Magaziner, J., & Cadigan, D. A. (1988). Community care of older women living alone. Women and Health, 14(3/4), 121-138.

This paper compares the formal and informal care used by women living alone and women living with others using data from a household survey of women over 65. In contrast to those living with others, who use few formal services and receive most of their care from the children they live with, those living alone rely on a diverse group of informal caregivers and formal services, many of which are provided in their homes. Women living alone also report using mechanical devices more often, and are less confident that assistance will be available in the event of illness. Results are discussed from psychological and organizational perspectives. (Journal abstract).

home health care, informal support networks, living alone, United States.

7. Magaziner, J., Cadigan, D. A., Hebel, J. R., & Parry, R. E. (1988). Health and living arrangements among older women: does living alone increase the risk of illness? Journals of Gerontology, 43(5), M127-M133.

This study compares the physical, mental, and functional health of aged women living alone to those living with a husband and to those living with others, and considers whether living arrangements lead to health problems or if health problems influence the choice of living arrangements. Data were collected in 1984 during the first wave of a prospective study of 807 women 65 years or older living in an area consisting of 20 contiguous census tracts in Baltimore, MD. Multivariate analyses demonstrate no particular disadvantage associated with living alone for this group of elderly women. After controlling for age and socioeconomic status, analyses indicate that it is those living with persons other than their husbands who are most impaired. In addition, poor health does not appear to result from living arrangement: rather, those who are sickest choose to live with others because of health problems. (Journal abstract).

functional health, health status, living alone, mental status, United States.

8. Magaziner, J., & Carigan, D. A. (1989). Community resources and mental health of older women living alone. Journal of Aging and Health, 1(1), 35-49.

The relationship between community resources and mental health was examined in a community sample of 807 women 65 years and older. Results indicate that those in other living arrangements, but they are less likely to believe someone will be available to assist them for a long or short time or in an emergency. In addition, those living alone who have more neighbours and more children in the neighbourhood are more likely to believe short and long-term community care will be available if needed. (Journal abstract).

informal support networks, living alone, mental health, United States.

9. Mahalski, P. A., Jones, R., & Maxwell, G. M. (1988). The value of cat ownership to elderly women living alone. International Journal of Aging and Human Development, 27(4), 249-60.

A survey of elderly women was carried out to discover their attitudes towards pet cats. The women were living in publicly-owned pensioner housing in two New Zealand cities. In one city cats were allowed in the pensioners' housing and in the other city they were not. Attitudes towards cats were more positive in the city where cats were allowed, and more positive if pensioners owned a cat, or wished to own one. As positive attitudes towards cats outweighed negative ones, the City Authority which had prohibited cats reversed its policy. There was conflicting evidence about the role of cats in reducing feelings of loneliness. It appears that "loneliness" signifies the loss of many aspects of social interaction and that pets may substitute for only some of these interactions. (Journal abstract).

living alone, loneliness, New Zealand, pets.

10. Mutchler, J. E. (1990). Household composition among the nonmarried elderly: a comparison of black and white women. Research on Aging, 12(4), 487-506.

Differences in household composition between Black and White women have often been explained as resulting from differences in the resources of the two groups, particularly economic differences. A competing viewpoint holds that living arrangements reflect the cultural context within which life choices are negotiated. The purpose of this article is to assess the relative merits of these arguments. In this analysis, the extensive data available in the 1984 panel of the Survey of Income and Program Participation are employed. Indicators of health, kinship, income, and wealth are included in the analysis of living arrangements among Black and White women aged 55 and over. The results indicate that these resources are associated with choice of living arrangements among members of the two groups, but that Black and White women respond differently to levels of wealth and health when making decisions about household composition. (Journal abstract).

Blacks, economic status, health status, racial differences, single, United States, Whites.

11. Timaeus, I. (1986). Families and households of the elderly population: prospects for those approaching old age. <u>Ageing and Society</u>, 6(3), 271-293.

Long-term demographic trends that determine the absolute and relative size of the elderly population also underlie changes in the proportions of older people with living spouses and children. Such changes have important implications for residential isolation, the provision of care and the overall quality of life of the old. Demographic trends influencing the family situations of older people in Britain are discussed and detailed projections presented for women reaching age 60 in the period 1971-96. Increases in the propensity to marry and bear children after about 1940, together with declining mortality, mean that the proportions of older women that are married and that have children are likely to increase until the second decade of the next century. It is often assumed that demographic ageing will result in an increase in the number of elderly women living alone. However, the increase in the proportion of them that are married offsets this trend. (Journal abstract).

England, future projections, marital status.

12. Wolf, D. A. (1990). Household patterns of older women: some international comparisons. <u>Research on Aging</u>, <u>12</u>(4), 463-486.

Comparative analyses based on aggregate data have shown that the percentage of older women living alone has risen dramatically during recent decades, a pattern repeated in many European and North American countries. This article investigates the correlates of the decision to live alone, using individual-level data from five countries and a parallel analytic approach. The major categories of factors analyzed here are kin availability, financial resources, and disability and health status. Several common patterns of findings emerge for the group of countries considered: Larger kin networks and the presence of severe disabilities reduce the probability of living alone. Despite these similarities in individual-level correlates, there remain some differences across countries in the levels of single-person households, and these might be attributable to macrolevel forces such as housing and social welfare policies. (Journal abstract).

living alone, international.

9.3   Relocation

1. Cheung, H. Y., & Liaw, K.-L. (1987). Metropolitan out-migration of elderly females in Canada: characterization and explanation. <u>Environment and Planning A</u>, <u>19</u>(12), 1659-1671.

This paper contains an analysis of the 1971-1976 out-migration pattern of Canadian elderly females from the 23 Census Metropolitan Areas (CMAs). Migration is conceptualized as a three-level choice process. The major findings are as follows:

Elderly females are substantially less migratory than young females but are slightly more mobile than elderly males. In addition, the elderly females in the more recently settled western region tend to be more mobile than those in other regions.

Elderly migrants show substantially less preference for the metropolitan destinations than the young migrants; however, among elderly, females have stronger preference for metropolitan areas than males.

The destination choice pattern of metropolitan-bound out-migrants is less dispersed for the elderly than for the young. Among the older persons, in most CMAs, female migrants have a larger dispersion than male migrants.

With respect to metropolitan-bound elderly migrants from the CMAs, the probability of choosing a particular destination is positively related to population size, brightness, and housing growth, and negatively related to the logarithm of distance, cultural dissimilarity, coldness, and gross rent.

Environmental variables are more important than the housing variables in determining the destination choice pattern of the elderly migrants. (Journal abstract).

Canada, gender differences, migration.

2. Hartwigsen, G. (1987). Older widows and the transference of home. <u>International Journal of Aging and Human Development</u>, <u>25</u>(3), 195-207.

A relocation pattern, as indicated by a sample of older widows as they relocated from homes previously shared with their husbands to a metropolitan Phoenix life care facility, is presented. The suggested pattern is illuminated with quotes at each identified stage, revealing the individuals' inner feelings and motivations at those times. Characterized by relatively high income and educational levels, personal independence and prior careers, the sample is more representative of future women than those of their own age cohort. It is felt that these attributes were conducive to their apparently successful relocation. (Journal abstract).

decision making, United States.

3. Kalymun, M. (1985). The prevalence of factors influencing decisions among elderly women concerning household possessions during relocation. Journal of Housing for the Elderly, 3(3/4), 81-99.

This study identified the prevalence of factors influencing elderly women's decisions concerning their living room items during relocation. The 36 participants lived alone in identical one-bedroom apartments and had relocated within one year prior to the time this study was initiated. A structured focused interview consisting of open-ended questions was used to collect the data. Responses to open-ended questions were tape-recorded, transcribed, and content-analyzed. The prevalence of factors influencing decisions to eliminate, retain, and acquire furniture, accessories, and decorative items pertained to the usefulness of items, spatial dimensions, building regulations, family attachments, gifts, and the decorative compatibility of items with the living room. (Journal abstract).

decision making, possessions, United States.

4. Lee, J. A. B. (1989). An ecological of aging: Luisa's plight. Journal of Gerontological Social Work, 14(1/2), 175-190.

A transactional view of aging highlights the need for attachments throughout the life course. It emphasizes the environment, its supports, its nutritive and non-nutritive or noxious qualities as critical to our understanding of the aging process. This article discusses the aging process from an ecological perspective. It includes an exploration of theoretical developments and service delivery needs. It also provides a case example of a homeless 75-year-old woman to illustrate the dehumanizing gaps in our service delivery systems that make the consolidation of a sense of ego integrity an unlikely outcome. (Journal abstract).

homeless, service needs, United States.

5. McCracken, A. (1987). Emotional impact of possession loss. Journal of Gerontological Nursing, 13(2), 14-19.

The purpose of a research study, conducted in 1983 and 1984, was to develop and test a multivariate relocation model to explain more fully the location process of elderly women. This article reports on one of the 15 variables examined, possession change. (Journal abstract).

possessions, self-identity, United States.

6. Redfoot, D. L., & Back, K. W. (1988). The perceptual presence of the life course. International Journal of Aging and Human Development, 27(3), 155-170.

Despite the recent popularity of the term, the degree to which the "life course" as such is experienced in everyday life is not clear. Explorations of this question have not been very satisfying because they tend to either eliminate biographical time (as in survey research) or assume its presence (as with clinical, biographical, and life historical research) through the methods used. Our exploratory research used the meanings of personal possessions as an indirect measure of the temporal framing of experiences among forty women who had moved into facilities for elderly persons. We found considerable variation in the relative frequency and importance of biographical references in descriptions of those possessions, which challenges the concepts that have been used to relate experiences of temporality to the self and the methods that have been used to explore these experiences. (Journal abstract).

life span, possessions, self-identity, United States.

7. Voges, W., & Pongratz, H. (1988). Retirement and the lifestyle of older women. Ageing and Society, 8(1), 63-84.

Change of residence from a private household to a residential care facility, implying the relinquishing of household activities, is as critical a life event for older women as retirement from employment outside a home is for older men. This transition terminates many of the activities that had structured the older women's lives for decades, and implies modification of patterns of lifestyle. Based on interviews with female residents of residential care facilities in the Munich area, a close relative who had observed the transition and an employee at the facility, the impacts of the move on dimensions/aspects of lifestyle were analysed, as well as the success with which adaptation to the new setting was made. The positive relationship posited by the continuity hypothesis between continuity in lifestyle and contentment with life situation were generally upheld, although the compensation for a dimension of lifestyle disrupted by the transition by another dimension often occurred. (Journal abstract).

institutionalization, relocation stress, West Germany.

Chapter 10

Informal Support Networks

10.1   General

---

1. Antonucci, T. C., & Akiyama, H. (1987). An examination of sex differences in social support among older men and women. <u>Sex Roles,</u> <u>17</u>(11/12), 737-748.

This paper is designed to empirically investigate sex differences in social support. Several types of sex differences are examined, including quantity and quality of support, the relationship between quantitative and qualitative measures of support, the number and source of support on well-being. The data are taken from the Supports of the Elderly, a national survey of older people (Kahn and Antonucci, 1984). Included in the present study are 214 men and 166 women ranging in age from 50 to 95 who are married and have at least one child. The analyses reveal that women have larger networks and receive supports from multiple sources, while men tend to rely on their spouses exclusively. Men report greater satisfaction with marriage than women. Quantitative supports are more related to qualitative supports for women than for men. For both sexes, the quality of support rather than the quantity of support has significantly greater effects on well-being; both the quantity and quality of social support have a greater impact on the well-being of women compared to men. (Journal abstract).

gender differences, marital satisfaction, national study, psychological well-being, United States.

2. Aronson, J. (1990). Women's perspectives on informal care of the elderly: public ideology and personal experience of giving and receiving care. <u>Ageing and Society,</u> <u>10</u>(1), 61-84.

Drawing on a qualitative study of thirty-two women aged between 35 and 85, this paper links women's experiences of giving and receiving care in the informal sphere to their wider social and ideological context. While subjects subscribed to cultural assumptions about families, responsibility, gender and old age, they experienced awkwardness in translating them into their own lives. Younger women and women looking back on their middle years experienced contradiction between the cultural imperative to be unburdensome and independent and their wish for security. Feelings of guilt and shame were associated with not living up to these expectations. They rendered subjects' concerns, individual failings and stifled expression of their needs. To facilitate such expression and work towards social policies that enhance women over the life course, it will be necessary to envision alternative types of supportive services and to challenge the ideological barriers to their use that the subjects of this study had so acutely internalised. (Journal abstract).

Canada, lifespan.

3. Brody, E. M. (1986). Filial care of the elderly and changing roles of women (and men). <u>Journal of Geriatric Psychiatry,</u> <u>19</u>(2), 175-201.

This paper will summarize the developments that led to parent care becoming a common phenomenon and the research information on filial care of the elderly. Selected information from the Philadelphia Geriatric Center studies will then be presented to highlight the interaction of caregivers' inner processes with values, situational factors, and the service environment. Case vignettes will illustrate that interaction. The paper will conclude with some comments about the inner processes at work when parent care becomes necessary and about women's (and men's) changing roles in such situations. (Journal abstract).

United States.

4. Hatch, L. R. (1991). Informal support patterns of older African-American and White women. <u>Research on Aging,</u> <u>13</u>(2), 144-170.

In this study of informal support patterns of older African-American and White women, a particular focus is the examination of potential interaction effects between race and variables representing three major areas of life experience: family, paid work, and religious participation. Specifically, for four dependent variables measuring dimensions of giving and receiving help, attendance at religious social events was more important in predicting the informal support patterns of older African-American women than those of older White women. These results provide support for Taylor's recommendation than formal service providers use the organizational structure of churches to more effectively provide services to African-American elderly. Results from this study also raise questions concerning whether the hierarchy of primary care providers reported in the caregiving literature is applicable to members of different racial or ethnic groups. (Journal abstract).

Blacks, employment, family relationships, national study, racial differences, religion, United States, Whites.

---

5. Kaden, J., & McDaniel, S. A. (1990). Caregiving and care-receiving: a double bind for women in Canada's aging society. Journal of Women and Aging, 2(3), 3-26.

Many aspects of aging are women's issues. Yet research on aging has, until recently, focussed little attention on gender differences in the experience of growing old. Older women are more likely than older men to be poor, widowed, living alone in poor health, receiving assistance from both formal and informal supports, as well as being institutionalized in long-term care facilities. This secondary analysis of data from the 1982 "Survey of the Elderly in the Waterloo Region" attempts to address a gap in our knowledge concerning gender differences in the giving and receiving of social support in later years. Gender differences in (1) need for social support, (2) turning to formal assistance, (3) amount of formal assistance used, (4) amount of informal assistance received were examined using analysis of variance and logistic regression procedures. The profile of social support that emerged suggests both similarities and differences in the way elderly men and women experience the giving and receiving of social support. Older women in this sample were found to be disadvantaged in the areas of income, health, years lived alone, and loneliness, relative to older men. Low-income was related to formal service use for older women, but not for older men. Yet the older women in the sample were more likely to turn to or use formal services than the older men, turning instead to the informal, family support system. Older men were more likely to be receiving informal assistance from wives; older women were more likely to be receiving informal assistance from children, principally daughters.

The implications of these findings centre around the concern that population aging, viewed as an economic burden to society, has negative connotations for the elderly and their caregivers who may increasingly become dependent upon formal social support programs. These negative implications may disproportionately affect women who are predominant on both sides of the caregiving equation. (Journal abstract).

Canada, gender differences.

---

6. Miller, D. B. (1985). Women and long term nursing care. Women and Health, 10(2/3), 29-38.

Women have played a significant role in long term care: formerly as volunteer caregivers and presently as volunteer and paid caretakers, as professionals working in the field and increasingly as old, old residents in nursing homes. The goal in long term care is helping people to function to their maximum level; it is based on a philosophy of care not cure. Family-patient relationships influence quality in long term care facilities where nursing is the matrix of professional services. Respite care is designed to provide relief to family caretakers for time limited periods and long term home health care is a non-institutional alternative where the nursing home therapeutic regime is brought into the patients' own home. Whatever the model, the female influence is pervasive. (Journal abstract).

United States.

7. Stone, R., Cafferata, G. L., & Sangl J. (1987). Caregivers of the frail elderly: a national profile. <u>Gerontologist</u>, <u>27</u>(5), 616-626.

The 1982 National Long-Term Care Survey and Informal Caregivers Survey provided data for the first national estimates of informal caregivers to noninstitutionalized disabled elders. The descriptive profile confirmed previous research findings that informal caregivers are predominantly female, that a sizeable proportion is over age 65, and that a minority use formal services. There also was evidence for competing demands: 21% reported child care responsibilities, 9% indicated that they had quit their jobs, and 20% reported other work conflict. (Journal abstract).

national study, United States.

8. Vinokur, A. D., & Vinokur-Kaplan, D. (1990). "In sickness and in health": patterns of social support and undermining in older married couples. <u>Journal of Aging and Health</u>, 2(2), 215-241.

The effects of gender, age, marital satisfaction, and physical impairment on patterns of giving and receiving social support and social undermining (e.g., personal criticism) were examined in two samples totaling 431 older married couples. In the first sample, data were collected from husbands and their wives, half of whom were long-term breast cancer (BC) survivors and half who constituted an asymptomatic, matched control group. The second sample included data from husbands and their wives who had recently been diagnosed to have breast cancer. Wives reported giving more social support to their husbands than they felt they had received from them; and they reported giving more support than their husbands reported receiving from them, except for the group of recently diagnosed BC. Advanced age was correlated with husbands' reports of receiving more social support, and in the two breast cancer groups, of also giving more social support and engaging in less social undermining. It was also found that among the women in the asymptomatic control group, those who were more physically impaired reported both giving and receiving less social support, and this was corroborated by husbands' reports. In contrast, there were no associations between wives' degree of impairment and social support in the breast cancer groups. The differential effects were hypothesized to result from the husbands' causally attributing their wives' impairment and difficulties to internal characterological factors versus to external ones beyond their control (i.e., the BC disease). (Journal abstract).

breast cancer, marriage, United States.

10.2   Caregivers

1. Barusch, A. S., & Spaid, W. M. (1989). Gender differences in caregivers: why do wives report greater burden? Gerontologist, 29(5), 667-676.

Women typically report greater burden associated with caregiving than do men. We used data from interviews with 131 older spouse caregivers to explore potential explanations for this difference. A linear regression model explained 35% of the varience in caregiver burden. The patient's cognitive and behavioural difficulties emerged as the most important predictor of burden, followed by caregiver age, unpleasant social contacts, caregiver sex, and overall coping effectiveness. Findings suggest that age differences in male and female caregivers contribute to the observed differences in burden. (Journal abstract).

age differences, caregiver burden, gender differences, United States.

2. Robinson, K. (1986). Older women and care giving. Nursing Success Today, 3(10), 28-33.

Older women as care givers has been demonstrated to be an area with rich potential for nursing in the future. Implications for social policy, as well as focus as a priority health concern, have been discussed. Other disciplines are also documenting the role of nursing and care giving. A focus on older women as care givers is an area of rich potential and one to which nursing can make great contributions in solving pressing problems of our present healthcare system. (Journal abstract).

social policy, United States.

3. Staight, P. R., & Harvey, S. M. (1990). Caregiver burden: a comparison between elderly women as primary and secondary caregivers for their spouses. <u>Journal of Gerontological Social Work</u>, <u>15</u>(1/2), 89-104.

The overall purpose of this research was to examine the burdens of caregiving on elderly women who serve as primary and secondary caregivers for their impaired spouses. Fifty women 60 years and older identified as spousal caregivers participated in an in-person structured interview. Data were analyzed to compare primary caregivers (caregivers living with their spouses) and secondary caregivers (caregivers of institutionalized spouses) on the following factors: loneliness, depression, time contraints, perceived health status, financial status and perceived life satisfaction.

Findings suggest that both groups of women are equally susceptible to the burdens inherent in caregiving. Time contrainsts were identified as the one major difference between caregiving groups. In addition, the results indicate the spousal caregivers, both primary and secondary, are an at-risk population and are especially vulnerable to loneliness, mild depression, financial worries and low life satisfaction. (Journal abstract).

caregiver burden, marriage, United States.

10.3   Care Recipients

---

1. Abel, E. K. (1986). Adult daughters and care for the elderly. <u>Feminist Studies</u>, <u>12</u>(3), 479-497.

This article addresses women's traditional roles are caregivers. Three issues are presented. First, this article examines the amount and nature of informal care women provide for aging parents and the costs they incur as a result. Second, this article describes women's special role in parental caregiving; for exampple, the difficulties that arise in mother-daughter relationships when the care giver-care receiver roles are reversed. And third, this article concludes with a discussion on dilemmas feminists face in framing appropriate policies for the care of the frail elderly. (Author abstract).

caregiver burden, caregivers, policy, United States.

2. Abel, E. K. (1989). Family care of the frail elderly: framing an agenda for change. <u>Women's Studies Quarterly</u>, <u>17</u>(1/2), 75-86.

This article describes family caregiving; the effect of gender, class and race on family caregiving experiences. As well, the negative consequences of caregiving are described, for example the financial and emotional impact of caregiving. And finally, this article describes some solutions including financial compensation, home health care services, training and counseling programs, and support groups. (Author abstract).

caregiver burden, caregivers, gender differences, racial differences, United States.

3. Abel, E. K. (1990). Informal care for the disabled elderly: a critique of recent literature. <u>Research on Aging</u>, <u>12</u>(2), 139-157.

Most studies of informal care for the disabled elderly are based on structured interviews, which are analyzed statistically, and they focus on two issues that lend themselves to quantification - the tasks caregivers perform and the stress they experience. The focus on chores restricts researchers' understanding of the experience of caregivers. Task-oriented research may be particularly inappropriate for an activity dominated by women. Because stress has critical implications for public health, researchers have attempted to identify caregivers most at risk of stress and to evaluate interventions. Although these studies have provided useful information for practioners, the preoccupation with stress compels researchers to miss essential aspects of the caregiving experience and restricts the range of policy recommendations. Researchers should employ qualitative, as well as quantitative, methodologies and should incorporate the theoretical insights of a wide range of disciplines. Because scholars in the field of women's studies have directed considerable attention to personal relationships and caregiving issues, their writings may be especially useful for charting an agenda for research. (Journal abstract).

caregiver burden, caregivers, research methodology, United States.

4. Aronson, J. (1990). Old women's experiences of needing care: choice and compulsion? <u>Canadian Journal on Aging</u>, 9(3), 234-247.

Drawing on a qualitative study of women as givers and receivers of care, this paper explores older women's experiences of needing care. Old women find themselves in a social context in which government services are kept in the background and families are generally regarded as the proper locus of assistance to old people. Respondents described contradictions between needing support and security and wanting to adhere to cultural values of independence and self-sufficiency. Their low expectations of public services and sense of marginality in their families exacerbated these dilemmas. The fallacy of understanding old women's conduct in this contrained context as the exercise of choice is elaborated, and attention is given to ways of fostering the conditions in which elderly women can shape the kinds of supportive environments they would like to see in the future. (Journal abstract).

Canada.

5. Brody, E. M., Kleban, M. H., Johnsen, P. T., Hoffman, C., & Schoonover, C. B. (1987). Work status and parent care: a comparison of four groups of women. Gerontologist, 27(2), 201-208.

Four groups of parent caring daughters were compared. Two groups were nonworkers: traditional homemakers and those who had quit jobs to help their mothers. Two groups were workers: the "conflicted," who had reduced their working hours or considered quitting and those who had not. The conflicted workers and women who had quit work had the most impaired mothers and more of them had experienced lifestyle disruptions and caregiving strain. Both groups of workers were more career-oriented; both groups of nonworkers held more traditional views of women's roles. (Journal abstract).

caregiver burden, caregivers, United States, widowed.

6. Gibeau, J. L., & Anastas, J. W. (1989). Breadwinners and caregivers: interviews with working women. Journal of Gerontological Social Work, 14(1/2), 19-40.

Until recently, studies of family caregivers for the elderly have not considered the work lives of caregivers. Based on interviews with 77 women who were working full-time while caring for an elderly family member, this study examined the strains experienced and supports needed to balance work and family responsibilities. One in 5 of the women interviewed had considered quitting work because of caregiving. The functioning of the elderly family member, the amount of caregiving work performed, and selected job factors affected absenteeism and the likelihood that a woman might consider quitting her job. Implications for the development of employee benefits to assist family caregivers are discussed. (Journal abstract).

caregivers, United States.

7. Goodman, C. C. (1990). The caregiving roles of asian American women. Journal of Women and Aging, 2(1), 109-120.

Asian Americans are the fastest growing subgroup of elderly in the United States. When Alzheimer's Disease strikes Asian American families, women are usually the caregivers. In depth interviews with Asian American caregivers and professionals reveal common themes of family centrality, balance of multiple obligations, and norms of reciprocity and competence. (Journal abstract).

caregivers, Chinese, dementia, Japanese, United States.

8. Gottlieb, B. H. (1989). A contextual perspective on stress in family care of the elderly. Canadian Psychology, 30(3), 596-607.

Responsibility for the care and support of the elderly is gender defined, largely assumed by wives and by female relatives of the succeeding generation. To understand the stress process that unfolds at the time of the transition to the caregiving role and over its course, a conceptual framework is presented which highlights several personal and contextual variables mediating the relationship between the objective and subjective burdens of intergenerational caregiving. Specifically, the framework highlights four sets of variables which mediate the impact of the caregiver's role on her well-being: the past and present quality of her relationship with the elderly recipient of care; the role's reverberations on other life spheres; the support available from the caregiver's social ecology; and a set of three social psychological variables colouring her reactions to the caregiving relationship. (Journal abstract).

Canada, caregiver burden, caregivers.

9. Greene, R. W., & Feld, S. (1989). Social support coverage and the well-being of elderly widows and married women. Journal of Family Issues, 10(1), 33-51.

The relationship between social support coverage and well-being was examined in four subgroups from a national sample of women ages 50 and older: first married (N=151), widows (N=144), widows within the last five years (n=60), and widows for longer than five years (n=84). The index of support coverage represented how many of six functions were carried out by at least one supporter. Two hypotheses were tested: (1) that support coverage is associated with well-being in all subgroups, and (2) that social support is more strongly associated with well-being in the subgroups experiencing higher stress, that is, widows more than married women and recent widows more than long-term ones. The hypotheses were not supported. Instead, the relationships between social support and well-being were positive in some groups and negative in others. The importance of considering the causal directions of links between social support and well-being and the possible negative consequences of receiving social support are discussed. (Journal abstract).

married, United States, well-being, widowed.

10. Hatch, L. R. (1990). Effects of work and family on women's later life resources. <u>Research on Aging</u>, <u>12</u>(3), 311-338.

This article reviews the current state of knowledge on how women's work and family experiences throughout the life course influence their economic and social resources. The article draws together literature on topics that usually have been treated as separate and distinct from one another. Although researchers increasingly are examining linkages between the "world of work" and the "world of family," most studies focus on one or the other. A broader picture is required to understand the separate and combined influences of work and family experiences on later-life resources. (Journal abstract).

economic status, employment, family relationships, United States.

11. Krause, N., & Keith, V. (1989). Gender differences in social support among older adults. <u>Sex Roles: A Journal of Research</u>, 21(9/10), 609-628.

The purpose of this study was to determine whether exposure to life stress can help explain gender differences in the use of social support. Findings from a longitudinal study suggest that as the number of stressful life events increase, elderly men and women are equally likely to become more involved in their social network, while gender differences emerge only in response to chronic finanical strain. Further analysis indicates that elderly women are more likely than elderly men to report that the support they received increased their feelings of personal control. (Journal abstract).

gender differences, longitudinal study, stress, United States.

12. Novero Blust, E. P., & Scheidt, R. J. (1988). Perceptions of filial responsibility by elderly filipino widows and their primary caregivers. <u>International Journal of Aging and Human Development</u>, <u>26</u>(2), 91-106.

This study assessed perceptions of filial responsibility among forty older Filipino mothers and their primary caregiver daughters from two urban and two rural barangays in the town Los Banos (39 miles southeast of Manila). Using parallel standard structured interview measures, perceptions of filial expectations and filial behaviors were gathered across five categories of parental support; financial and material aid; personal care; service provision; respect; and warmth and affection. Intragenerational comparisons (analyses of variance) showed that widows' reports of actual amount of support received significantly exceeded their expectations for most forms of aid. In contrast, daughters' expectations for level of parental support exceeded their behaviors, but only for the more instrumental forms of aid. Intergenerational comparisons (t-test analyses) revealed that daughters held reliably higher filial expectations for almost all forms of support than did their mothers. Comparisons of reports of actual support showed intergenerational consensus on the whole. Implications of these data for research and intervention in this area are discussed. (Journal abstract).

caregivers, Philippines, widowed.

13. O'Bryant, S. (1985). Neighbors' support of older widows who live alone in their own homes. Gerontologist, 25(3), 305-310.

Recent older widows who live alone are a vulnerable group that needs both social and instrumental support. This study compared the neighbour support given to 226 widows who were categorized into three groups - those who had one or more children in the same city, those who had children who resided elsewhere, and those who were childless. Multivariate analyses revealed differences among these groups on various measures of neighbour support. Results are discussed among these groups on various measures of neighbor support. Results are discussed in terms of the hierarchical-compensatory and task-specific models of informal support along with widow's social activity patterns, work histories, and neighbor attitudes. (Journal abstract).

adult children, childless, United States, widowed.

14. O'Bryant, S. L. (1988). Self-differentiated assistance in older widow's support systems. Sex Roles, 19(1/2), 91-106.

It was proposed that today's older women, who are a low-fertility cohort, have deficiencies in their informal support systems due to small families, and consequently, the absence of either sons or daughters in those families. Respondents (N=225) were recent widows, ages 60-89, who resided in a large metropolitan area in the Midwest. Each widow was personally interviewed regarding 10 areas of support that are provided by adult children, other kin, or friends/neighbors. Findings indicated significant differences in the receipt of traditionally male types of support for widows with sons, as compared to those without sons (p<.01), but no differences in the receipt of traditionally female types of support for widows without daughters. In addition, the extent to which persons other than children perform sex-differentiated types of support was explored. Directions for future research are suggested. (Journal abstract).

gender differences, United States, widowed.

15. O'Bryant, S. L., & Morgan, L. A. (1990). Recent widow's kin support and orientations to self-sufficiency. Gerontologist, 30(3), 391-398.

This paper examines two issues: the role of the adult child network in task support to widows, and whether widow's attitudes toward independence result in lower levels of task support. Data on recently widowed women suggest that many are quite self-sufficient; however, in those areas where support is needed, they largely rely on children. Widows' past experiences and attitudes toward independence influence the amount of overall help they receive, whereas income, number of children, and perceived willingness of children to help affect the proportion of help that comes from children. (Journal abstract).

United States, widowed.

16. Pratt, C. C., Jones, L. L., Shin, H. Y., & Walker, A. J. (1989). Autonomy and decision making between single women and their caregiving daughters. Gerontologist, 29(6), 792-797.

We examined perceptions of decisional autonomy and decision-making processes among 64 elderly, single mothers and their caregiving daughters. Mothers were highly involved in decisions affecting their lives, ranging from daily care to major health decisions; daughters were particularly influential over major health, financial and housing decisions. Mothers' level of personal care dependency was negatively associated with both mothers' and daughters' confidence in the mothers' decision-making abilities. (Journal abstract).

caregivers, decision making, single, United States.

17. Sherman, S. R., Ward, R. A., & LaGory, M. (1988). Women as caregivers of the elderly: instrumental and expressive support. Social Work, 33(2), 164-167.

This study investigates two types of social support among elderly men and women: 1) instrumental support defined as tangible aid and service referral, 2) expressive support defined as role models and confidents who provide a form of sharing. A sample of 1185 well elderly were interviewed. Social support was analysed by elderly and caregivers' age and gender. In brief, results indicate that women are central to instrumental and expressive support for both elderly men and women. Results are discussed in terms of social work implications. (Author abstract).

age differences, caregivers, gender differences, United States.

18. Spitze, G., & Logan, J. (1989). Gender differences in family support: is there a payoff? Gerontologist, 29(1), 108-113.

National data for respondents over age 65 revealed that, although women are less likely to be living with a spouse, living arrangements of unmarried women and men are similar. Women live closer to children, receive more phone calls, have marginally more contact but do not receive more mail. Women's receipt of more informal assistance is largely explained by greater need levels, particularly for the unmarried. These findings are discussed in relation to women's roles as family caretaker and kinkeeper at earlier life cycle stages. (Journal abstract).

gender differences, living arrangments, national study, United States.

19. Storm, C., Storm, T., & Strike-Schurman, J. (1985). Obligations for care: beliefs in a small canadian town. Canadian Journal of Aging, 4(2), 75-85.

A combined questionnaire and interview procedure was used to explore the perceptions and obligations to assist a frail old person with physical care, financial aid, and psychological support. Subjects for the interview were 80 women aged 18-25, 30-45, 50-65, and 65-85 years, all residents of a small town in Maritime Canada. The questionnaire was omitted in the case of the oldest group. The results showed that children were perceived to have a strong obligation to assist, substantially reduced, however, by circumstances such as geographical distance or financial exigency. The obligation of government was also strong for all but psychological needs. Siblings, friends, and the church were perceived to be common sources of assistance, particularly psychological, but with significantly less moral obligation compared to other sources. Differences between age groups were small. The interviews, however, showed the youngest group to be less realistic and more absolute about children's responsibilities for old people than were old people for themselves. Similarly, the oldest subjects were more likely than younger subjects to stress the responsibility of the old person for his/her own welfare. (Journal abstract).

age diferences, Canada.

20. Thompson, J. (1989). The elderly and their informal social networks. Canadian
Journal on Aging, **8(4), 319-332.**

A sample of 334 people aged 56 and over living in the Capital Regional District of B.C.
(Greater Victoria) were interviewed about their supportive social network. Four social
supportive roles were investigated: caretaker, helper, confidant, and advisor.

Most of the sample had network members to fulfill these roles, however, in the lives of
about one-fifth of the respondents, support in one or more of these areas was not available.
Although most of the respondents in excellent or good health felt no need for more people
in certain supportive roles, more people with fair or poor health expressed a need for more
people in their supportive networks.

This research supports earlier findings about the vulnerability of women who are widowed
and over 74 years old. They are the group most in need of socially supportive networks.
(Journal abstract).

Canada, gender differences.

21. Thompson, M. G., & Heller, K. (1990). Facets of support related to well-being:
quantitative social isolation and perceived family support in a sample of elderly
women. Psychology and Aging, **5(4), 535-544.**

The purpose of this study was to examine the independent and interactive relationships of
measures of network embeddedness and perceived social support with mental and physical
health measures from responses of a sample of 271 community-dwelling elderly women.
Quantitative social isolation was measured as the co-occurence of low network
embeddedness with family and with friends. There was a threshold effect such that
quantitatively isolated participants had poorer psychological well-being and functional
health than did nonisolated participants. This effect was independent of perceived support
levels. The pattern was different for perceived social support. Elderly women with low
perceived family support had poorer psychological well-being regardless of perceived
support from friends or network embeddedness. Implications are discussed for several
unanswered questions in the social support literature, including possible interventions for
the quantitatively isolated and for those with low levels of perceived support. (Journal
abstract).

physical health, psychological well-being, United States.

22. Walker, A. J., & Allen, K. R. (1991). Relationships between caregiving daughters and their elderly mothers. <u>Gerontologist</u>, <u>31</u>(3), 389-396.

In this qualitative study of 29 pairs of widowed mothers and their caregiving daughters, we employ social exchange theroy to identify three relationship types: intrinsic (45%), ambivalent (34%), and conflicted (21%). These types differ in the extent to which the women receive rewards from interacting with their partner, experience costs in their interaction, handle conflicts that arise in their relationships, and express feelings of concern for each other. They also differ in that daughters in intrinsic pairs have fewer children and shorter caregiving histories than daughters in ambivalent or conflicted pairs. (Journal abstract).

daughters, relationship satisfaction, United States.

23. Walker, A. J., & Pratt, C. C. (1991). Daughters' help to mothers: intergenerational aid versus caregiving. <u>Journal of Marriage and the Family</u>, <u>53</u>(1), 3-12.

Following the convoy model (Kahn and Antonucci, 1980), this study compares aid given by adult daughters to self-sufficient elderly mothers (n=43) with that given by adult daughters to elderly mothers who are dependent for aid (n=139). While daughters with dependent mothers reported more time spent in aid-giving, daughters with self-sufficient mothers gave aid in the same categories that daughters with dependent mothers did. Daughters did not differ on money spent giving aid. The study suggests that caregiving is an intensification of a preexisting pattern of aid-giving that is evident by female intergenerational relationships. (Journal abstract).

intergenerational relationships, United States.

24. Wister, A. V., & Strain, L. (1986). Social support and well-being: a comparison of older widows and widowers. <u>Canadian Journal on Aging</u>, 5(3), 205-220.

This paper investigates several dimensions of the informal support network and well-being among widows and widowers. Using subsets of two random samples of older people living in Winnipeg. Manitoba collected in 1980, one group who were using home care services and another who were not, widowed men and women are contrasted on a number of support network variables. While significant differences arise in length of widowhood, functional ability and some components of the support network, no gender differences are found for the measures of well-being for either sample, even after introducing control variables. Implications for future research and practice are discussed. (Journal abstract).

Canada, gender differences, widowed.

Chapter 11

Physical Health and Illness

11.1   General

---

1. Lempert, L. B. (1986). Women's health from a woman's point of view: a review of the literature. <u>Health Care for Women International</u>, 7(3), 255-275.

This review of the literature on current women's health problems clarifies the conditions and updates the current understanding of women's health within the context of medical and social research. The negative health effects of traditional socialization and women's secondary status within the society is confirmed. The conditions of women's health are presented through chronological life stages: prepubescence, puberty, young womanhood, reproduction, middle age, and aging. Also discussed are those women's health problems reflecting both internal and external abuse. (Journal abstract).

lifespan, review, United States.

2. Leslie, L. A., & Swider, S. M. (1986). Changing factors and changing needs in women's health care. <u>Nursing Clinics of North America</u>, 21(1), 111-123.

During the last few decades, the roles of women in society have undergone tremendous changes. These changes have occurred in the occupational realm and in the home and have far-reaching consequences for women's health. In addition, improvements and modifications in health care technology and delivery have affected the general health status of women. These changes are reflected in the health, social, and economic status indicators available from a variety of sources. (Journal abstract).

economic status, health status, social relationships, United States.

3. Older Women's League. (1988). The picture of health for midlife and older women in America. <u>Women and Health</u>, 14(3/4), 53-74.

This report overviews the major health problems of middle aged and older women and health care access issues. The relationship of labor force involvement to health status and insurance benefits is considered. Other payment sources such as Medicaid and Medicare

are critiqued for their failure to finance needed prevention and other services. (Journal abstract).

cancer, dementia, cardiovascular disease, gender differences, long term care, Medicare, osteoporosis, review, United States.

4. Pearson, B. P., & Beck, C. M. (1989). Physical health of elderly women. <u>Journal of Women and Aging</u>, 1(1/2/3), 149-174.

With the many advances of medical science in reducing mortality from major diseases in America, women are experiencing a "mixed blessing." While there is rejoicing at the prospect of a longer life, there is fear that they will experience major health problems with which they will be unable to cope. Health is a major determinant of the quality of life and is intricately connected to the social, environmental, and economic aspects of the lives of elderly women, including a historical overview of health concerns of elderly women, including a historical overview of health care advances for the elderly, physical changes normally occurring with the aging process, and future projections concerning the health and services needed to promote the highest quality of life for elderly females in our society. (Journal abstract).

cancer, cardiovascular disease, musculoskeletal disorders, review, sensory disorders, United States.

11.2 Breast Cancer

---

1. Akhter, S. S., Allan, S. G., Rodger, A., Chetty, U. D. I., Smyth, J. F., & Leonard, R. C. F. (1991). A 10-year experience of tamoxifen as primary treatment of breast cancer in 100 elderly and frail patients. <u>European Journal of Surgical Oncology</u>, <u>17</u>, 30-35.

Between 1977 and 1983 100 elderly women (median 76.3 years) with breast cancer were treated with tamoxifen as primary therapy. The median follow-up is 59 months. Sixty-eight responded (40 CR and 28 PR) with median response durations of 47 months and 26 months respectively. Twenty-two patients had disease stabilization for a median of 15.5 months and 10 had progressive disease. The median time to best response was 13.5 weeks for patients achieving CR and 14 weeks for those with PR. Estrogen receptor values were obtained in 37 patients of which two patients had no ER detectable. Sixty-seven percent of

ER-unknown patients responded compared with 74% of ER-rich. Likelihood of response did not appear to depend upon T-stage or age. Survival was better than that of an unmatched historical group treated with surgery/radiotherapy and compares favourably with recent reports. Although 35% have died of breast cancer, 25% died of other causes and 22% remained free of recurrence at the time of reporting or death. Only 11% underwent subsequent mastectomy/ lumpectomy and the most frequent subsequent treatments were radiotherapy to the breast (32%) and further hormonal therapies (40%). Tamoxifen is a practical primary therapy of breast cancer in the elderly and frail women obviating the need for surgery in a high proportion of cases. (Journal abstract).

mortality, Scotland, treatment.

2. Chu, J., Diehr, P., Feigl, P., Glaefke, G., Begg, C., Glicksman, A., & Ford, L. (1987). The effect of age on the care of women with breast cancer in community hospital. <u>Journals of Gerontology</u>, 42(2), 185-190.

We studied the process of care received by 1,680 female cancer patients treated in 17 community hospitals. The probability of receiving various diagnostic, consultation, therapy, or rehabilitation services was almost significantly associated with patient age or more disease stages. Most often there was a linear trend for older patients to receive fewer services (e.g. biopsies prior to definitive treatment, number of lymph modes examined, chemotherapy, radiation therapy) but other age patterns also were found. Age was not significantly associated with clinical staging or estrogen receptors. (Journal abstract).

age differences, health care, United States.

3. Dupont, W. D., & Page, D. L. (1991). Menopausal estrogen replacement therapy and breast cancer. <u>Archives of Internal Medicine</u>, 151(1), 67-72.

We conducted a meta-analysis of the literature concerning breast cancer and estrogen replacement therapy. The overall relative risk of breast cancer associated with this therapy was 1.07. However, the variation of the estimated risks among the studies was far greater than could plausibly be explained by chance alone. To explain this variation, we looked at the effects of type, duration, and dosage of treatment. Overall, women who took 0.625 mg/d or less of conjugated estrogens had a risk of breast cancer that was 1.08 times that of women who did not receive this therapy (95% confidence interval [CI], 0.96 to 1.2). The relative risks from these individual studies of low dosage therapy did not differ significantly from each other. Women who took 1.25 mg/d or more of conjugated estrogens had a breast cancer risk of 2.0 or less in all studies. However, the variation in observed risks at the higher dosage was significant. This implies that other risk factors varied among these studies, making it difficult to estimate the overall risk associated with this dosage. The relative risk of breast cancer associated with estrogen replacement therapy among women with a history of benign breast disease was 1.16 (95% CI, 0.89 to 1.5). The combined results from multiple studies provide strong evidence that menopausal therapy consisting of 0.625 mg/d or less of conjugated estrogens does not increase breast cancer risk. (Journal abstract).

therapy, United States.

4. Henderson, B. E., Paganini-Hill, A., & Ross, R. K. (1991). Decreased mortality in users of estrogen replacement therapy. Archives of Internal Medicine, 151(1), 75-78.

In a retrospective study of 8881 postmenopausal female residents of a retirement community in southern California, we evaluated in detail the relationship between estrogen use and overall mortality. After 7 1/2 years of follow-up, there had been 1447 deaths. Women with a history of estrogen use had 20% lower age-adjusted, all-cause mortality than lifetime nonusers (95% confidence interval, 0.70 to 0.87). Mortality decreased with increasing duration of use and was lower among current users than among women who used estrogens only in the distant past. Current users with more than 15 years of estrogen use had a 40% reduction in their overall mortality. Among oral estrogen users, relative risk of death could not be distinguished by specific dosages of the oral estrogen taken for the longest time. Women who had used estrogen replacement therapy had a reduced mortality from all categories of acute and chronic arteriosclerotic disease and cerebrovascular disease. This group of women had a reduced mortality from cancer, although this reduction was not statistically significant. The mortality from all remaining causes combined was the same in estrogen users and lifetime nonusers. (Journal abstract).

mortality, therapy, United States.

5. Satariano, W. A., Ragheb, N. E., Branch, L. G., & Swanson, G. M. (1990). Difficulties in physical functioning reported by middle-aged and elderly women with breast cancer: a case-control comparison. Journals of Gerontology, 45(1), M3-M11.

Levels of physical functioning reported by women aged 55 to 84 with incident breast cancer were compared to those reported by women of the same age without the disease. A total of 422 breast cancer patients, identified through the Metropolitan Detroit Cancer Surveillance System, were interviewed 3 and 12 months after diagnosis. Interviews with 478 controls of the same age, identified through telephone random-digit dialing, were conducted twice during the same time period. At 3 months, patients aged 55-64 and 65-74 reported greater difficulty than controls in completing tasks requiring upper-body strength. Little difference was shown between cases and controls aged 75 to 84. After one year, patients aged 65-74 still reported higher than expected levels of difficulty in light lifting as well as pushing and lifting heavy objects. Among cases aged 55-64, only pushing and lifting heavy objects remained problematic. Estimates of the prevalence of physical difficulty will be useful in planning future breast cancer treatment and rehabilitation services. (Journal abstract).

physical functioning, United States.

11.3   Dementia

1. Brayne, C., & Calloway, P. (1989). Epidemiological study of dementia in a rural population of elderly women. British Journal of Psychiatry, 155, 214-219.

A study of 365 women aged 70-79 in a rural community was carried out using the Cambridge Examination of Mental Disorders in the Elderly (CAMDEX). Prevalence rates of dementia are reported by severity for the 70-74 and 75-79 age groups. Differential diagnosis was made according to CAMDEX guidelines. Senile dementia of Alzheimer type accounted for half the dementia cases. The prevalence rates overall did not differ from those reported in other recent studies, but the rates for levels greater than mild/moderate were lower, despite the inclusion of subjects in institutions. (Journal abstract).

Alzheimer's disease, England, rural community.

2. Kawai, M. J., Miyamoto, M., & Miyamoto, K. (1990). Five elderly dementia patients who played with dolls. Journal of Women and Aging, 2(1), 99-107.

It is said that the study of Psychopathology in the elderly ultimately led to the understanding of normal ageing. In our paper, the authors interest focused on the attitudes of demented patients toward dolls and tried to understand the meaning of those attitudes. In this paper, dolls were regarded as playing a role to reduce or eliminate existence anxiety. The authors pointed out the importance of understanding the way elderly dementia patients insist on the existence of themselves in the background of attitudes which are commonly superficially regarded as childish phenomena. (Journal abstract).

Alzheimer's disease, Japan.

3. Mant, A., Saunders, N. A., Eyland, A. E., Pond, C. D., Chancellor, A. H., & Webster, I. W. (1988). Sleep-related respiratory disturbance and dementia in elderly females. Journals of Gerontology, 43(5), M140-M144.

Sleep-related respiratory disturbance was studied with a microprocessor-based portable monitoring system in female residents of a retirement village aged > or = 75 years. Comparisons were made between 29 demented subjects Mini-Mental State Examination Score (MMSE) <21 and 48 controls (MMSE>25). Respiratory disturbance index (RDI, the number of apnea and hyponea/hour of total sleep time) was higher in the demented subjects: mean RDI (+/-SD) 18.5 vs 7.3 +/- 10.8, p=.004. The number of minutes per hour of sleep spent with disturbed breathing was greater in demented subjects than in controls (p=.01). These differences between demented subjects and controls persisted after adjustment for age and relevant medical history. Other possible confounders, namely body mass index and use of sedatives, were not significant. We conclude that respiratory disturbance during sleep is more prevalent in elderly demented female than in controls. (Journal abstract).

respiration, sleep, United States.

11.4   Exercise

---

1. Foster, V. L., Hume, G. J. E., Byrnes, W. C., Dickinson, A. L., & Chatfield, S. J. (1989). Endurance training for elderly women: moderate vs low intensity. Journals of Gerontology, 44(6), M184-M188.

This investigation evaluated the efficacy of training at moderate-60% Maximal Heart Rate Reserve, HRRmax (MOD) and low-40% HRRmax (LOW) intensities in a population of older American women (N = 16, mean age = 78.4 years). Prior to and immediately following a 10-week training program consisting of exercising at the prescribed heart-rate intensity with a caloric expenditure of 100 calories, the following measurements were performed: Maximal oxygen consumption (VO2 max). Maximal Lactate Production (HLAmax), Maximal Heart Rate (HRmax). Maximal Workstage (WSmax), Total Cholesterol (TOTC), High Density Lipoprotein Cholesterol (HDLC), and Rate Pressure Product Max (RPPmax). Significant differences, p < .05 were noted pre- to post-training for measures of VO2max, whether expressed in 1-min 1 or ml kg1 min1, and WSmax. No statistical differences existed between the groups pre- or post-training for these measures. The results suggest that the low-intensity exercise prescription provides an adequate training stimulus for older women who have been sedentary and who might be at higher risk for cardiac or musculoskeletal injury, particularly at the initiation of an exercise program. (Journal abstract).

training program, United States.

2. Hopkins, D. R., Murrah, B., Hoeger, W. W. K., & Rhodes, R. C. (1990). Effect of low-impact aerobic on the functional fitness of elderly women. Gerontologist, 30(2), 189-192.

To determine the effect of low-impact aerobic dance on sedentary elderly women (N=53) functional fitness was measured by items from the proposed American Alliance of Health, Physical Education, Recreation, and Dance (AAHPERD) fitness test for older adults. After 12-weeks of low-impact aerobic dance, the group improved significantly on all functional fitness components except motor control/coordination, including cardiorespiratory endurance, strength/endurance, body agility, flexibility, body fat, and balance. (Journal abstract).

physical fitness, United States.

3. Kolanowski, A. M., & Gunter, L. M. (1988). Do retired career women exercise? Geriatric Nursing, 9(6), 350-352.

This study examined health, morale and exercise in 43 retired career women. Results indicate that exercise did not play a role in the health status or morale of this group. (Author abstract).

health status, United States.

4. O'Brien, S. J., & Vertinsky, P. A. (1990). Elderly women, exercise and healthy aging. Journal of Women and Aging, 2(3), 41-65.

The persistent view of old age as a time for accepting an inevitable decline in health and vigour continues to shape the exercise patterns of elderly women, despite rapidly accumulating evidence that what has formerly been perceived as "normal aging" is, in part, the deficit of disuse and inactivity. While the risks associated with increased physical activity are not to be overlooked, more attention is being given to the overwhelming benefits of adequate exercise for the elderly, both in terms of short and long-term contributions to enhanced physical, social and emotional well-being. Conditioned to believe that being old and female is a sort of "double jeopardy" requiring restraint in physical activity, elderly women have been slow to respond to the new view of exercise as a crucial part of healthy aging. So long as elderly women do not readily perceive the advantages to be accrued from regular exercise patterns and do not believe they are capable of vigourous physical activity, government policies and plans to disseminate information about health and exercise are unlikely to generate large scale action toward health promotion. (Journal abstract).

health promotion, physical activity, United States, well-being.

5. O'Brien, S., & Vertinsky, P. A. (1991). **Unfit survivors: exercise as a resource for aging women.** Gerontologist, 31(3), 347-357.

Some researchers have suggested that about 50% of aging decline is preventable through improved life-style habits such as participation in regular exercise, yet exercise as a resource for healthier survival is being ignored by many aging women. Though recent research findings highlight regular physical activity as a potent factor in combatting hypokenesis (the disease of inactivity), numerous real and perceived barriers to exercise stand between the older women and her ability to achieve a better quality of life. Among strategies that have been developed to overcome these barriers are social empowerment initiatives that may encourage women to combat disability by engaging in regular exercise. (Journal abstract).

health promotion, longevity, United States.

6. Rikli, R., & Busch, S. (1986). **Motor performance of women as a function of age and physical activity level.** Journals of Gerontology, 41(5), 645-649.

In Study 1, simple and choice reaction time, balance, sit and reach flexibility, shoulder flexibility, and grip strength of older active women were compared with older inactive women, and active and inactive younger women. Except for grip strength, cores of older active women on all measures were significantly better than older inactive women, and much more like those of the younger women. In Study 2, scores of avid women golfers were compared with the older active and inactive women from Study 1. On all variables, the scores of golfers were significantly better than those of the older inactive women, but not significantly different from the older active women. Findings were consistent with previous research on men, indicating that motor performance tends to be more highly related to lifelong physical activity level than to age. (Journal abstract).

age differences, cognitive processing, physical activity, United States.

7. Weiss, C. R., & Jamieson, N. R. (1987). Affective aspects of an age-integrated water exercise program. <u>Gerontologist</u>, <u>27</u>(4), 430-433.

Queried were 88 female participants (90.7%) of a community-based age-integrated water exercise program designed to enhance comfort and social interaction. Affective measures, such as motivation to enroll and to continue, as well as viewing the membership as a support group, elicited few differences by age. Members endorsed having adults of all ages in classes and there was little indication that subgroups of different ages formed spontaneously. (Journal abstract).

support group, United States.

11.5   Health Status

---

1. Engle, V. F., & Graney, M. J. (1985/86). Self-assessed and functional health of older women. <u>International Journal of Aging and Human Development</u>, <u>22</u>(4), 301-313.

This study examines the contributions made by functional health, age self-concept, and attitudes, and demographic variables toward explaining health self-assessments in a sample of older women. The participants in the study were a simple random sample of white females (114) over age sixty years and who were residents in five apartment complexes for the aged in a large Midwestern City. Significant correlations to self-assessment of health were found among measures of functional health, self-concept and attitudes, and demographic variables. Multiple regression analysis using five variables (self-assessment of speed, emotional behavior, age self-concept, body care and movement, and occupation) explained almost 40 percent of variance in self-assessment of health data. (Journal abstract).

functional health, self-concept, United States.

2. Gunter, L. M., & Kolanowski, A. M. (1986). Promoting healthy lifestyles in mature women. <u>Journal of Gerontological Nursing</u>, <u>12</u>(4), 6-13.

The purposes of this article were to discuss the relationship of life events and perceived health status in retired career women, and the use of a series of structured letters as research methodology to study life events or life history in older women. The sample consisted of 50 volunteers from a women's club. (Journal abstract).

retirement, United States.

3. McElmurry, B. J., & LiBrizzi, S. J. (1986). The health of older women. <u>Nursing Clinics of North America</u>, 21(1), 161-171.

This article addresses the health of older women from both a professional (i.e., nursing) and research approach. Topics include evaluating health status, dimensions of health status, measuring health status, profile of a healthy women. (Author abstract).

United States.

4. Svanborg, A., Sixt, E., Sundh, V., & Thorton, J. E. (1988). Subjective health in relation to aging and disease in a representative sample at ages 70, 75 and 79. <u>Comprehensive Gerontology A</u>, 2(3), 107-113.

This study explores the relationship between perception of health in 70-79-year-olds and documented functional ability/disability well as prevalence of definable disorders. Two thirds of both men and women declared themselves healthy at age 70, 2/3-3/4 at age 75 and 3/4 at age 79. Subjective health correlated significantly with the results of an extensive clinical examination for men at age 75 and for women at ages 75 and 79. In both sexes the correlation coefficients between the number of definable diseases and subjective health scoring was statistically significant as well as between mortality and subjective health. Some correlations were also found between subjective health and certain parameters of organ system functions. Contrary to objective findings, the proportion of those who declared themselves health was not decreasing by increasing age, and sex differences in consumption of care was not reflected in any sex difference in subjective health. The correlation between subjective health and number of disorders illustrates that the subjective health answers were influenced by knowledge obtained at previous clinical examinations and from drug prescriptions. Many elderly with functional disorders and drug treatment reported, however, that they were well. Subjective evaluation of health seemed to be markedly influenced by their willingness to accept impairment, disability and handicaps as being normal for their age. (Journal abstract).

age differences, functional health, gender differences, Sweden.

11.6   Longevity

1. Kastenbaum, R. (1990). The age of saints and the saintness of age. <u>International Journal of Aging and Human Development</u>, <u>30</u>(2), 95-118.

The image of the saint as an old person is a familiar one. Does this mental association have any basis in fact? This article reports a study examining the age of saints, and includes a discussion of the saint as a possible model for the old person. The sample of 487 saints (118 females, 369 males) was drawn from reference sources to meet the criteria of a) actual historical person, and b) established dates (year) of birth and death. Those who died as martyrs were analysed separately. Martyrdom was twice as common among males. Almost all female martyrs died young; males were more likely to be put to death in their forties. Saints whose lives were not brought to an abrupt end by martyrdon were studied more extensively. Male saints, combining all historical periods, had a mean longevity of 69.9 years: literally the proverbial "three score and ten!" Female saints had a mean longevity of 58.1. A series of quasi-comparisons suggests that saints, especially the males, have had a longevity advantage throughout most of history. However, a time trend was noted among the males: the number of very old saints has diminished markedly in recent times, and centenarians, in particular, have been absent for more than seven hundred years. The data suggest that interactions exist between gender and historical period. Four alternative hypothesis about the possible age-saint relationship are examined in light of the present findings, and the saint is explored as a possible model for coping with he burdens and trials of age, contrasted with current age-based health rationing concepts. (Journal abstract).

gender differences, religion, United States, women religious.

2. Lewis, M. (1985). Older women and health: an overview. <u>Women and Health</u>, <u>10</u>(2/3), 1-16.

Older women's health issues are unique. There are more older women than ever before. They are living increasingly longer than men. They are disproportionally represented in nursing homes, since many women are alone: twenty-five percent aged 70 or over have no living children and over 60 percent of older women are widowed, divorced or single. Older women have fewer personal financial resources for health care than men. Health care reimbursement does not meet their needs for financial coverage of chronic outpatient and nursing home care. They face age and sex discrimination on the part of many health care providers and are subject to a growing tendency to be seen as "burdens" and "problems" in the American health care system. (Journal abstract).

gender differences, health care, United States.

3. Markides, K. S. (1989). Consequences of gender differentials in life expectancy for Black and Hispanic Americans. International Journal of Aging and Human Development, 29(2), 95-102.

Increased survival by Blacks and Hispanics is causing a widening of the sex imbalance of the elderly population much like we have observed in the general population. These demographic trends point toward greater widowhood among minority women and continuing high rates of poverty. In addition, we can expect increased rates of disability in minority elderly women, increased dependency worsening intergenerational relationships, and higher rates of institutionalization. (Journal abstract).

Blacks, Hispanics, longevity, United States, widowhood.

4. Markides, K. S. (1990). Risk factors, gender and health. Generations, Summer, 17-21.

This article focuses on documenting gender differences in health, particularly in the middle and older years, and explores factors associated with these differences. More specifically, we present data on mortality and life expectancy, leading causes of death, major impairments and disabilities, and other physical health indicators. Where data are available, we also document differences by race and ethnicity. (Journal abstract).

gender differences, longevity, racial differences, United States.

5. Veevers, J. E., & Gee, E. M. (1986). Playing it safe: accident mortality and gender roles. Sociological Focus, 19(4), 349-360.

One dimension of sex differences which has received little attention is the fact that males have substantially higher rates of accidental death than females. In the United States in 1960, among persons aged 10-24 years, accidental deaths among males outnumbered deaths among females by more than four to one. This discrepancy, which contributes to differential mortality by sex, is due, in large part, to the hazardous aspects of the traditional male role. Gender differences in socialization perpetuate an association of masculinity with risk-taking. In addition, differences in the division of labor, in alcohol use, and in recreational pursuits tend to place males in relatively greater jeopardy. If significant changes have occurred in gender roles, it would be expected that the sex mortality ratio (SMR) for accidental deaths would decrease. Data on mortality rates in the United States in 1960 are compared with 1979 data. Over this time period, the SMR declined from 4.35 to 3.47 for persons aged 10-24. The data are further analyzed in terms of five specific causes of accidental deaths. The SMRs have declined substantially for motor vehicle accident deaths and deaths due to drowning. The implications of these data for the study of gender roles are discussed with reference to the social import of risk-taking and the high cost of "playing it safe." (Journal abstract).

age differences, gender differences, mortality, national study, social roles, United States.

11.7 Miscellaneous

1. Campbell, A. J., Borrie, M. J., & Spears, G. F. (1989). Risk factors for falls in a community-based prospective study of people 70 years and older. Journals of Gerontology, 44(4), M112-M117.

We investigated factors associated with falls in a community-based prospective study of 761 subjects 70 years and older. The group experienced 507 falls during the year of monitoring. On entry to the study a number of variables had been assessed in each subject. Variables associated with an increased risk of falling differed in men and women. In men, decreased levels of physical activity, stroke, arthritis of the knees, impairment of gait, and increased body sway were associated with an increased risk of falls. In women, the total number of drugs, psychotropic drugs and drugs liable to cause postural hypotension, standing systolic blood pressure of less than 110 mmHg, and evidence of muscle weakness were also associated with an increased risk of falling. Most falls in elderly people are associated with multiple risk, many of which are potentially remediable. The possible implications of this in diagnosis and prevention are discussed. (Journal abstract).

falls, gender differences, New Zealand.

2. Celestin-Roux, C., Hale, W. E., Perkins, L. L., & Stewart, R. B. (1987). Anemia: an evaluation of age, sex, disease and medications in a geriatric population. Journal of Geriatric Drug Therapy, 1(4), 63-86.

A geriatric health screening program (Dunedin) was used to evaluate the incidence, prevalence and risk factors leading to the development of anemia. At the fourth annual visit the incidence of anemia was 8.4% of the participants and this percentage decreased over the next four years to 4.3%. Men had a significantly higher incidence of anemia at each of the five annual periods evaluated (p < 0.0001). The prevalence of anemia at all eight visits for men and women combined ranged between 19.8% and 25.3%. Overall prevalence of anemia for all visits and age groups was 3.7 times greater in men than women. The number of medical disorders reported by these subjects did not correlate with hemoglobin or hematocrit. After adjusting for age no specific medical disorders or drugs were found to correlate with anemia. (Journal abstract).

anemia, drug use, gender differences, United States.

3. Cook, N. R., Evans, D. A., Funkenstein, H. H., Scherr, P. A., Ostfeld, A. M., Taylor, J. O., & Hennekens, C. H. (1989). Correlates of headache in a population-based cohort of elderly. Archives of Neurology, 46(12), 1338-1344.

Data from a community-based study of 3811 persons aged 65 years and older were used to describe the characteristics of headache in the elderly. Subjects were asked whether they experienced headache in the past year, the frequency and severity of their headaches, and whether they experienced three symptoms of migraine: unilaterality, nausea or vomiting, an aura preceding the headache. Prevalence of headache in those aged more than 65 years declined with age in both men and women; women had a higher prevalence in each age group. The same was true for frequent, severe, and migrainous headache. We examined age- and sex-adjusted correlations of headache with several medical and social factors. Prevalence of any headache was strongly associated with joint pain, depression, bereavement, waking during the night, use of eyeglasses, symptoms of temporomanidibular joint dysfunction, and self-assessment of health. Similar variables were associated with frequency, severity, and migrainous symptoms, and thus could not be distinguished among these various types. (Journal abstract).

age differences, gender differences, headaches, United States.

4. Gee, M. I., Ko, S. Y. Y., & Hawrysh, Z. J. (1988). Nutritional health of elderly women: evidence of a relationship between dietary intake and taste perception. <u>Canadian Home Economics Journal</u>, <u>38</u>(3), 142-147.

Suprathreshold taste perception and nutrient intake were assessed quantitatively for 30 elderly (70-79) and 30 young (29-29 years) women living independently in the community. Both taste intensity and taste pleasantness were evaluated by magnitude estimation (ME) for two taste qualities (sourness; saltiness) in each of two systems (aqueous; food). Dietary intakes (4 days) were assessed by a combination of dietary recall and food records. Comparison of ME for six suprathreshold concentrations by elderly and young revealed loss of taste perception with aging. The elderly had poorer diets than the young.

For the elderly, significant positive correlations were noted between percent risk of vitamin A deficiency and the slopes of all the taste intensity functions. The elderly subgroup with steeper slopes of taste intensity was at greater nutritional risk than the subgroup with flatter slopes. For some of the elderly women, deficits in taste perception were related to poor dietary intake. (Journal abstract).

Canada, nutrition, taste perception.

5. Goldman, J. J. (1988). Prader-Willi syndrome in two institutionalized older adults. <u>Mental Retardation</u>, <u>26</u>(2), 97-102.

As Prader-Willi Syndrome is believed to lead to medical complications causing death by early adulthood, its course has not been studied beyond that point. This is not always the case, however. Two women, ages 54 and 69 years, were described in this paper. Professionals should be familiar enough with the characteristics of the syndrome to recognize it among adults, particularly residents of institutional settings. Implications for altered management of such persons and for planning/funding for as much as an 80-year life expectancy were discussed. (Journal abstract).

Prader-Willi syndrome, United States.

6. Linville, S. E., & Fisher, H. B. (1985). Acoustic characteristics of women's voices with advancing age. <u>Journals of Gerontology</u>, <u>40</u>(3), 324-330.

The purpose of this study was to increase current understanding of acoustic characteristics of women's voices with advancing age. Phonated and whispered/ae/vowel productions by 75 women at three age levels (25 to 35, 45 to 55, 70 to 80 years) were assessed on acoustic measures related to fundamental frequency standard deviation, decreased with advanced age in women, suggesting that laryngeal and/or respiratory control of phonation shows some deterioration with age. Second, spectral analysis of phonated and whispered/ae/vowel productions revealed significant lowering of the frequency of the first format (F1) with advanced age, suggesting age-related changes in vocal tract dimensions, or positioning of speech structures. (Journal abstract).

age differences, speech, United States.

7. Lowik, M. R. H., Wedel, M., Kok, F. J., Odink, J., Westenbrink, S., & Meulmeester, J. F. (1991). Nutrition and serum cholesterol levels among elderly men and women (Dutch Nutrition Surveillance System). Journals of Gerontology, 46(1), M23-M28.

Associations of serum cholesterol with relevant dietary intake variables (assessed with the dietary history method) and body mass index were investigated in elderly men (n=199) and women (n=180) 65-79 years old. All subjects were apparently healthy, nondiabetic, and not on a dietary regimen. The associations were studied separately for men and women using linear regression analysis and all possible subsets regression analysis. Among men, body mass index (kg/m2) and intake of monounsaturated fat and of alcohol were positively and consistently associated with serum cholesterol. Among women, intake of alcohol and of saturated fat were positively associated, and intake of polysaccharides was inversely associated with serum total cholesterol. The intake of monounsaturated fatty acids was highly (r>.60) positively correlated with the intake of total fat and saturated fatty acids, and inversely carbohydrates. HDL-cholesterol was positively associated with alcohol intake (significant for men only), and inversely with body mass index (women only). The results indicate that the effect of dietary factors on serum cholesterol levels is probably not age-limited. Elderly people may potentially benefit from weight reduction or control, moderate alcohol consumption, and avoidance of too much dietary fat. These suggestions are in fair accordance with general population-based guidelines for a healthy diet. However, as our study was cross-sectional, causation as well as the public health impact remains to be proven. (Journal abstract).

cholesterol, Netherlands, nutrition.

8. Pollak, C. P., Perlick, D., Linsner, J. P., Wenston, J., & Hsieh, F. (1990). Sleep problems in the community elderly as predictors of death and nursing home placement. Journal of Community Health, 15(2), 123-135.

In 1984-85, 1855 elderly residents of an urban community responded to a comprehensive baseline interview that included questions regarding an extensive set of sleep characteristics and problems. During the subsequent 3 1/2 years of follow-up, 16.7% of the respondents died and 3.5% were placed in nursing homes. The predictive significance of each sleep characteristic for mortality and for nursing home placement was determined separately for males and females, using Cox proportional hazards models. Selected demographic and psychosocial variables were also entered into the models. Age, problems with activities of daily living (ADL), self-assessed health, income, cognitive impairment, depression and whether respondents were living alone were controlled for statistically.

Of the many variables analyzed, in males insomnia was the strongest predictor for both mortality and nursing home placement. For mortality, the relative hazard associated with insomnia exceeded the hazards associated with age, ADL problems, fair-poor health and low income. For nursing home placement, the hazard associated with insomnia exceeded that associated with cognitive impairment. The relationships of insomnia to mortality and nursing home placement were U-shaped, with a worse outcome if insomnia complaints over the preceding 2 weeks were either prominent (numerous or frequent) or absent. For females, insomnia was a borderline predictor of mortality and did not predict nursing home placement at all. Symptoms of the restless legs syndrome predicted mortality for females in some Cox regression models. Reported sleep duration, symptoms of sleep apnea and frequent use of hypnotic drugs did not predict mortality or nursing home placement in either sex. (Journal abstract).

death, gender differences, institutionalization, longitudinal study, mortality, United States.

11.8   Osteoporosis

---

1. Albers, M. M. (1990). Osteoporosis: a health issue for women. Health Care for Women International, 11(1), 11-19.

Osteoporosis is a debilitating disease, most of whose victims are women. This disease results when bone resorption lags behind bone formation, resulting in a net loss of bone. Although the underlying mechanisms have yet to be identified, we know that both aging and decreased estrogen levels promote osteoporosis. The weakened bone is susceptible to fracture and contributes to the morbidity and mortality rates of women over the age of 40. Nonmodifiable risk factors for the development of osteoporosis include being female; having a small, thin body build; and having lighter skin pigmentation. Modifiable risk factors include estrogen and calcium deficiencies, a sedentary lifestyle, smoking, excessive alcohol intake, and certain medical conditions. Restoring estrogen to premenopausal levels results in slowing of bone loss and maintenance of bone levels for most women for whom estrogen replacement therapy is desirable. Of the treatments available, this one shows the most powerful and protective effect on bone. Because treatment cannot reverse the condition, considerable energy must be directed toward prevention of osteoporosis.

Recommendations for prevention have been made on the basis of modifiable risk factors. (Journal abstract).

health promotion, treatment, United States.

2. Christiansen, C., & Riis, B.J. (1990). 17 Beta-estradiol and continuous norethisterone: a unique treatment for established osteoporosis in elderly women. Journal of Clinical Endocrinology and Metabolism, 71(4), 836-841.

Forty women aged 64.7 + 5.1 yr with established postmenopausal osteoporosis were blindly allocated to 1 yr's treatment either with either continuous combined estrogen/progestrogen therapy (2 mg estradiol + 1 mg norethisterone acetate + 500 mg calcium daily) or placebo + 500 mg calcium daily. In the group treated with hormones bone mineral density in the spine (dual photon absorptiometry) increased highly signifcantly by 8-10% during the 1 yr of treatment. Bone mineral content in the mid-shaft of the forearm (single photon absorptiometry) and the total body bone mineral (dual photon absorptiometry) increased by 3-5% when compared to that in the placebo group, which showed virtually unchanged values at all measurement sites. Seven of the women treated with hormones were examined after a further year of treatment. BMC increased by another 3-6%, reaching a 12% increase in bone mineral density in the spine after 2 yr of treatment.

Biochemical estimates of bone resorption (fasting urinary calcium and hydroxyproline) and bone formation (serum alkaline phosphatase and plasma osteocalcin), decreased significantly ($P < 0.001$) in the group treated with hormones, but remained unchanged in the placebo group. The reduction in indices of bone resorption was more pronounced than that in bone formation after one year, indicating a positive bone balance. No further changes were seen in these bone turnover parameters during the second year of treatment. In the group treated with hormones, serum levels of triglycerides, total cholesterol, and low density lipoprotein cholesterol decreased by about 12% ($P < 0.05$-$P < 0.01$), whereas high density lipoprotein cholesterol decreased by about 8% ($P < 0.01$). The high density lipoprotein cholesterol/low density lipoprotein cholesterol ratio was unchanged. The hormone treatment did not produce any major side effects, and only minor bleedings were experienced by a few women.

The present study demonstrates that treatment with female sex hormones in this particular combination is a realistic approach to the treatment of women with established postmenopausal osteoporosis. (Journal abstract).

Denmark, treatment.

---

3. Riggs, B. L. (1991). Overview of osteoporosis. <u>Western Journal of Medicine</u>, <u>154</u>(1), 63-77.

Osteoporosis is a common age-related disorder manifested clinically by skeletal fractures, especially fractures of the vertebrae, hip, and distal forearm. The major cause of these fractures is low bone mass, although an increase in trauma due to falls in the elderly also contributes. There are multiple causes for low bone mass which, in any given individual, may contribute differently to the development of the osteopenias. The most important groups of causes are failure to achieve adequate peak bone mass, slow bone loss due to processes relating to aging, the menopause in women, and a variety of sporadic behavioral, nutritional, and environmental factors that affect bone mass in some but not in other individuals. The most important approach is prevention. Drugs and behavioral factors known to cause bone loss should be eliminated and perimenopausal women should be evaluated for possible preventive administration of estrogen. For patients with fractures due to established osteoporosis, the only drugs approved by the Food and Drug Administration are the antiresorptive agents calcium, estrogen, and calcitonin. Formation-stimulating regimens, however, are being developed and may be available for clinical use in the forseeable future. These regimens may be capable of increasing bone mass to above the fracture threshold, thereby resulting in a clinical cure of the osteoporosis. (Journal abstract).

review, United States.

4. Roberto, K. A. (1990). Adjusting to chronic disease: the osteoporotic woman. <u>Journal of Women and aging</u>, 2(1), 33-47.

The physical, psychological, and social components of the lives of 115 older women were examined in order to gain a better understanding of the impact of living with osteoporosis. Adjustments made in the women's lives included the use of supportive devices, changes in sleep and rest patterns, not being able to carry out household tasks, less involvement in social activities, and a greater reliance on family member for assistance. Results are discussed in terms of issues facing the older women in the adjustment process. (Journal abstract).

coping, United States.

5. Roberto, K. A. (1988). Stress and adaptation patterns of older osteoporotic women. <u>Women and Health</u>, <u>14</u>(3/4), 105-119.

This study explored the ways in which osteoporosis affected the lives of 115 community-dwelling older women. Stress and adjustment patterns were the main variables examined.

The women perceived more stress in their lives since being diagnosed with osteoporosis than before the diagnosis. Pain, loss of roles, and other limitations placed on the women due to their condition contributed to their feelings of stress. Both short and long term coping strategies were developed by the women to help them adapt to their illness. (Journal abstract).

coping, stress, United States.

6. Roberto, K. A. (1988). Women with osteoporosis: the role of the family and service community. <u>Gerontologist</u>, <u>28</u>(2), 224-228.

Older women (n=115) diagnosed with osteoporosis reported their major problems to be pain and inability to do housework. Most viewed their family as being supportive since they have had osteoporosis. They frequently received help from their children, with those who had lower incomes and specific fractures receiving the most help. The use of community services, however, was surprisingly low. (Journal abstract).

informal support networks, service utilization, United States.

Chapter 12

Policy

12.0 Policy

1. Faulkner, A. O., & Micchelli, M. (1988). The aging, the aged and the very old: women the policy makers forgot. Women and Health, 14(3/4), 5-19.

The nation's policy on aging has not adequately addressed the disjuncture between the compelling increase in the number of aged and the changing family and social roles of women. There is a continuum of mid-life, aged and very old women engaged in inter-generational exchange of care, who have unmet needs both as care givers and care receivers. Shortcomings in public policy arrangements are discussed, along with proposals for a national policy on aging that focuses on the family as a caring unit. (Journal abstract).

Canada, informal support networks.

2. Hess, B. B. (1986). Antidiscrimination policies today and the life chances of older women tomorrow. Gerontologist, 26(2), 132-135.

In the absence of enforcement of existing statutes, and given the structural changes in the economy, women's economic disadvantages in the workplace will continue through this century, despite increased educational attainment and labor force participation. This is especially true for women of color and Hispanic origin, but all women run the risk of outliving their resources. Proposed remedies such as earnings sharing and pay equity have received no support from the current administration. (Journal abstract).

employment, racism, sexism, United States.

3. Hudson, R. B., & Gonyea, J. G. (1990). A perspective on women in politics: political mobilization and older women. Generations, summer, 67-71.

Older women are victims of ageism, sexism, and racism. Despite the size of the population of elderly women, elderly women have been politically ignored. Neither the women's movement nor the old-age movement have centrally addressed the concerns of older women. The author encourages working towards developing a more selective political identity. (Author abstract).

United States.

4. Jackson, J. J. (1988). Aging black women and public policies. <u>Black Scholar</u>, <u>19</u>(3), 31-43.

I have selected three key issues about the social aging, or patterned or systematic changes in the statuses and roles that are associated with the aging of adults, of the changing populations of elderly black women now and during the past few decades. The selection of key issues is hampered greatly by the considerable heterogeneity of elderly black women. When it comes to aging, all elderly black women are not in the same boat. These three issues are: 1) how valid and reliable is the currently dominant characterization of old black women, and how does it affect their well-being?, 2) what are the major issues surrounding the social, economic, and health conditions of meaningfully identified subgroups of aging black women?, 3) what should be the substantive content of advocatory efforts in behalf of older black women? (Journal abstract).

Blacks, economic status, health care, racism, United States.

5. Jorgensen, L. A. B. (1989). Women and aging: perspectives on public and social policy. <u>Journal of Women and Aging</u>, 1(1/2/3), 291-315.

This article addresses how social policy has treated elderly women in the past, present and future. (Author abstract).

United States.

6. Moon, M. (1990). Public policies: are they gender neutral? <u>Generations</u>, <u>Summer</u>, 59-63.

This article briefly explores how public programs treat men and women differently, what the implications are for fairness, and raises some possibilities for change. Before looking at how public programs are constructed and interact by gender, however, it is instructive to set the stage with a brief look at how older men and women differ by some critical socioeconomic factors. (Journal abstract).

gender differences, health care, Medicaid, Medicare, poverty, Social Security, supplemental security, United States.

7. Muller, C. (1988). Medicaid: the lower tier of health care for women. <u>Women and Health</u>, <u>14</u>(2), 81-103.

Being poor in the United States means being exposed to the Medicaid system, whose characteristics, as determined by both federal and state policy, affect access to health care.

This paper examines those aspects of the Medicaid system which have a desperate impact on women because they are overrepresented in certain social strata, as well as some aspects which affect the ability of both sexes to utilize the health care system. Owing to the problems of women in society, women make up two-thirds of the Medicaid clientele. Thus the burdens created by the limitations of Medicaid are a significant gender issue. Policies regarding AFDC coverage and pregnancy particularly concern younger women, many of whom have problems related to marriage, childbirth, and absence of economic support from fathers which place them at risk for poverty. Regulations as to income and assets of elderly persons requiring long-term care are among the policies that affect older women whose spouses have become disabled. Mandating less restrictive eligibility standards and coverage during transition of Medicaid clients to work would help address the twin problems of inferiority and uncertainty with regard to health care. (Journal abstract).

gender differences, health care, Medicaid, United States.

8. Padgett, D. (1988). Aging minority women: issues in research and health policy. <u>Women and Health</u>, <u>14</u>(3/4), 213-225.

This paper presents an overview of current knowledge about the economic, psychosocial and cultural dimensions of the aging process among minority women in the U.S. Attention is directed to the shorter life span of minority women and its implications for understanding aging, the reality of "quadruple jeopardy" hypothesis, and the adaptive advantages minority women may have in dealing with growing older. The need to consider cohort effects and ethnic diversity in future research on minority women is stressed. (Journal abstract).

ethnicity, health care, United States.

9. Quadagno, J., & Meyer, M. H. (1990). Gender and public policy. <u>Generations</u>, <u>Summer</u>, 64-66.

While some analysts believe that gender inequality in old age is merely a function of market-derived inequities that accumulate during the productive years, we will argue that the rules that determine benefits are political decisions and not the inevitable consequence of inexorable forces. To the extent that women are penalized by the eligibility rules for public and private pensions, those penalties are the result of political choices we, as a nation, have made. (Journal abstract).

gender differences, Medicaid, Medicare, pensions, Social Security, United States.

10. Rathbone-McCuan, E. (1985). Health needs and social policy. <u>Women and Health</u>, <u>10</u>(2/3), 17-27.

This article describes demographic and economic factors that impinge on the health care of elderly women. Policies that control access to and utilization of health and long term care services are discussed. Some of the shortcomings of past policies are noted and current social reform efforts aimed at greater policy equity for elder women are reviewed. (Journal abstract).

demography, economic status, service utilization, United States.

11. Rodeheaver, D. (1987). When old age became a social problem, women were left behind. <u>Gerontologist</u>, <u>27</u>(6), 741-746.

Suggested is that social policies and programs for the aged are characterized by failure to recognize that females predominate among elderly people. Masculine bias toward independence and corresponding disregard for feminine values of relatedness have been considered in relation to studies of the interdependence of elderly people, their families, and communities. The foundations of this bias are seen in the history of old age as a social problem. (Journal abstract).

gender differences, social roles, United States.

12. Sofaer, S., & Abel, E. (1990). Older women's health and financial vulnerability: implications of the medicare benefit structure. <u>Women and Health</u>, <u>16</u>(3/4), 47-67.

Elderly women and men have different patterns of disease and utilize health services differently. This essay examines the extent to which medicare covers the specific conditions and services associated with women and men. Elderly women experience higher rate of poverty than elderly men; consequently, elderly women are especially likely to be unable to pay high out-of-pocket costs for health care. Using a new method, simulating out-of-pocket costs, the Illness Episode Approach, the essay shows that medicare provides better coverage for illnesses which predominate among men than for those which predominate among women. In addition, women on medicare who supplement their basic coverage by purchasing a typical private insurance "Medigap" policy do not receive as much of an advantage from their purchases as do men. The calculations also show that the Medicare Catastrophic Coverage Act would have little impact on the gender gap in financial vulnerability. (Journal abstract).

economic status, gender differences, health care, Medicare, United States.

13. Zones, J. S., Estes, C. L., & Binney, E. A. (1987). Gender, public policy and oldest old. <u>Ageing and Society</u>, 7(3), 275-302.

Those 85 years of age and older are the fastest growing subpopulation in the United States. Because they represent a very small proportion of the population (just 1% in 1980), the oldest old have not been studied until recently. Much of the interest in this group is related to their growth (over 50% per decade in the past 50 years) coupled with their disproportionate use of public resources, particularly health and social services. Women are strikingly overrepresented among the oldest old, with a gender ratio of approximately 44 males for every 100 females age 85 and older.

This paper examines the convergence of an expanding population of very elderly women, many of whom live alone and in poverty, with a political climate of diminishing resolve to respond to needs that cannot be met within the family. The economic position, health status and living arrangements of women 85 and older are viewed as outcomes of historical and social factors that have affected them as a group throughout the lifespan. Likewise, policy toward the elderly, in particular very elderly women, is seen as a process of social construction, linked to broad historical and contemporary social structural issues. Policy options for the elderly now under consideration in the United States are presented with respect to the degree to which they address both the immediate economic, health and long term care needs of very old women as well as enduring prospects for their well being. (Journal abstract).

demography, health care, informal support networks, United States.

Chapter 13

Psycho-Social Aspects

> ## 13.1 General

1. Beck, C. M., & Pearson, B. P. (1989). Mental health of elderly women. <u>Journal of Women and Aging</u>, 1(1/2/3), 175-193.

The mental health of elderly women has only recently become a focus of study and public concern, so the amount of knowledge specific to this area is limited. Therefore, much of what is presented here is an extrapolation of information from the literature on women and mental health and the literature about the aged and mental health.

A brief historical overview of mental health of aging women will be presented, followed by information on the incidence of mental illness in aged women and their utilization of mental health services. Then several factors influencing older women's mental health will be addressed. Finally, some of the major mental health problems of elderly women will be discussed. (Journal abstract).

depression, drug abuse, elder abuse, loneliness, service utilization, suicide, United States.

2. Gaylord, S. (1989). Women and aging: a psychological perspective. <u>Journal of Women and Aging</u>, 1(1/2/3), 69-93.

A psychological perspective on aging and women is potentially broadened in scope and addresses not only the behavior of older women, but the behavior of others toward them. This article provides a brief overview of research findings and issues in some but not all of the relevant areas. First, the history of psychological study of older women is overviewed. Next, psychological study is placed in the context of biological, social and cultural factors. A brief discussion follows concerning the need for circumspect interpretation of the research literature to be presented. The main body of the article covers aspects of the wide-ranging psychological literature pertaining to older women. Topics include information processing and cognition, intelligence, creativity, personality, and life satisfaction. Some major topics are not discussed here because they are addressed by other authors in this volume. Omitted are descriptions of sensory changes with age, issues of stereotyping, sexuality, and mental health, as well as the large body of psychoanalytic literature. (Journal abstract).

coping, life satisfaction, memory, self-esteem, stress, social roles, United States, well-being.

3. George, L. K. (1990). Gender, age and psychiatric disorders. <u>Generations, summer</u>, 22-27.

This article comments on research on psychiatric disorders. Of particular interest is the relationships among gender, age and psychiatric disorders. (Author abstract).

age differences, gender differences, research methodology, United States.

4. Grau, L. (1988). Mental health and older women. <u>Women and Health</u>, <u>14</u>(3/4), 75-91.

Currently it is estimated that up to 25 percent of the elderly manifest symptoms of mental disorder. The recognition of the seriousness of the problem has lead to a growing body of research in the field of geriatric mental health. This paper presents an overview of early gerontological studies of life satisfaction and morale of older persons and of the two most prevalent mental health problems of the aged, depression and dementia. Mental health service delivery and utilization are also considered. (Journal abstract).

Alzheimer's disease, dementia, depression, life satisfaction, service utilization, United States.

5. McDaniel, S. A. (1989). Women and aging: a sociological perspective. <u>Journal of Women and Aging</u>, 1(1/2/3), 47-67.

In this article, an overview of the sociological approach to women and aging is provided. To set the stage for understanding women and aging in contemporary society, the situation of older women in the past is briefly reviewed. The basic orientation of the sociological perspective is highlighted, with particular attention to the similarities and differences between the sociologies of aging and of women. Recent steps toward integration into a sociology of women and aging are discussed and a critical assessment of the "state of the art" of this emerging subfield is provided. The article concludes with speculation about what the future holds for older women in society, as well as for enhanced sociological understanding of women and aging and of women's situations in an aging society. (Journal abstract).

Canada.

6. Rodeheaver, D., & Datan, N. (1988). Challenge of double jeopardy: toward a mental health agenda for aging women. <u>American Psychologist</u>, <u>43</u>(8), 648-654.

The elderly may be considered a group at risk with regard to mental health and the mental health system. Aging women experience a double jeopardy arising from social, economic, and psychological conditions surrounding age and gender-in particular, poverty, widowhood, and the dynamics of family caregiving. This double jeopardy translates into a vulnerability within the mental health system that is seen in issues of service utilization, therapist-client interactions, and diagnosis, most notably in diagnoses of Alzheimer's disease, alcohol and drug misuse, and depression. The failure of the mental health system to consider elderly individuals as psychological survivors further suggests an implicit assumption that mental decline is a normative part of the aging process. Recommendations for change include addressing gender and age interactions in mental health policy and in psychological research, training, and practice. (Journal abstract).

Alzheimer's disease, depression, drug abuse, drug misuse, service utilization, United States.

13.2   Coping

---

1. Conway, K. (1985/1986). Coping with the stress of medical problems among black and white elderly. <u>International Journal of Aging Human Development</u>, <u>21</u>(1), 39-48.

This is a preliminary study looking at the coping responses of a group of black and white urban elderly women to the stressful event of a medical problem. Cognitive and active coping responses, as well as social support, were explored. Findings revealed these women were similar in many of the ways in which they responded to the stress of medical problems. However, there were some definite racial differences. These included level of social support, use of prayer in coping, and use of nonprescription drugs; the black elderly engaged in these latter behaviors more frequently. (Journal abstract).

Blacks, drugs, informal support networks, physical health, racial differences, religion, stress, United States, Whites.

2. Downe-Wamboldt, B. (1991). Stress, emotions, and coping: a study of elderly women with osteoarthritis. <u>Health Care for Women International,</u> <u>12</u>(1), 85-98.

My purpose in conducting this study was to identify and describe the illness-related stressors and emotions experienced by elderly women with osteoarthritis and the coping strategies they used to manage these situations. The theoretical framework for the investigation was based on a process theory of stress and coping developed by Lazarus and Folkman (1984). In a home interview, 90 women completed a demographic profile and identified concerns, feelings, and coping strategies used to manage problems associated with osteoarthritis. Descriptive statistics and content analysis of data indicated that the stress of osteoarthritis involved physical, social and psychological aspects of life and evoked both positive and negative feelings. The women used a broad repertoire of coping behaviors, including problem- and emotion-focused strategies to manage the problems associated with osteoarthritis in their day-to-day life. This information has implications in both treatment and prevention areas for health professionals who provide services for this group of people. (Journal abstract).

arthritis, Canada, stress.

3. Essex, M. J., & Klein, M. H. (1989). The importance of the self-concept and coping responses in explaining physical health status and depression among older women. <u>Journal of Aging and Health,</u> 1(3), 327-348.

This study examined a model specifying the links among the physical, functional, and subjective components of physical health status and depression among older women, and assessed the effects of the self-concept (i.e., health confidence and self-esteem) and coping responses (i.e., direct action, positive cognitive, and passive cognitive coping) at each point in the model. Based on cross-sectional interview data with 274 older women, a series of regression analyses indicated that the self-concept and coping responses were significantly involved at each step of the health process but that the specific effects of the self-concept were different earlier than later in the model. Earlier in the model, self-esteem and physical health status indirectly influenced subsequent health status through their effects on health confidence and cognitive coping responses. At the final point in the model, physical health status continued to operate indirectly through health confidence and the cognitive coping responses; however, health confidence and positive cognitive coping responses then directly affected self-esteem which, together with health confidence, subsequently had direct negative effects on depression. These results were interpreted within a social psychological framework that incorporated self-concept theory with cognitive theories of depression. (Journal abstract).

depression, health status, self-concept, United States.

---

4. Hubbs-Tait, L. (1989). Coping patterns of aging women: a developmental perspective. Journal of Women and Aging, 1(1/2/3), 95-121.

This article addresses women's psychological coping patterns as they age beyond midlife. There are three main sections. The first section presents developmental theories proposed by Erikson, Thomae, Gilligan Bakan, and Block. The second section presents stressful life events. Physical and social challenges include physical health deterioration, retirement, stereotyping and living alone. The third section presents research on coping. Several questions are addressed: is there an increase in active coping after mid-life?, are aging women who integrate aging and communion better adjusted?, is there an increase in integrity as women age?, is the perception of stress related to coping in the elderly? (Author abstract).

lifespan, stress, United States.

13.3   Death and Dying

---

1. Caserta, M. S., Lund, D. A., & Dimond, M. F. (1989). Older widows' early bereavement adjustments. Journal of Women and Aging, 1(4), 5-27.

Using the sample of 242 older widows at 2-3 months following the death of their spouse, the following research questions were examined: (1) What are the interrelationships among older widows' personal resources and their bereavement outcomes? (2) Do levels of these outcomes and personal resources differ according to age? (3) Is age related to both outside employment and income, and if so, do outcomes and personal resources differ according to these factors? Significant correlations were observed among many of the indicators with some of the strongest being between the resources of self-esteem and competencies. With the exception of ease of contact, social support played a minimal role on affecting outcomes. Those who worked outside the home reported higher self-esteem and fewer days sick while income was the most predictive of perceived health, depression, and competencies. Age by itself had little effect on both bereavement outcomes and resources. Differences were more easily explained by the relationship of age with employment status and income. (Journal abstract).

bereavement, economic status, employment status, informal support networks, self-esteem, United States.

2. Dessonville-Hill, C., Thompson, L. W., & Gallagher, D. (1988). The role of bereavement in older women's adjustment to widowhood. Gerontologist, 28(6), 792-796.

Older widows (n=95) were evaluated at 2 months, 6 months, and 1 year following the death of their spouse. Hypothesized was the widows who expected the death of their spouse would adjust better to bereavement than those who did not expect the death. Results revealed, however, that expectancy of death was not related to adjustment to bereavement. Widows who had rehearsed the role of widowhood fared no better in their adjustment to bereavement than widows who did not rehearse. (Journal abstract).

anticipatory grief, bereavement, United States.

3. Kinderknecht, C. H., & Hodges, L. (1990). Facilitating productive bereavement of widows: an overview of the efficacy of widow's support groups. Journal of Women and Aging, 2(4), 39-54.

Because of gender and socialization differences, widowhood is primarily a women's issue. Bereavement associated with widowhood is generally considered to be a difficult life event replete with a myriad of complex emotions that are often further complicated by the inability of family, friends, and society to productively assist the widow through the bereavement process. Productive grieving should include the undiluted outpouring of grief, providing the widow with the opportunity and enough time to express her loss and then, to eventually accept and adjust to the loss. An overview of the literature reveals that widow's support groups provide a safe, nurturant, and mutually supportive environment which can facilitate a healthy grieving process. (Journal abstract).

bereavement, review, support groups, United States.

4. Lund, D. A., Caserta, M. S., & Dimond, M. F. (1986). Gender differences through two years of bereavement among the elderly. Gerontologist, 26(3), 314-20.

The bereavement process of elderly male and female surviving spouses was compared in a 2-year longitudinal study. Bereaved persons (n=192) between the ages of 50 and 93 completed mailed and interview questionnaires at six periods following the spouse's death. MANOVA tests with repeated measures were carried out on five global outcome scales derived by factor analysis and on depression and life satisfaction. No statistically significant differences at any of the time periods indicated that their bereavement processes were characterized more by similarities than differences. (Journal abstract).

bereavement, depression, gender differences, life satisfaction, longitudinal study, United States.

5. Quinn, P. K., & Reznikoff, M. (1985). The relationship between death anxiety and the subjective experience of time in the elderly. International Journal of Aging and Human Development, 21(3), 197-210.

The present study explored the relationship between participants' level of anxiety about death and both their sense of purposefulness in life and their personal experience of time controlling for the effects of participants' general anxiety and social desirability set. Participants were 145 women aged sixty to eighty-five, members of senior citizens clubs in suburban New Jersey, who agreed to complete a booklet of questionnaires at home and return them anonymously. As hypothesized, respondents high in measured death anxiety were found to be more likely to express less sense of purposefulness to their lives, an inclination to procrastinate and be inefficient in their use of time, and a reported disposition towards being inconsistent. For the most part, the relationship between death anxiety and the other variables was found to hold even when the effects of general anxiety and social desirability were partialed out. (Journal abstract).

death anxiety, United States.

13.4   Depression

---

1. Cwikel, J., & Ritchie, K. (1989). Screening for depression among the elderly in Israel: an assessment of the short geriatric depression scale (S-GDS). Israel Journal Medical Sciences, 25(3), 131-137.

Depression is a common source of distress in the elderly. Screening for depression allows for accurate diagnosis and treatment by clinicians and enables prevalence estimates to be used for monitoring morbidity and health services. A screening instrument is required that is both easily administered and has been validated among the heterogeneous population of community-dwelling elderly in Israel. This study assesses the suitability of a short screening test with high face validity, the Short Geriatric Depression Scale (S-GDS), in a Jerusalem community sample (n=285). The test yielded a 34% prevalence rate for depression, which is similar to rates found in community studies elsewhere. The screening test correctly classified 72% (95% confidence interval, 60 to 84%) of those with depression in a diagnosed subsample of 71 subjects. The specificity was only 57% (95% confidence interval, 44 to 70%) which was probably due to confounding with early dementia. The S-GDS was more likely to classify as depressed those with no formal education, those of Middle Eastern origin, and women. Higher levels of sensitivity and specificity can be obtained by calibrating the cutoff score based on the level of education. The internal consistency of the test was adequate for the community sample as a whole, as well as among various demographic subgroups. The stability of test responses was also significant. Guidelines for the development of an instrument more appropriate for the Israeli population are suggested. (Journal abstract).

dementia, Israel, measurement tools, screening tests.

2. Davis-Berman, J. (1989). Physical self-efficacy and depressive symptomatology in older women: a group treatment approach. Journal of Women and Aging, 1(4), 29-40.

This article presents an outline of a practice model geared toward alleviating depressive symptomatology in older women. Based in Bandura's (1977) self-efficacy theory, and on empirical data reported in this article, the focus of the practice model is on physical self-efficacy as a cognitive mediator of depressive symptoms in older women. Through the use of group treatment approach, an attempt is made to raise levels of physical self-efficacy, and to determine the concomitant changes in depressive symptoms. Finally, the importance of continued research, and the further refinement of practice of practice methods based in theory is stressed. (Journal abstract).

treatment, United States.

3. Essex, M. J., Klein, M. H., Lohr, M. J., & Benjamin, L. S. (1985). Intimacy and depression in older women. Psychiatry, 48(2), 159-178.

This study examines the effects of the qualities of intimate relationships on depression in older women. The data are from a study of women over 50, randomly selected from five census tracts in Madison, Wisconsin, who were given questionnaires about depression and the quality of their intimate relationships on two occasions (summer of 1978 and summer of 1979). The results showed that some dimensions of the relationships that the women described with their most significant others predicted depression. The more depressed the women were, the more they felt that (1) the relationship was less friendly, (2) their friendly feelings were not reciprocated by the significant other, (3) their relationship was less consistent and predictable, and (4) there was less time spent with the significant other in the best state. These findings are discussed as partially consistent with Seligman's arguments on the comparability of his "learned helplessness" model and depression and with the focus of cognitive theories of Beck and others on the role of perceptions and expectations in depression. (Journal abstract).

learned helplessness, relationship satisfaction, United States.

---

4. Fiorot, M., & Boswell, P. (1990). Personality and response to psychotherapy in depressed elderly women. <u>Behavior, Health and Aging</u>, 1(1), 51-63.

Samples of pure or compulsive personality types in elderly depressed women showed that, as predicted, compulsive types did not respond to psychotherapy as well as dependent types. Compulsive dropped out more and did not improve as much as dependents. Previous work suggested that dependent types were more concerned about social support and compulsive types about success. However, in this sample of elderly women there were no differences between the two personality types in measures of affiliation and achievement concerns, with both groups predominantly affiliation oriented. Earlier work did not take gender, age cohort, and developmental factors into account. (Journal abstract).

therapy, United States.

5. Krames, L., England, R., & Flett, G. L. (1988). Role of masculinity and femininity in depression and social satisfaction in elderly females. <u>Sex Roles</u>, <u>19</u>(11/12), 713-721.

Several recent meta-analyses indicate a relation between masculinity and psychological adjustment, but there is little correlation between femininity and adjustment. The present study examined the generalizability of this finding in a sample of elderly women. Thirty women ranging in age from 68 to 97 years were administered a battery of questionnaires including the Personal Attributes Questionnaire, the Geriatric Depression Scale, the Hopelessness Scale, and three subscales from the Self-Evaluation of Life Function Scale. Consistent with previous meta-analytic results, correlational analyses revealed significant negative relations between masculinity and the cognitive measures of depression (i.e., hopelessness and self-esteem), and no correlation between femininity and these same cognitive measures. Femininity, however, was correlated with social satisfaction and symptoms of aging. Masculinity was unrelated to these social and physical indices of depression. The implications of these findings for the androgyny and masculinity models of mental health are discussed with particular reference to the role that femininity may play in potentiating or exacerbating depression. (Journal abstract).

Canada, gender differences.

6. Lalive d'Espinay, C. J. (1985). Depressed elderly women in Switzerland: an example of testing and of generating theories. <u>Gerontologist</u>, <u>25</u>(6), 597-604.

Results of a Swiss study revealed that a high proportion of farm women were depressed. Their depression is accounted for through the development of a theory of culture shock which is based upon the conflict between traditional values and the realities of everyday life. The importance of using life histories to supplement survey data in theory development is illustrated. (Journal abstract).

Switzerland.

7. Lennon, M. C. (1987). Is menopause depressing? An investigation of three perspectives. Sex Roles, 17(1/2), 1-16.

This study examines three perspectives in the literature about menopausal depression. According to one, the physiological changes of menopause result in increased psychological distress. Another approach proposes that menopause is most depressing for women who occupy traditional female gender roles. The third asserts that menopause is not especially depressing for most women. This study empirically examines three perspectives using data from two community surveys. These analyses suggest menopausal status may not be associated with depressive symptomatology, either directly or indirectly through traditional gender roles. (Journal abstract).

menopause, United States.

8. Maiden, R. J. (1987). Learned helplessness and depression: a test of the reformulated model. Journals of Gerontology, 42(1), 60-64.

The old model of learned helplessness and depression was compared with the reformulated model. Fifty elderly depressed / nondepressed women were exposed to a number guessing task and were given nonveridical feedback as to their success or failure on the task. As predicted by the reformulated model, significant interaction effects were found. Depressed women attributed failure to lack of ability; they attributed success to luck. In contrast, nondepressed women attributed failure to bad luck and success to high ability. In the second part of the study, the reformulated model's hypothesis was tested regarding personal and universal helplessness. Although it only approached significance it was consistent with the hypothesis; depressed women saw themselves as personally helpless when compared with others for failure outcomes; non-depressed women saw themselves as universally helpless (i.e. everyone would fail the task). A revised clinical treatment model was proposed suggesting an interactionist strategy in treating depression. (Journal abstract).

learned helplessness, treatment, United States.

9. Newmann, J. P., Engel, R. J., & Jensen, J. (1990). Depressive symptom patterns among older women. <u>Psychology and Aging</u>, 5(1), 101-118.

The structure of depressive symptom patterns was investigated in a community sample of 244 women between the ages 51 and 92 who were administered the SCL-90-R Depression and Additional Symptoms Scales. Confirmatory factor analysis was used to test alternative measurement hypotheses implied by clinical formulations of depressive symptom patterns among elderly persons. The findings show support for the hypothesis that 2 somewhat different depressive syndromes, along with 4 more delimited forms of distress, underlie symptom-reporting patterns. Implications of these findings for future research on the relation between aging and depression are discussed. (Journal abstract).

United States.

13.5   Life Satisfaction

---

1. Bearon, L. B. (1989). No great expectations: the underpinnings of life satisfaction for older women. <u>Gerontologist</u>, <u>29</u>(6), 772-778.

Interviews with 30 older women (age 65-75) and middle-aged women (age 40-50) revealed that, although having the same average global life satisfaction, the two groups differed significantly in salient sources of satisfaction and dissatisfaction and in the aspirations on which they based their judgements about satisfaction. Health was more salient for older than middle-aged women. Material well-being was important to the satisfaction of both groups, but was more often cited as a future aspirations of the middle aged. Older women strove to maintain the status quo or prevent fears from being realized, while middle-aged women looked forward to achievements and acquisitions. (Journal abstract).

age differences, United States.

---

2. Huyck, M. H. (1991). Predicates of personal control among middle-aged and young-old men and women in middle America. <u>International Journal of Aging and Human Development</u>, <u>32</u>(4), 261-275.

These analyses explore relationships between the conscious general sense of control and: 1) personal evaluations of major life domains (health, spouse's health, marriage, parenting, work, leisure): and 2) spouse's evaluation of life domains, within groups defined by gender and age. Respondents include 101 men and 127 women; all are Caucasian; they reside in a middle-class community in the midwestern United States; they are aged forty-three to seventy-six (M=56); they are all in long-term marriages, with an average of 4.4 children; and 73 percent had at least one child living at home. Evaluations of life domains included self-report satisfaction and investment scales completed after personal interview questions about the domain. There were no gender differences and minimal age differences in levels of sense of control or evaluations of the life domains. However, as expected, multiple regression analyses indicated that the evaluations that contribute to a sense of control vary by gender and by age group within gender group. For men, the sense of control is linked to experiences in work; for younger middle-aged men, satisfaction with health is important; and for older men, investment in marriage is important. Younger middle-aged women's sense of mastery s tied to satisfaction with mothering and investment in their own health; older women's sense of control is linked to satisfaction with marriage, health and leisure. Age group patterns may reflect both developmental and cohort effects. (Journal abstract).

age differences, gender differences, United States.

3. Lohr, M. J., Essex, M. J., & Klein, M. H. (1988). **Relationships of coping responses to physical health status and life satisfaction among older women. Journals of Gerontology,** 43(2), P54-P60.

This study examined a model specifying the causal links between the physical, functional, and subjective components of physical health and life satisfaction among older women, and assessed the effects of three coping responses (direct-action, positive-cognitive, and passive-cognitive coping) at each point in the process. Based on interview data with 281 older women, a series of regression analyses indicated that, before the inclusion of the coping variables, physical conditions directly contributed to functional impairment, and both indirectly lowered life satisfaction through their direct negative effects on subjective health assessments. Further analyses indicated that positive-cognitive coping buffered the effects of physical conditions at each point in the model, the passive-cognitive coping generally had deleterious effects on health status, although it prevented negative health assessments from lowering life satisfaction, and that direct-action coping had little effect. These findings emphasize the importance of a multidimensional conceptualization of physical health status in understanding its relationship with life satisfaction as well as the specific functions of coping at different points in the process for older women. (Journal abstract).

coping, health status, physical function, United States.

4. Magee, J. J. (1987). Determining the predictors of life satisfaction among retired nuns: report from a pilot project. <u>Journal of Religion and Aging</u>, 4(1), 39-49.

The life satisfaction of older nuns, or religious women, is a pressing consideration for the communities to which they belong. Congregations of women religious have been rapidly "greying" for the past two decades. The number of younger women joining congregations have profoundly decreased while the number of members over 65 years of age has been increasing. Congregations are confronted with the task of responding to the needs of their older members at a time when these members are no longer involved in full-time assignments and careers. For some, retirement has also involved a relocation to age-segregated residence, attenuation of ties in valued relationships, and an unanticipated variety of activities available to them in their newfound leisure time. (Journal abstract).

retirement, United States, women religious.

5. Riddick, C. C. (1985). Life satisfaction for older female homemakers, retirees, and workers. <u>Research on Aging</u>, 7(3), 383-393.

An examination of a nationally representative sample of 403 homemakers, 698 retirees, and 119 workers revealed that employment status had a significant effect on older women's life satisfaction. Older women who were currently employed had greater life satisfaction than members of their cohort who were homemakers or retirees. Furthermore, based on path analyses leisure activity emerged as an important predictor of life satisfaction for homemakers and retirees. Income and health problems also had meaningful effects on the life satisfaction of all three groups. Implications of the findings for theory development and future research are discussed. (Journal abstract).

economic status, employment status, health status, United States.

6. Thomas, B. L. (1988). Self-esteem and life satisfaction. <u>Journal of Gerontological Nursing,</u> <u>14</u>(12), 25-30.

This study anticipated that the acquisition of meditation / relaxation skills would provide the elderly with an independent vehicle for coping with the stresses of age, loss of social and work-related roles, as well as negative responses of reactions from society. (Journal abstract).

Blacks, coping, self-esteem, United States.

13.6	Loneliness

1. Andersson, L. (1985). Intervention against loneliness in a group of elderly women: an impact evaluation. Social Science and Medicine, 20(4), 355-364.

An intervention program, based on an interpretation of everyday loneliness as consisting of two parts - emotional and social estrangement - is discussed. The main variables were (1) availability of a confidant, (2) social comparison and (3) personal control (the CCC-design). The intervention took the form of a small group meetings. The sample consisted of elderly women living in Stockholm and interviews were held before, and 6 months after the participation in the program. Results showed that subjects had less feelings of loneliness, and also less feelings of meaninglessness, more social contacts, higher self-esteem, greater ability to trust and lower blood pressure (both systolic and diastolic) after the intervention. Analyses showed that women with several years of adult employment on the same job experienced the greatest decrease in feelings of loneliness. Also, women who had much contact with their grandparents, and women who had experienced a serious or protracted illness in the family during childhood, had the greatest decline in blood pressure. It was concluded that change in blood pressure operates through some other mechanism than the one which effects feelings of loneliness. Finally, a model is presented for distinguishing between different levels of intimacy. (Journal abstract).

blood pressure, Sweden, treatment.

2. Beck, C., Shultz, C., Walton, C. G., & Walls, R. (1990). Predictors of loneliness in older women and men. Journal of Women and Aging, 2(1), 3-31.

Loneliness is an emotion which evolves from cognitive processes when there is a discrepancy between desired and available relationships (Peplau, Micelli & Morasch, 1982). Older women and men are especially vulnerable to loneliness due to the significant changes in relationships which occur in old age. The literature which addresses loneliness in older adults is incomplete, especially in regard to differences between women and men. This pilot study explores whether factors which predispose people to loneliness, and factors which precipitate in loneliness differ in women and men.

Univariate comparisons on the study variables reveals no significant differences between women and men. Hopelessness was found to be a significant predictor of loneliness in both women and men. In addition there was a trend for spiritual well-being (existential) and education to have a smaller effect in women than in men. Additional studies with larger samples are needed to look at multiple predictors of loneliness in older women and men. (Journal abstract).

gender differences, hopelessness, United States.

3. Essex, M. J., & Nam, S. (1987). Marital status and loneliness among older women: the differential importance of close family and friends. Journal of Marriage and the Family, 49(1), 93-106.

This study examines the marital status differences in the frequency and sources of loneliness among older women. Using structured interview data from a sample of 356 older women interviewed in 1979, the analyses show that loneliness for married women revolves around the marital relationship, whereas the amount of time since the marital dissolution and the quality of the closest friendship are critical for formerly married older women. Never-married women are not as affected by relationship with family and friends but are lonely if their health is poor. These results are discussed from a life-cycle perspective and interpreted on the basis of the desolution hypothesis and symbolic interactionism. (Journal abstract).

marital satisfaction, marital status, relationship satisfaction, United States.

4. Moon, J.-H., & Pearl, J. H. (1991). Alienation of elderly Korean American immigrants as related to place of residence, gender, age, years of education, time in the U.S., living with or without children, and living with or without a spouse. International Journal of Aging and Human Development, 32(2), 115-124.

Dean's Alienation Scale (DAS) was administered to 137 Korean immigrants, aged sixty years or older, who had resided in the United States for at least one year but not more than fifteen ears. The study was made in order to determine the relationship of alienation to the independent variables of place of residence (an ethnically homogeneous Korean community in Los Angeles vs. ethnically heterogeneous communities in Oklahoma), gender, age, years of education, time in the United States, living with or without children, and living with or without a spouse. Significant relationships ($p < .01$) were found between one or more of the subscales of the DAS (powerlessness, normlessness, social isolation, and total alienation) and place of residence, age, time in the United States, and whether living with or without a spouse. Simultaneous regression analyses were performed to determine the relative contribution of the independent variables to each of the subscales. (Journal abstract).

age differences, education, gender differences, isolation, Korean, living arrangements, United States.

13.7   Memory

---

1. Beaton, S. R. (1991). Styles of reminiscence and ego development of older women residing in long-term care settings. International Journal of Aging and Human Development, 32(1), 53-63.

Styles of reminiscence used in life stories, rather than being outcomes of life review undertaken in old age, may be the characteristic ways in which individuals at particular levels of ego development, think about, relate to, and recount the stories of their lives. To investigate the contention that differences in the styles of reminiscence of older persons could be explained by their levels of ego development, seventy-five women residing in long term care facilities responded to the Washington University Sentence Completion Test and told the stories of their lives. A trend from higher to lower levels of ego development was associated with styles of reminiscence in the direction predicted. Women with Affirming styles had higher levels of ego development than women with Negating and Despairing styles. Resilience seemed the most likely explanation for cases that did not fit the predictions. Life stories are suggested for routine data gathering and foster a different level of engagement than do conventional data gathering techniques. (Journal abstract).

ego development, reminiscence, United States.

2. Gregory, M. E., Mergler, N. L., & Durso, F. T. (1988). Cognitive reality monitoring in adulthood. Educational Gerontology, 14(1), 1-13.

This experiment assessed adult age differences for cognitive reality monitoring (attributing a memory to either an internal or external source) as a function of whether the terminal position in a sentence was completed with an externally presented or internally generated word. Older adults (mean age = 72.3 years) made slightly more accurate attributions than younger adults (mean age = 18.5 years) even though the younger adults accurately recognized a higher proportion of target words than older adults. Subjects were able to discriminate either type of target from distractor, but when an attribution error was made, it was made in favor of external origin. In this experiment, older adults' common complaints about memory source confusions seem without firm basis. Results suggest that the manner in which younger and older adults process and discriminate between sources of information is invariant across the life span. (Journal abstract).

age differences, cognitive reality monitoring.

3. Markson, E. W. (1985/1986). Gender roles and memory loss in old age: an exploration of linkages. International Journal of Aging and Human Development, 22(3), 205-214.

A framework relating gender roles, role loss, and memory is presented. For the now-old woman, her identity has usually been defined by her roles within the family; other personal touchstones have been less legitimate. In old age, when key family roles dwindle, many women who have relied on their families as sources of identity are placed in an anomic situation, especially women with limited resources. When few meaningful social roles exist in the present, memory becomes increasingly important as a link to develop and maintain the self. It is proposed that, without meaningful present roles to frame one's past experience, memory is likely to be characterized by a high frequency of nonintegrated, relatively meaningless relationships, in turn leading to a narrowing of horizons and inability to take the role of the other. Episodic memories may decay since present events have no interest and generic memory becomes impaired. A case study approach is used to examine the relationship between self-preoccupation, group affiliation, object relations, and memory loss among three older working-class women. Their speech patterns, specifically pronoun use, were analyzed and support the postulate that a high frequency of self-references indicates memory loss and paucity of present experience. (Journal abstract).

memory loss, social roles, United States.

13.8   Religion

---

1. Hoch, C. C., Reynolds, C. F., Kupfer, D. J., Houck, P. R., Berman, S. R., & Stack, J. A. (1987). The superior sleep of healthy elderly nuns. International Journal of Aging and Human Development, 25(1), 1-9.

The nocturnal sleep structure of ten healthy elderly nuns was compared to that of ten healthy age-matched female controls. The nuns fell asleep more quickly and had less early morning awakening, as well as greater REM sleep time. These differences may reflect the more highly entrained life style of the nuns, including modest habitual sleep restriction (and thus accumulated sleep debt) of about one hour each night. The current findings, reviewed in relation to the sleep and aging literature, tend to support the concept that some of the effects of aging on sleep can be offset by attention to good "sleep hygiene," including careful entrainment of sleep schedule and modest habitual sleep restriction. However, age-related decrements in slow-wave sleep and sleep maintenance were not significantly better in the nuns. (Journal abstract).

sleep, United States, women religious.

2. Pressman, R., Lyons, J. S., Larson, D. B., & Strain, J. J. (1990). Religious beliefs, depression, and ambulation status in elderly women with broken hips. American Journal of Psychiatry, 147(6), 758-760.

The authors studied the relationship between religious belief and psychiatric and medical status in 30 elderly women recovering from the surgical repair of broken hips. Religious belief was associated with lower levels of depressive symptoms and better ambulation status. (Journal abstract).

depression, surgery, United States.

3. Sered, S. S. (1990). Women, religion, and modernization: tradition and transformation among elderly Jews in Israel. American Anthropologist, 92(2), 306-318.

Modernization affects the religious lives of women in diverse and dramatic ways. On the one hand, women may find increased arenas for religious involvement, both inside and outside of traditional religious frameworks. Simultaneously, women's rituals and beliefs are often especially vulnerable to attacks from the forces of modernization. This paper focuses on the experience of elderly Jewish women of Asian origin who now live in modern Israel. The author suggests that the very nature of women's religion - domestic, personal, hidden, and flexible - explains its tenacity and creativity in the face of modernization. These findings are examined within a broad, cross-cultural context. (Journal abstract).

Asian, gender differences, Israel.

4. Wolf, M. A. (1990). The crisis of legacy: life review interviews with elderly women religious. Journal of Women and Aging, 2(3), 67-79.

This study examines the life-satisfaction of a group of elderly women religious (Catholic sisters). It focuses on the life-long development experienced by the women and presents their self perceptions as women aging in a community with few young members.

The findings indicate that certain common factors influenced the women's early life decisions to enter the convent, that their worklives are important to their personal development, and their retirement is that of the nontraditional woman. In terms of late life satisfaction, the women rated high in health, family involvements and spiritual achievement. There is concern, however, for the legacy that they leave: this is resolved through passive mastery. Excerpts from the in-depth interviews provide the context for discussion. (Journal abstract).

life satisfaction, United States, women religious.

5. Wolf, M. A. (1986). Growth and development with older women religious: an exploration in life review. Lifelong Learning, 9(4), 7-10.

This article discusses an educational protocol conducted with a group of older women in religious life. Sixty women, ages 60 and above, members of a Roman Catholic religious order, participated in a series of educational workshops during 1983 and 1984. They explored their own personal growth and development through exercises in values, clarification, lifeline, and life review. Within a personal framework, this article discusses these learners and the pedagogical implications for conducting life review workshops with older individuals whose lives have followed divergent patterns. It finds life review a useful tool for unlocking problematic issues and as a means of looking at psychosocial development. As an exploratory paper, the author makes observations and raises questions. (Journal abstract).

life review, United States, women religious.

6. Woodworth, D. L. (1985). Patterned religious meanings: orientations expressed by a sample of elderly women. <u>Journal for the Scientific Study of Religion</u>, <u>24</u>(4), 367-383.

Sociological research has tended to neglect the meaning for respondents, particularly the elderly, of religious issues, beliefs, concepts, and practices. In this study, religious meanings were elicited, through open-ended and structured questions, from 40 elderly, female nursing-home residents. The open-ended responses, reported here, were subjected to computer contextual content analysis, and additional understanding was gained through the use of factor and cluster analyses. Two major ideas - Cognition and Conduct - were identified, and the subthemes contained in these categories were explored, using verbal examples from conversations. Responses were profiled along both ideas and then cross-classified in order to draw out dominant meaning patterns or orientations running through the responses. Four such themes were identified: 1) Choice within Ambiguity, 2) Normative Certainty, 3) Goodness and Trust, and 4) Normative Uncertainty. Classification in these categories was then compared to denominational membership, which suggested that the religious meaning orientations were related to but distinct from specific belief systems. The utility of these findings for understanding other social behaviors and attitudes is also explored. (Journal abstract).

United States.

13.9   Sexuality

---

1. -----. (1989). Sexual problems in the elderly, II: men's vs. women's. <u>Geriatrics</u>, <u>44</u>(3), 75-86.

As men and women age, each sex finds a particular type of sexual dysfunction becoming more prevalent. For each dysfunction, furthermore, the primary care physician has a management role. The major dysfunctions and what to do about them is reviewed by an expert panel. The second installment in a two-part discussion. (Journal abstract).

gender differences, physical health, United States.

---

2. Bernhard, L. A., & Dan, A. J. (1986). Redefining sexuality from women's own experiences. Nursing Clinics of North America, 21(1), 125-136.

Traditionally women's sexuality has been defined and described using narrow and socially prescribed concepts. In the past 20 years new ideas about women's sexuality have emerged. At the same time, sexuality has become a legitimate concern for health professionals. Nurses and their clients can benefit from learning about the emerging women-centered concepts of sexuality. Women's sexuality is not primarily a response to men's sexuality but has its own characteristics. A women's sexuality is an expression of mutuality, involving not only sexual gratification but also a sense of herself as a women in the context of her life, her relationships, and emotions.

Several groups of women whose sexual needs have traditionally been unmet by nurses and other health care professionals include adolescents, physically disabled women, lesbians and older women. A self-care framework differentiates socially constructed definitions of sexuality from lived experience and suggests the importance of attending to individual women's experiences throughout life. (Journal abstract).

United States.

3. Litz, B. T., Weiss, A. M., & Davies, H. D. (1990). Sexual concerns of male spouses of female Alzheimer's disease patients. Gerontologist, 30(1), 113-116.

Little is known about the impact of dementia on sexuality. The attendant cognitive changes that occur in the Alzheimer's patient present the caregiver with many, often conflicting, challenges to a couple's sexual functioning. This case study highlights these issues by describing a man who reported an erectile dysfunction directly stemming from stressful changes that had occurred in his relationship to his wife who had Alzheimer's disease. General themes and relevant hypotheses are derived and clinical practice implications are explored. (Journal abstract).

Alzheimer's disease, United States.

4. Mooradian, A. D., & Greiff, V. (1990). Sexuality in older women. Archives of Internal Medicine, 150(5), 1033-1038.

A host of biological and psychosocial factors play an important role in age-related changes of female sexuality. The most important of these are the availability of a sexually active partner and presence of concurrent illnesses. Some of the age-related changes in physiological indicators of sexual function, such as vaginal blood flow, are the result of estrogen deficiency, and as such are essentially reversible. Despite the inherent limitations of many studies in female sexuality, a significant degree of objective measurements has been reported in the literature. Future research should focus on developing appropriate techniques for quantitative estimation of sexual response in women. The need for love and sexual intimacy does not diminish with age, and sexual history should be part of the clinical evaluation of older patients. (Journal abstract).

physical health, United States.

5. Rice, S. (1989). Sexuality and intimacy for aging women: a changing perspective. Journal of Women and Aging, 1(1/2/3), 245-264.

This article overviews sexuality and intimacy of elderly women. Topics that are addressed include: defining sexuality, issues that affect sexuality, physical changes related to sexuality, intervention to enhance sexuality and intimacy, professional contracts with older women, and future tends. (Author abstract).

review, United States.

6. Rienzo, B. A. (1985). The impact of aging on human sexuality. Journal of School Health, 55(2), 66-68.

Review of gerontological and medical literature reveals the need for education for lay persons and professionals about the effects of the aging process on human sexuality. Primary prevention of psychosocial problems and sexual dysfunction could be abated by including accurate information about sexuality and aging and effective communication techniques in sexuality education and programs, including those with young adults. In addition, professional preparation of health educators must include the skills and knowledge needed in this area. (Journal abstract).

education, gender differences, United States.

7. Rotberg, A. R. (1987). An introduction to the study of women, aging and sexuality. Physical and Occupational Therapy in Geriatrics, 5(3), 3-12.

Therapists are confronted with an increasing number of older clients, which necessitates focusing our attention to the knowledge base of normal aging. Sexuality is an integral aspect of older people's lives. This paper confronts some of the myths and misconceptions of "old sex." In addition, a general review of sexuality and the elderly highlights several research studies: the Kinsey Reports of 1948 and 1953; the Masters and Johnson Report of

1966; the Starr-Weiner Report of 1981; and the Consumers Union Report of 1984. The biological, psychological, and sociological factors of female aging are examined as they relate to female sexuality. Sexuality and the older woman and friendship between older women concludes this article. As therapists, we owe our clients a sensitivity to their sexual needs and desires. We owe ourselves an honest approach to our personal feelings about growing old. (Journal abstract).

United States.

8. Schumacher, D. (1990). Hidden death: the sexual effects of hysterectomy. <u>Journal of Women and Aging</u>, 2(2), 49-66.

While there has been some positive changes in American attitudes toward the sexuality and reproductive life of young women, little attention is paid to preserving aging women's sexuality. The tragic effects of this neglect appear in the case of hysterectomy, which every year deprives hundreds of thousands of women of normal sexual response. (Journal abstract).

hysterectomy, United States.

Chapter 14

Social Relationships

14.1   Adult Children

1. Bulcroft, K. A., & Bulcroft, R. A. (1991). The timing of divorce: effects on parent-child relationships in later life. <u>Research on Aging</u>, 13(2), 226-243.

The National Survey of Families and Households was used to assess the effects of marital status on contact with adult children (N=1,929). Respondents were 55 years of age or older, had been married at least once, and had a biological child aged 19 years or older from the first marriage, who was not residing in the home. As hypothesized, divorce had a negative effect on interaction with adult children, and this effect is much greater for men than women. In particular, those men who divorced when their children were younger had the lowest rates of interaction. These data suggest that the long-term effects of divorce for men are particularly deleterious in terms of interaction with their children. (Journal abstract).

divorce, family relationships, gender differences, national study, United States.

2. Gallin, R. S. (1986). Mothers-in-law and daughters-in-law: intergenerational relations within the Chinese family in Taiwan. <u>Journal of Cross-Cultural Gerontology</u>, 1(1), 31-49.

This paper examines the relations of mothers-in-law and daughters-in-law in a Taiwanese village that has changed over the past 25 years from an economic system based primarily on agriculture to one founded predominantly on off-farm employment. Using ethnographic data, it explores Amoss and Harrell's (1980:5) proposition that the position of old people is a function of a "cost/contribution balance" compounded by resources controlled. It concludes that economic development shifts power between women in different generations. (Journal abstract).

Taiwan.

3. Gee, E. M. (1990). Demographic change and intergenerational relations in Canadian families: findings and social policy implications. Canadian Public Policy, 16(2), 191-199.

This paper provides estimates of the demographic parameters of parent-child relations in Canada, using an historical framework. Four birth cohorts are chosen (1860, 1910, 1930, and 1960) and are examined from two points of view - as children (particularly adult children) and as parents. The analysis highlights the ways in which demographic change influences the intergenerational context of family life. Four major social policy implications of the data are outlined, focussing upon care-giving and care-receiving in an aging society. (Journal abstract).

Canada, informal support networks, national study, policy.

4. Reinhardt, J. P., & Fisher, C. B. (1988). Kinship versus friendship: social adaptation in married and widowed elderly women. Women and Health, 14(3/4), 191-211.

The qualities of daughter versus same-sex friend relationships were described by 151 married and widowed elderly women. The relationship of these qualities to life satisfaction was assessed. Relationship qualities predicted life satisfaction in widowed women but not in married women. Significant predictors of life satisfaction for widows included the emotional support of daughters, the instrumental support of friends and kinship strength. In a comparison of the relationship qualities, both married and widowed respondents described daughters as providing more stimulation, ego support and utility than friends. Married women described relationships with both daughters and friends as more stimulating than widowed women. The value of assessing qualitative indices of later life relationships is discussed. (Journal abstract).

life satisfaction, married, peer relationships, relationship satisfaction, United States, widowed.

5. Rogers, L. P., & Markides, K. S. (1989). Well-being in the postparental stage in Mexican-American women. Research on Aging, 11(4), 508-516.

There has been limited research documenting the effects of the postparental stage of the family cycle in Mexican-American women. This study compared to the psychological and physical well-being of the middle-aged Mexican-American women from San Antonio who had children present in the home with those who no longer had any children present in the home (postparental). The findings are consistent with the results from studies with other groups that indicate that the postparental stage does not appear to have negative consequences on the psychological and physical well-being of women. However, employment appears to be associated with higher well-being regardless of the stage in the life cycle. (Journal abstract).

employment, Mexican, United States, well-being.

6. Scharlach, A. E. (1987). Relieving feelings of strain among women with elderly mothers. Psychology and Aging, 2(1), 9-13.

I hypothesized that feelings of strain experienced by an adult daughter are likely to interfere with the nature of her relationship with her aging mother and to have a potentially deleterious effect on the mother. To test this proposition, I devised a study that examined the impact of two brief interventions on 37 middle-aged women and 24 of their elderly mothers: (a) a cognitive-behavioral presentation designed to reduce the daughter's unrealistic feelings of responsibility and (b) a supportive-educational presentation designed to increase the daughter's awareness of her mother's needs. I found that the first procedure was more effective than the second in reducing the daughter's burden, improving the mother-daughter relationship, and decreasing the loneliness experienced by the elderly mother. (Journal abstract).

informal support networks, loneliness, relationship satisfaction, United States.

7. Scharlach, A. E. (1987). Role strain in mother-daughter relationships in later life. Gerontologist, 27(5), 627-631.

A role theory perspective was utilized to examine how women's perceived filial role strain can affect their relationships with their elderly mothers. Data from 40 middle-aged women and 24 of their mothers demonstrated that women who reported greater role strain had poorer quality mother-daughter relationships. Suggested by the findings is that social policies and programs which relieve the role strain experienced by adult daughters may also benefit their elderly parents. (Journal abstract).

informal support networks, relationship satisfaction, United States.

8. Synge, J. (1988). Avoided conversations: how Parents and children delay talking about widowhood and dependency in late life. Ageing and Society, 8(3), 321-335.

This paper draws on a 1980 sample survey of middle-aged and elderly residents of a medium-sized Canadian city (N=464). Few parents and grown-up children discussed in advance what might happen should parents become seriously ill or unable to look after themselves. However, most respondents did feel these matters should be discussed in advance, and most felt that parents should be the ones to raise these issues. This was true for both the middle-aged and the elderly. Elderly men rarely discussed their wives' futures with their children. Both the middle-aged and the elderly rarely talked with siblings or friends about the possibility of their own or their parents' dependency. Discussions that took place were often precipitated by illness. However, children expressed a great deal of concern for parents, especially in older parents. A variety of possible contributing explanations are suggested. These range from unwillingness to acknowledge changing family structure and mortality to parents' view on non-family-provided services. (Journal abstract).

Canada, informal support networks, widowhood.

9. Talbott, M. M. (1990). The negative side of the relationship between older widows and their adult children: the mothers' perspective. Gerontologist, 30(5), 595-603.

Possible reasons that relationships between older parents and their adult children do not contribute to the well-being of the older parents are explored in this qualitative study of 55 older widowed mothers. Some older mothers feel unappreciated by their children. Some older mothers provide substantial goods and services to their children, at great personal cost. The older mother-adult child relationship may be characterized by a power differential, such that some older mothers feel subordinate to their adult children. Exchange theory is applied to these phenomena. (Journal abstract).

informal support networks, relationship satisfaction, United States.

10. Uhlenberg, P., & Cooney, T. M. (1990). Family size and mother-child relations in later life. Gerontologist, 30(5), 618-625.

What effect does family size have on mother-child relationships in later life? From the child's perspective, does sibsize affect the level of interaction and quality of the relationship? From the mother's perspective, does family size affect the amount of contact with and support received from children? These questions are examined using data from the National Survey of Families and Households conducted in 1987-88. The findings show the family size does make a difference, both for adult children and for older mothers. (Journal abstract).

informal support networks, relationship satisfaction, United States.

14.2   Childlessness

1. Goldberg, G. S., Kantrow, R., Kremen, E., & Lauter, L. (1986). Spouseless, childless elderly women and their social support. <u>Social Work</u>, 31(2), 104-112.

A study of spouseless, childless elderly women living in a metropolitan area included women who had never married, women who were widowed, and women who were divorced or separated. Although potentially at risk with regard to attaining social supports, most of the women had developed substitute supports for the close kin they lacked. Most respondents were younger elderly - aged 65 to 74 - who considered themselves in good health. (Journal abstract).

divorced, informal support networks, never married, single, United States, widowed.

2. Houser, B. B., Berkman, S. L., & Beckman, L. J. (1984). The relative rewards and costs of childlessness for older women. <u>Psychology of Women Quarterly</u>, 8(4), 395-398.

Currently married or widowed women aged 60-75 (N=719), either childless or with one or more children, were interviewed about advantages and disadvantages of childlessness and about other family-related and social areas. Results indicate that childless older women did not conform to a stereotype of unhappiness and dissatisfaction. Respondents with and without children valued the rewards of their particular lifestyle and perceived costs to the other. (Journal abstract).

adult children, married, United States, widowed.

3. Huseby-Darvas, E. V. (1987). Elderly women in a Hungarian village: childlessness, generativity, and social control. <u>Journal of Cross-Cultural Gerontology</u>, 2(1), 15-42.

This study considers the meaning of biological and cultural continuity, and the changing roles of older women in general and childless elderly women in particular in a Hungarian rural community, Cserepfalu. Data gathered from participant observation, life histories, and formal and informal interviews are supplemented with statistical, archival, secondary, and other documented material. After a glance at how childlessness is conceptualized in Cserepfalu, an overview of the social history, economy, demography, and ideology of the village is given. The women's roles in the domestic economy, courting customs, and reproductive strategies are examined from a diachronic perspective. Finally it is suggested that, increasingly during the past four decades of radical, community-threatening social change, older women, including the childless, assumed the generative role of Kulturtrager (upholder, perpetuator of culture). They endeavor to guard selected meaningful events from the past, labor to govern the present, and thus attempt to guide the young thereby ensuring the future of their community. (Journal abstract).

Hungary, rural community.

14.3   Grandparenthood

1. Gladstone, J. W. (1987). Factors associated with changes in visiting between grandmothers and grandchildren following an adult child's marriage breakdown. Canadian Journal on Aging, 6(2), 117-127.

This paper identifies some factors associated with changes in face-to-face contact between grandmothers and grandchildren following a child's marriage breakdown. A qualitative analysis showed that geographic mobility, the appeal of a grandmother's home, employment status of the adult child, and the absence of the child-in-law were related to increases in visiting. Unresolved conflict and difficulties re-negotiating post-breakdown relationships were related to decreases in visiting. These findings as well as implications for service delivery are discussed. (Journal abstract).

Canada, marriage breakdown.

2. Gladstone, J. W. (1989). Grandmother-grandchild contact: the mediating influence of the middle generation following marriage breakdown and remarriage. Canadian Journal on Aging, 8(4), 355-365.

This paper focuses on ways that adult children and children-in-law mediate contact between grandmothers and grandchildren, following marriage breakdown and remarriage in the middle generation. A qualitative analysis of face-to-face contact between 110 grandmothers-grandchild pairs was conducted. Findings showed that adult children have a more direct influence on visiting, by arranging or obstructing visits between grandmothers and grandchildren. The influence of first or second children-in-law was found to be more indirect. By preventing an estranged spouse from seeing his or her child, custodial children-in-law could also be preventing a grandmother's access to her grandchild, if she depended on her noncustodial child to bring the grandchild to see her when he or she exercised visiting rights. Children-in-law could also act as intermediaries through their absence as well as through their presence. These findings, as well as ways that grandparents can negotiate relationships with adult children and children-in-law, are discussed. Especially noted is the value of monitoring communication exchanges, maintaining friendly relationships with children-in-law and step-grandchildren, and acting as resources to the family. (Journal abstract).

Canada, marriage breakdown, remarriage.

3. Gladstone, J. (1988). Perceived changes in grandmother-grandchild relations following a child's separation or divorce. Gerontologist, 28(1), 66-72.

When 80 grandmothers were queried about interaction pre- and post-marital breakdown, contact between them and their grandchildren was perceived to increase, as well as participation in commercial recreation and provision of certain types of support, such as babysitting, teaching family history and tradition, and proffering advice on personal problems. Geographic proximity and the custodial status of adult children were important factors mediating perceived changes in contact and support. (Journal abstract).

Canada, marriage breakdown.

4. Thomas, J. L. (1986). Age and sex differences in perceptions of grandparenting. Journals of Gerontology, 41(3), 417-469.

This study considered age and sex differences in grandparenting satisfaction and in perceived grandparenting responsibilities. Two hundred seventy-seven grandparents in three age groups (45 to 60, 61 to 69, 70 to 90) completed measures of perceptions of grandparenting experience. An Age group x Sex multivariate analysis of variance indicated that younger grandparents expressed greater responsibility for disciplining, caretaking, and offering childrearing advice. Grandfathers also expressed greater responsibilities for caretaking and offering childrearing advice, but less satisfaction with grandparenting. When number of grandchildren and grandchildren's were statistically controlled, younger grandparents and grandfathers expressed greater responsibility for caretaking for offering childrearing advice; grandfathers also expressed greater responsibility for caretaking but less satisfaction with grandparenting. Findings are discussed with respect to possible development changes in grandparenting and cohort differences in perceptions of grandparenting. (Journal abstract).

age differences, gender differences, relationship satisfaction, United States.

5. Thomas, J. L. (1986). Gender differences in satisfaction with grandparenting. Psychology and Aging, 1(3), 215-219.

Grandmothers (n = 177) and grandfathers (n = 105) completed mail questionnaires covering demographic and family background, and grandparenting satisfaction and perceived responsibilities (disciplining, caretaking, helping, advising). Grandmothers' satisfaction scores significantly exceeded those of grandfathers, and different variables predicted men's and women's satisfaction scores. Discussion focuses on possible sources of these gender differences, and consequences of these differences for further research. (Journal abstract).

gender differences, relationship satisfaction, United States.

6. Wentowski, G. J. (1985). Older women's perceptions of great-grandmotherhood: a research note. Gerontologist, 25(6), 593-596.

In an exploratory anthropological study nineteen older women gave their perceptions of great-grandmotherhood. They modeled their behaviour on their earlier role of grandmother, but advanced age and lack of geographic proximity restricted their ability to carry it out in the same way. They also felt more removed from the fourth generation. Great-grandmotherhood was significant for symbolic and emotional rather than social and instrumental reasons. (Journal abstract).

United States.

14.4 Lesbians

1. Deevey, S. (1990). Older lesbian women: an invisible minority. Journal of Gerontological Nursing, 16(5), 35-37.

The purpose of this study was to describe the older lesbian woman. Seventy-eight older lesbian women completed a mail survey consisting of Almig's questionnaire on lesbian life experiences, and Muhlenkamp's Personal Lifestyle Questionnaire (on health behaviors). Results are discussed in terms of their implications toward nursing approaches. (Author abstract).

physical health, United States.

2. Galassi, F. S. (1991). A life-review workshop for gay and lesbians elders. Journal of Gerontological Social Work, 16(1/2), 75-86.

A Life-Review Model to serve the specific needs of Gay and Lesbian Elders has been very much needed. A workshop has been developed through which the gay and lesbian elderly community may articulate both its personal and collective history, and its current psychological and physical health priorities. The workshop model reveals formerly undisclosed data which can be utilized in printed, audio and video cassette presentations by geriatric practitioners, social workers, medical school faculties and community service administrators on behalf of gay and lesbian elders. (Journal abstract).

life review, United States.

3. Kehoe, M. (1986). Lesbians of 65: a triply invisible minority. Journal of Homosexuality, 12(3/4), 139-152.

Questionnaire responses from 50 lesbians, 65 to 85 years of age, were used to describe their present status, their educational background, their economic and occupational condition, their personal and psycho/social concerns, as well as their perception of their own physical and mental health. The data suggests that the 65+ lesbian is a survivor, a balanced personality, coping with aging in a satisfactory manner. (Journal abstract).

economic status, education, employment status, mental health, physical health, United States.

4. Kehoe, M. (1988). Lesbians over 60 speak for themselves. Journal of Homosexuality, 16(3/4),

This special issue reports the findings of the first nationwide study of elderly women whose emotional and or sexual preferences are for other women. A sample of 100 elderly lesbians were administered an 87 item questionnaire. The questionnaire was designed to measure life-style satisfaction, social life, services for older adults, family relationships, relationships with older women, sexuality, health and background information. The study is presented in six chapters: the project (history, purpose, method, limitations), the background (lifestyles, careers, roles), family and other social relationships (parents, siblings, children, husband, peers, organizations, life satisfaction), lesbian relationships and homosexuality (lesbian identity, bisexuality, couples), the present (physical health, emotional health, attitudes toward elderly lesbians), lesbians and gay men over 60 (gender differences). (Author abstract).

employment status, family relationships, gender differences, life satisfaction, loneliness, mental health, national study, peer relationships, physical health, sexuality, United States.

5. Kehoe, M. (1986). A portrait of the older lesbian. Journal of Homosexuality, 12(3/4), 157-161.

Little attention is given to the aging lesbian; women, elderly and lesbians are often hidden or ignored. This article describes the older lesbian. (Author abstract).

United States.

6. Tully, C. T. (1989). Caregiving: what do midlife lesbians view as important? Journal of Gay and Lesbian Psychotherapy, 1(1), 87-103.

This study describes the caregiving needs of 73 midlife lesbians perceived as important to their ability to maintain themselves in their communities as they age. It examines to whom they turn for care currently and from whom they expect care in the future if they become frail. Pertinent concerns for therapeutic interventions specific to midlife lesbians are discussed. While the data suggest that basic biopsychosocial caregiving needs and personal desires of aging lesbians are similar to other aging persons, this minority has special caregiving needs because of its sexual orientation. (Journal abstract).

care recipients, United States.

14.5 Marriage and Remarriage

1. Boellhoff Giesen, C. (1989). Aging and attractiveness: marriage makes a difference. International Journal of Aging and Human Development, 29(2), 83-94.

In order to explore women's agreement with the double standard of aging, thirty-two women ranging in age from twenty-eight to sixty-three were asked to share their definitions of attractiveness, femininity, and sexual appeal. They were then asked if they had changed these definitions over time and if they perceived themselves as growing more or less attractive, feminine, and sexually appealing as they grew older. The findings showed that attractiveness was defined primarily by appearance, femininity by behavior and inferred traits, and sexual appeal by both. More single than married women had changed definitions of these terms, and more single women perceived themselves as having grown more attractive, feminine, and sexually appealing as they grew older. Age differences in these evaluations were found among the group of married women, but few age differences were found among single women. The findings suggest there may be qualitatively differing experiences between single and married women that are reflected in their evaluations of attractiveness and sexual appeal. (Journal abstract).

age differences, single, United States.

2. Burch, T. K. (1990). Remarriage of older Canadians: description and interpretation. Research on Aging, 12(4), 546-559.

The remarriage experience of Canadian men and women aged 55 and over at time of survey are described using data from the Canadian Family History Survey, carried out in 1984 by Statistics Canada. Data pertain to approximately 1,300 women and 1,100 men. Remarriage is put in the context of total life cycle experience by means of a simple decomposition of the lifetime probability of remarriage (due to high rates of widowhood) but their lower remarriage rates compared to men. The sex differential in remarriage remains when age at dissolution is controlled. A major regional differential is found in remarriage patterns in Canada, with residents of Quebec showing appreciably lower remarriage rates following divorce than the rest of the country. An interpretation of the observed patterns suggests the need for more attention to motivation in the study of remarriage behaviour. (Journal abstract).

Canada, gender differences, national study, remarriage.

3. Cassidy, M. L. (1985). Role conflict in the postparental period: the effects of employment status on the marital satisfaction of women. Research on Aging, 7(3), 433-454.

A theory of role conflict is developed in order to predict how the marital satisfaction of 190 postparental women might vary depending on their employment status (employed or retired) and their husbands' employment status (employed or retired), while controlling for number of demographic factors. The data used to test the hypotheses are obtained from a statewide survey of Washington state residents age 55 and over in 1980. The results of the first multiple regression analysis indicate that only the prestige associated with wives' present or former occupations (SEI) and husbands' present or former occupations (SSEI) have significant effects on marital satisfaction. However, when analyzed separately by wives' employment status, SEI and SSEI, along with chronological age, are found to significantly affect the marital satisfaction of employed women, but not retired women. Possible implications of the findings are discussed. (Journal abstract).

employment status, marital satisfaction, United States.

4. Gentry, M., & Shulman, A. D. (1988). Remarriage as a coping response for widowhood. Psychology and Aging, 3(2), 191-196.

Consideration and use of remarriage as a response to cope with the death of a husband was examined in 39 women who had been widowed and had subsequently remarried, 192 widows who had considered remarriage but had not yet remarried, and 420 widows who had not considered remarriage. Controlling for age, we found that women who had remarried reported fewer current concerns than did the other two groups. Furthermore, we found that women who retrospectively recalled the most concerns immediately after the death of the spouse were the ones who eventually remarried. The remarried group believed that they were experiencing significantly fewer concerns now than they had after the spouse's death; the women who had not considered remarriage believed that they were experiencing the same number of concerns now as before; and those women who had considered remarriage believed that they were experiencing significantly more concerns.

Implications for remarriage as a coping mechanism for widowhood and the relation of age to remarriage decisions are discussed. (Journal abstract).

bereavement, coping, remarriage, United States, widowhood.

5. Goldscheider, F. K. (1990). The aging of the gender revolution: what do we know and what do we need to know? <u>Research on Aging</u>, <u>12</u>(4), 531-545.

Over the last decade, research on the elderly family has been glowing, portraying strong marital and family relationships. But the currently elderly, while they have benefited from the demographic and economic transformations of modernity, did not anticipate in the family revolutions that have followed. Cohorts who will become the elderly of the 21st century have been on the leading edge of the family revolution, the rapid growth of labor force participation among women, the tremendous rise in divorce and in childrearing out of marriage, and the overall decline in marriage and remarriage. Increasingly, the elderly will not be married or not in their first marriage. Research has focused on women and children as the sufferers from divorce, but in old age, as family relationships based on marriage and parenthood grow in importance, it is males who are at risk. This article presents a series of research findings that specify these risks. (Journal abstract).

adult children, divorce, economic status, marital status, remarriage, United States.

6. Klinger-Vartabegian, L., & Wispe, L. (1989). Age differences in marriage and female longevity. <u>Journal of Marriage and the Family</u>, <u>51</u>(1), 195-202.

Analysis of 1968 mortality data and comparable 1970 census data for women showed that women married to younger men tended to live longer than expected, while women married to older men tended to die sooner than expected. Representing fluctuation from the base rate of 100, the summary SMR (standard mortality ratio) for women with spouses 4 years older to 14 years older was 125. Thus the mortality risk associated with marriage to a younger man was clearly less than that associated with marriage to an older man. Two possible explanations are discussed: (a) mortality outcomes are predetermined by mate selection, or (b) psychological, social, and/or biological interaction within marriage influences longevity. (Journal abstract).

age differences, longevity, national study, United States.

7. Lee, G. R. (1988). Marital intimacy among older persons: the spouse as confidant. Journal of Family Issues, 9(2), 273-284.

This article reports on a study of the choice of confidant among a sample of married persons aged 55 and over. Although 85% of the women and 70% of the men reported having a confidant, less than 30% of the women and 40% of the men reported confiding in their spouses. Those who do confide in their spouses have markedly higher levels of marital satisfaction than others and also generally score higher on measures of overall emotional well-being. In many cases, the estimated negative effects of confiding in someone other than one's spouse are as large as or larger than the negative effects of not having a confidant. These indicate the import of identity of the confidant for both marital and general well-being. (Journal abstract).

gender differences, marital satisfaction, peer relationships, United States, well-being.

8. Preston, D. B., & Dellasega, C. (1990). Elderly women and stress: does marriage make a difference? Journal of Gerontological Nursing, 16(4), 26-32.

This study examined the relationship between marital status and stress. A sample of 900 non-institutionalized elderly were interviewed and measured subjectively for health, stress and mental health status. Results indicate no gender differences in stress/health relationship for married elderly respondents. However, gender differences were found for married respondents; for elderly men, there is no relationship between stress and health status, whereas for married women, there is a strong relationship. In fact, married women experienced the poorest health and highest stress among the four groups in this sample. Results are discussed in terms of women's life span development: physiologic, self concept and role performance, and interdependence. As well, nursing implications are provided. (Author abstract).

gender differences, health status, mental status, stress, United States.

9. Siegel, R. J. (1990). Love and work after 60: an integration of personal and professional growth within a long-term marriage. Journal of Women and Aging, 2(2), 69-79.

An exploration of growth and change involving external crisis and internal shifts of awareness during a therapist's transition from midlife to old age. Focus is on the continuing need to balance and renegotiate work and family within a framework of creativity, professional opportunities, aging, spouse's illness, and changing social climate. (Journal abstract).

employment, lifespan, United States.

---

10. Steitz, J. A., & Welker, K. G. (1990). Remarriage in later life: a critique and review of the literature. Journal of Women and Aging, 2(4), 81-90.

Remarriage for women in later life is becoming a more popular life option, yet little is known about the psychological adjustment factors or the common stressors during this time. This article critiques and reviews what is known about remarriage for women in later life and discusses the areas where further information is needed. The role of health status, marital satisfaction, life satisfaction, the potential stressors in a remarriage situation, and the lower remarriage rates for women as compared to men are explored. (Journal abstract).

gender differences, health status, life satisfaction, marital satisfaction, remarriage, review, stress, United States.

> ## 14.6   Peer Relationships

---

1. Adams, R. G. (1985/1986). Emotional closeness and physical distance between friends: implications for elderly women living in age-segregated and age-integrated settings. International Journal of Aging and Human Development, 22(1), 55-76.

The author discusses the need for a better theoretical understanding of friendship in order for its role in the lives of elderly people to be understood. The applicability to friendship of Simmel's approach to the study of social relationships is outlined. From this perspective, types of friendship are determined by the physical distance separating friends and the emotional closeness bringing them together. The data consist of seventy in-depth interviews of senior, unmarried women in a middle-class community bordering on Chicago. Qualitative data are reported to support quantitative analyses. There were positive relationships between emotional closeness and physical distance, duration and emotional closeness, and frequency of interaction and proximity. The author describes the implications for elderly women of the tendency for their close, old friends to be physically separated from them and their neighbors to be casual friends, but constant companions. The author discusses the effects of the age-density of residential context and life history on the types of friends the women had. (Journal abstract).

living arrangements, single, United States.

2. Adams, R. G. (1987). Patterns of network change: a longitudinal study of friendships of elderly women. <u>Gerontologist</u>, <u>27</u>(2), 222-227.

Old age is a period during which people have an opportunity to alter their friendship patterns. The data were in-depth interviews and observations of white, non-married, elderly women who lived in a middle-class suburb in 1981 and mail questionnaires and telephone interviews with 42 of the same women in 1984. Three independent dimensions of network evolution were identified. The patterns of change on these dimensions varied across middle-class status groups, but the members of each group tended to have reversed their middle-aged friendship pattern. (Journal abstract).

longitudinal study, single, United States.

3. Adams, R. G. (1985). People would talk: normative barriers to cross-sex friendships for elderly women. <u>Gerontologist</u>, <u>25</u>(6), 605-611.

A normative explanation for elderly women's lack of male friends is developed by showing that cross-sex friendship is defined as romance, that there are norms inhibiting romance during old age, and that other norms encourage them to reject potential mates who can no longer meet traditional sex role demands. The data were derived from in-depth interviews and observations of 70 non-married, white, elderly women who lived in a middle-class Chicago suburb. It can be expected that future cohorts of elderly women who will have been exposed to models of non-romantic cross-sex friendships early in their lives will have more of these friendships during old age. (Journal abstract).

single, United States.

4. Adams, R. G. (1986). Secondary friendship networks and psychological well-being among elderly women. <u>Activities, Adaptation and Aging</u>, 8(2), 59-72.

This study investigates primary and secondary friendships. Primary friendships are intimate relationships one shares with only a few people, whereas secondary friendships are current relationships and tend to keep a person active within the larger community. A sample of 70 non-married elderly women were measured for friendship and psychological well-being. Results indicate that secondary friendships are related to positive affect, and primary friendships may be slightly related to negative affect. (Author abstract).

psychological well-being, single, United States.

---

5. Adams, R. G. (1988). Which comes first: Poor psychological well-being or decreased friendship activity? <u>Activities, Adaptation and Aging,</u> <u>12</u>(1/2), 27-41.

Research has shown there is a positive relationship between friendship activity and psychological well-being. The common interpretation of this correlation is that an increase in friendship activity improves psychological well-being. This article shows any of the following three interpretations are more plausible: (1) good psychological well-being causes an increase in friendship activity, (2) the relationship is spurious, or (3) the system is nonrecursive. The theoretical and practical implications of the findings are discussed.

This article is based on a 1981-1984 longitudinal study of white, nonmarried, elderly women who lived in a middle-class suburb of Chicago. Cross-lagged panel analysis is used to interpret the relationships between aggregate measures of friendship activity and Bradburn's affect balance scale. (Journal abstract).

longitudinal study, psychological well-being, single, United States.

6. Babchuk, N., & Anderson, T. B. (1989). Older widows and married women: their intimates and confidants. <u>International Journal of Aging and Human Development,</u> <u>28</u>(1), 21-35.

Interview data obtained from 132 women sixty-five and older reveals that the widows and married women have a comparable number of primary friends. Being over age seventy-four influences the size of the friendship network for widows but not married women. The primary friendships of widows and married women parallel each other in terms of endurance and stability. Primary ties with men are the exception rather than the norm, for both widows and married women. Widows do differ from married women in that the former rely on confidant friends to a greater extent. Ties between older women and their confidants are characterized by norms of reciprocity. (Journal abstract).

married, United States, widowed.

7. Chin-Sang, V., & Allen, K. R. (1991). Leisure and the older black woman. <u>Journal of Gerontological Nursing,</u> <u>17</u>(1), 30-34.

This study investigated the thoughts and feelings about leisure and the leisure activities of older black women. Thirty women were interviewed for their: loneliness; church, worship and duty; affiliative activities; and solitary activities. These women described: 1) the narrowing of their family circles and the broadening of extra-familial relationships; 2) the importance of solitary activities to provide their physical, spiritual and emotional health; 3) the role of self-help practices and informal assistance to others in maintaining independence. (Author abstract).

Blacks, family relationships, informal support networks, leisure activities, United States.

8. Jacobs, R. H. (1990). Friendships among old women. Journal of Women and Aging, 2(2), 19-32.

Because of widowhood, divorce, retirement, and prejudice against them, old women are in special need of friendships with older women. Old women's friendships have many valuable functions. It is dangerous to depend on just one friend. There are impediments to making friendships in old age including projection of negativity about aging on other older women, lack of resources and transportation, fears of loss, invasion of privacy, obligations, and preference for males. Some women settle for paid therapists as friends or for self help groups. Communities can provide activities fostering friendships, and women themselves can learn how to make connections. (Journal abstract).

relationship satisfaction, United States.

9. Lewittes, H. J. (1988). Just being friendly means a lot - women, friendship, and aging. Women and Health, 14(3/4), 139-159.

This article examines friendship patterns and interaction skills among older, noninstitutionalized women. It draws on two studies, one quantitative, and the second qualitative, of friendship undertaken by the author. Friendship is viewed in relation to age, related socio-environmental transitions and psychological growth in later life including the issues of intimacy, reciprocity and relational identity. (Journal abstract).

lifespan, United States.

10. Roberto, K. A., & Scott, J. P. (1984-1985). Friendship patterns among older women. International Journal of Aging and Human Development, 19(1), 1-10.

This study examined the friendship patterns of older women. The participants in the study were white, middle-class, urban women, sixty-five years of age or older. Results indicated the older widowed women received more help from their friends than did married older women. In addition, significant differences in the morale of the older women were found according to the equity of helping behaviors with friends. Specifically, those equitably benefited women had a higher mean morale score than over benefited women. The under benefited women also had a higher mean morale score than the over benefited women. Discussion centered on the importance of friends in the lives of older women as well as on implications for friendship support systems in late life. (Journal abstract).

informal support networks, married, relationship satisfaction, United States, widowed.

11. Roberto, K. A., & Scott, J. P. (1986). Friendships of older men and women: exchange patterns and satisfaction. <u>Psychology and Aging</u>, 1(2), 103-109.

In this study we examined the relation between perceived equity of exchanges and friendship satisfaction for a sample of 110 older men and women. Respondents were interviewed concerning their relationship with their best friend and one other friend in their support network. Perceived equity was a significant predictor of friendship satisfaction only in the case of the other friend. In addition, results showed that men were involved in more equitable friendships than were women. Discussion focuses on the importance of equity consideration and gender differences in the friendships of older adults. (Journal abstract).

gender differences, relationship satisfaction, United States.

14.7   Single, Widowed and Divorced

---

1. Bulcroft, R. A., & Bulcroft, K. A. (1991). The nature and functions of dating in later life. <u>Research on Aging</u>, 13(2), 244-260.

Using the National Survey of Families and Households, logistic regression analyses were conducted to identify factors that are significant predictors of dating for persons aged 60 years and older. Stepwise regressions were also conducted to determine the effects of dating on psychological well-being of older daters. The strongest predictor of the propensity to date in later life is gender, with men significantly more likely to engage in dating. In particular, age and social role involvement tend to influence older men's likelihood of dating, while health and mobility were significantly associated with dating among older women. (Journal abstract).

dating, gender differences, national study, psychological well-being, United States.

2. Cain, B. S. (1988). Divorce among elderly women: a growing social phenomenon. Social Casework, 69(9), 563-568.

This exploratory study highlights key psychosocial dimensions of later-life divorce among elderly women. The author discusses three variables - the mourning process, the aging process, and generational attitudes - that make divorce especially difficult for elderly women. (Journal abstract).

bereavement, coping, divorce, marital satisfaction, United States.

3. Keith, P. M. (1985). Work, retirement, and well-being among unmarried men and women. Gerontologist, 25(4), 410-416.

The unmarried will be an increasing proportion of the aged retired population in the future. Longitudinal data were used to investigate factors associated with evaluations of work, retirement, and well-being of 1, 398 never-married, widowed, and divorced/separated men and women. Factors associated with evaluations tended to be similar across the three marital statuses. Formerly married women, however, especially seem to warrant the attention of practitioners who plan pre-retirement programs. (Journal abstract).

divorced, gender differences, longitudinal study, national study, never married, retirement, United States, well-being, widowed.

4. Pennington, J. (1989). The economic implications of divorce for older women. Clearinghouse Review, 23(4), 488-493.

As a review of all of the studies and research indicates, women, and especially older women, have been short-changed in the divorce process. A great deal of the problem was caused by sexist and stereotypical attitudes of the court system as a whole. But part of the blame must be assessed to the representatives and advocates for older women, who have settled for too little. Many attorneys now consider spousal support a lost cause, and so encourage clients to bargain it away. We must advocate for it in every case, and appeal low awards when the circumstances require it, or else spousal support may disappear. Older women themselves are so conditioned by society to be "ladylike" that they do not want to appear "greedy" or "bitchy," and wish to preserve their dignity at the expense of their health and well-being. Therefore, education and enlightenment are, as always, an important part of the equalization process. (Journal abstract).

divorce, economic status, review, United States.

5. Stirling, K. J. (1989). Women who remained divorced: the long-term economic consequences. <u>Social Science Quarterly</u>, <u>70</u>(3), 549-561.

This examination of the economic experiences of long-term divorced women finds that in the initial years of divorce economic well-being declines by more than 30 percent and remains at that same low level, a more serious decline than suggested in other studies. This study, unlike others, follows a cohort over time and uses the last three years of marriage as its basis for comparison. Changes in divorced women's economic behavior include increased labor force participation, but not further schooling. (Journal abstract).

divorce, economic status, employment, longitudinal study, United States.

6. Uhlenberg, P., Cooney, T., & Boyd, R. (1990). Divorce for women after midlife. <u>Journals of Gerontology</u>, <u>45</u>(1), S3-S11.

In spite of widespread interest in both aging and divorce, relatively little research has joined these topics. This study used data from the U.S. Census, Vital Statistics, and Current Population Survey to determine current divorce patterns for women aged 40+, project marriage and divorce experiences of future cohorts of elderly women, and consider the socioeconomic correlates of divorce for middle-aged and older women. Given current marriage, divorce, and widowhood rates, the findings indicate a marked decline in the proportion of future elderly women who will be married or widowed, and a dramatic increase in the proportion who will be divorced. Further, the data show that the socioeconomic well-being of divorcees is significantly below that of widowed or married women. (Journal abstract).

divorce, economic status, national study, United States.

7. Wolf, D. A. (1988). Kinship patterns and household composition: older unmarried Hungarian women, 1984. <u>European Journal of Population</u>, 4(4), 315-337.

Household composition of older unmarried women in Hungary is analyzed using data from the 1984 microcensus. The principal determinants of household composition investigated are kinship availability - the number of living children, siblings, and parents - health status, marital status, age and income. A multinominal logit model distinguishing among five household types reveals that number of children, severe disabilities, age and income are all strongly related to household composition. Trends in fertility and mortality patterns suggest that kinship patterns will change in coming years; these results imply that household composition will, in turn, change as well. (Journal abstract).

adult children, divorced, economic status, health status, Hungary, living arrangements, national study, never married, widowed.

Author Index

Author index

Keyword Index

Gender differences 3, 4, 13, 15, 18, 19, 24, 28, 30, 31, 32, 34, 35, 37, 38, 39, 40, 41, 42, 47, 50, 51, 52, 53, 57, 58, 62, 73, 74, 76, 77, 78, 81, 87, 92, 94, 96, 98, 101, 103, 104, 105, 106, 109, 117, 118, 119, 120, 121, 124, 131, 132, 133, 137, 141, 144, 147, 150, 151, 154, 155, 157, 160, 167, 169, 171, 173, 174, 178, 179

Germany 7

Group therapy 62, 63, 65

Headaches 121

Health care 15, 22, 24, 36, 110, 119, 131, 132, 133, 134

Health promotion 62, 76, 11, 125 (see also Screening Tests, Chapter 8.3 - Health Promotion and Disease Prevention)

Health status 22, 23, 24, 54, 57, 74, 78, 81, 82, 84, 85, 108, 114, 139, 147, 148, 173, 174, 181 (see also Chapter 11.5 - Health Status)

Higher education 47, 48 (see also Education, Chapter 6.0 - Education)

Hispanics 15, 69, 119

Home health care 24, 60, 61, 62, 74, 76, 77, 78, 84 (see also Chapter 8.4 - Home Health Care)

Homeless 80, 88

Hopelessness 150 (see also Depression)

Hospitalization 74, 75, 76, 77, 78 (see also Chapter 8.5 - Hospitalization)

Housing 22 (see also Chapter 9.0 - Housing)

Hungary 165, 181

Hysterectomy 158

Income 43 (see also Chapter 5.1 - Income)

Incontinence 64, 73

Informal support networks 23, 55, 71, 84, 85, 127, 130, 134, 138, 140, 161, 162, 163, 164, 177, 178 (see also Social Support Networks, Chapter 10.0 - Informal Support Networks)

Institutionalization 24, 60, 61, 62, 74, 90, 124 (see also Chapter 8.6 - Institutionalization)

Intergenerational relationships 14, 106 (see also Adult Children, Grandparenthood, Chapter 14.1 - Adult Children, Chapter 14.3 - Grandparenthood)

Marriage   96, 97 (see also Marital Satisfaction, Married, Chapter 14.5 - Marriage and Remarriage)

Marriage breakdown   165, 166 (see also Marital Satisfaction)

Married   52, 54, 55, 101, 161, 164, 176, 178 (see also Marriage, Chapter 14.5 - Marriage and Remarriage)

Measurement tools   13, 25, 143

Medicaid   60, 61, 71, 131, 132

Medicare   60, 61, 71, 109, 131, 132, 133

Memory   136 (see also Cognitive Processing, Decision Making, Chapter 13.7 - Memory)

Memory loss   152

Menopause   14, 67, 145

Mental health   85, 169

Mental status   84, 173

Mexicans   32, 162

Migration   87

Military personnel   57

Mortality   22, 110, 111, 120, 124

Movies   4

Musculoskeletal disorders   109

National study   19, 22, 41, 92, 93, 95, 104, 120, 160, 161, 169, 171, 172, 178, 179, 180, 181

Native Indians   15

Netherlands   123

Never married   164, 179, 181 (see also Single, Chapter 14.7 - Single, Widowed and Divorced)

New Mexico   10

New Zealand   85, 120

Nutrition   122, 123

Teacher's notes

Information text

Objectives

- Decide why and when we consult information texts
- Learn the typical features of information texts
- Locate specific details
- Learn what topic sentences are and how to use them
- Learn what skimming a text means

Prior knowledge

Students need to recognise some conventions of information texts such as headings, sub-headings, captions, index and glossary.

English Framework links

Yr7 Sentence level 13 a); Yr7 Reading 2, 6; Yr8 Word level 7b)

Scottish attainment targets

English Language – Reading
Strand – Reading for information
Level D
Strand – Knowledge about language
Level D

Background

Though some information texts are used for browsing, they are more often consulted for specific purposes. The writing is largely factual, written in the present tense and contains technical vocabulary. Typically, an information text is accompanied by pictures, maps and other visual features to engage the reader and present the information clearly. Headings and sub-headings also make the information more user-friendly. An index and sometimes a glossary are included. Remind the students of **keywords** mentioned in Prior knowledge.

Starter activity

Ask the students to bring in a piece of information text and examine it for the features mentioned in the Background. Show the students an example of an index and establish whether they know how to use it to find information. Note whether any of the texts have a glossary and whether the students are familiar with the vocabulary contained within.

Resource sheets and Activity sheets

The first Resource sheet, an information text entitled 'Are you playing games? (1)', should be used with the Activity sheet, 'A quick read', which focuses on sub-headings and topic sentences as a means of gaining a quick overall understanding of the text. It therefore introduces students to skimming and should be used before reading the whole text on the Resource sheet.

The second Resource sheet, 'Are you playing games? (2)', is an annotated version of the text, which shows other features that aid reading. Refer students to the Activity sheet 'Some features' to reinforce this.

Before students begin the Activity sheet, 'Fact and opinion', ensure that they understand the difference between a fact and an opinion. Some students may find the task difficult, particularly when a popular or long-held opinion can appear to be fact. Discuss the significance of separating the two. Students also need to identify the overall opinion being expressed in the paragraph entitled 'Problems, of course'. The others listed are only examples of this point.

Plenary

Conclude by asking students spot questions to see if they understand the text, for example: *Under which sub-heading can you find out about …?; What have you learned about …?* and so on. Finally, ask students what the features of a good information book would be. They should think of six or seven and agree on these. Then ask the students to place them in rank order and sum up the three most important features.

Are you playing games? (1)

Other worlds

Playing a computer game is rather like being in a story. Games are often about other worlds. There are aliens, monsters, dragons and spaceships. Players are part of the story and they must find their way out of trouble. To do this they need speed and skill.

Who's playing?

Not only young people play games. Adults do too. The average age is 23. Men and boys play most of all. One reason for this is that men create most games. When women create games, girls as well as boys choose to play.

Stars in your eyes

Some people play games for a living. They play in gaming championships, or they play on-line, or they travel from place to place playing with the public. Sometimes they give master classes. In the USA famous players are treated like stars.

How do you play?

Games are often played on a games console. It links to a television, or it has its own screen. Some games have more features than others. For example, one game can have many more places to visit. Another may have more than one ending.

Problems, of course

There are problems with games. Some are too violent. Others are unsuitable for children. Another problem is how long you spend playing. Too many hours can vanish staring at the screen – and all play and nothing else makes Jack a dull boy!

Are you playing games? (2)

Heading

Sub-heading tells you about the paragraph.

Opening paragraph on the topic.

Other worlds

Playing a computer game is rather like being in a story. Games are often about other worlds. There are aliens, monsters, dragons and spaceships. Players are part of the story and they must find their way out of trouble. To do this they need speed and skill.

Who's playing?

Fact

Not only young people play games. Adults do too. The average <u>age is 23</u>. Men and boys play most of all. One reason for this is that men create most games. When women create games, girls as well as boys choose to play.

Technical word to do with the topic.

Picture gives information.

Stars in your eyes

Some people play games for a living. They play in gaming championships, or they play <u>on-line</u>, or they travel from place to place playing with the public. Sometimes they give master classes. In the USA famous players are treated like stars.

How do you play?

Games are often played on a games console. It links to a television, or it has its own screen. Some games have more features than others. For example, one game can have many more places to visit. Another may have more than one ending.

Problems, of course

There are problems with games. Some are too violent. Others are unsuitable for children. Another problem is how long you spend playing. Too many hours can vanish staring at the screen – and all play and nothing else makes Jack a dull boy!

A quick read

The sub-heading gives you clues about what the paragraph is about.

The first sentence is a topic sentence. It tells you even more about the paragraph.

Other worlds

<u>Playing a computer game is rather like being in a story.</u> Games are often about other worlds. There are aliens, monsters, dragons and spaceships. Players are part of the story and they must find their way out of trouble. To do this they need speed and skill.

1. Read each sub-heading and each topic sentence in 'Are you playing games? (1)'. You are skimming through the text.

2. Write new sub-headings for each paragraph. They must fit the subject of each one.

....

....

....

....

....

3. Now give the information text a new title.

....

Some features

Information texts often have pictures or
diagrams.

1. What does the picture in 'Are you
    playing games? (1)' show?

2. Which paragraph does it link to?

3. Pictures may have captions
    underneath. These give us more
    information. For example:

    ●   Write a caption to go with the
        picture in 'Are you playing games? (2)'.

Dragus from *Dragon Pit* is no walkover!

Technical words

Information texts often have special words to do with the topic.
A list of these words is called a glossary.

Work with a partner. Make a glossary.

1. Find five technical words in 'Are you playing games?'.

2. Write them in alphabetical order below.

3. Take it in turns to explain what each word means.

4. Check the meaning of words you don't know.

Glossary

Fact and opinion

'Are you playing games?' is mainly an information text. But it also has opinions.

> **Remember**
> A fact is true.
> An opinion is someone's point of view.

☞ Here are two paragraphs from the text. Read them again.

How do you play?
Games are often played on a games console. It links to a television or it has its own screen. Some games have more features than others. For example, one game can have many more places to visit. Another may have more than one ending.

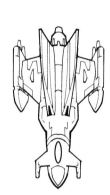

Problems, of course
There are problems with games. Some are too violent. Others are unsuitable for children. Another problem is how long you spend playing. Too many hours can vanish staring at the screen – and all play and nothing else makes Jack a dull boy!

1. Which paragraph has facts? Which has opinions? Mark which is which.
2. Underline in blue three facts.
3. Underline in red three opinions.
4. What is the *general* opinion being made? Choose *one* from the following and tick it:

   ● people spend too long playing games
   ● games are too violent
   ● games can cause problems
   ● children should not play games.

English Reading for meaning © Folens (copiable page)

Teacher's notes

Persuasion

Objectives

- Understand that adverts are persuasive texts
- Understand that language is used to persuade the reader
- Understand that the layout of written adverts is designed to influence the reader and to make information accessible

Prior knowledge

Students need to have had some experience of reading adverts in different contexts. They should be able to read an advert and express an opinion about it.

English Framework links

Yr7 Sentence level 13 e); Reading 2, 8, 10, 11; Yr8 Reading 6, 7, 9; Yr9 Reading 4

Scottish attainment targets

English Language – Reading
Strand – Knowledge about language
Level D
Strand – Awareness of genre
Level E

Background

Many types of writing rely on persuasion in one way or another. Arguments, reviews, articles that adopt a point of view and travel writing all seek to persuade. The most obvious, however, is advertising, since its primary focus is to sell goods. It is distinguished by emotive language and/or bold layout. It may cajole or amuse, or it may arouse feelings of guilt, for example in the case of charity advertising. Whatever technique is used, advertising is highly successful at influencing choices in a society dominated by consumption.

Starter activity

Ask students to bring in examples of a range of adverts from newspapers and magazines. Discuss what the adverts are seeking to do. Students should focus on the target audience and which adverts are the most persuasive. Ask them to compare these adverts with radio and television adverts and the techniques used (for example, the use of jingles). Work with them to complete the Activity sheet, 'Adverts spidergram', focusing on two or three adverts. (Students need to recognise the overall effectiveness of advertising, since some may claim not to be influenced by it.)

Resource sheets and Activity sheets

Read the Resource sheet 'Calling all texters – adverts' with the students. (Each student should keep a copy to annotate later.) Ensure that they grasp its intention. Then take students through the features in the Resource sheet, 'Calling all texters – layout'. Ask them to explain each label. Clarify for them as necessary. Students should grasp the importance of layout. Draw attention in particular to the small print, ensuring that they understand it. Ask them why they think such important information is set out in this way.

Return to the Resource sheet, 'Calling all texters – advert', then go through the questions on the Activity sheet, 'What is it saying?'. Students can mark and make notes on the Resource sheet. They should then work in pairs or groups of three to discuss the following point: *Would teenagers buy the phones in 'Calling all texters' or not and why?* They will need to consider the advert's strengths and weaknesses, such as how far it fits with current trends, whether there are drawbacks and so on.

As a class or group, students should then complete the writing frame, 'Our views', as a guide to reporting back. They can work through the Activity sheet, 'Adverts spidergram', again if necessary.

Plenary

Ask students to report back from their discussions and try to reach a consensus across pairs or groups. Then ask them to think of current teenage adverts and consider those that are most successful and why. Recap some of the main features that adverts use.

Adverts spidergram

☞ Complete the spidergram for each advert you look at.

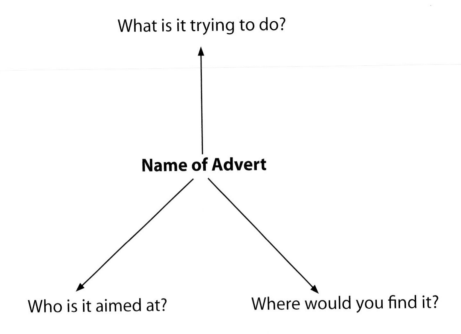

What is it trying to do?

Name of Advert

Who is it aimed at?   Where would you find it?

☞ Adverts like this seem to work. Why? Think of three points.

1.

2.

3.

English Reading for meaning   © Folens (copiable page)

Calling all texters – advert

Calling all texters

Choose from a truly mind-boggling range of the very best mobiles. Stylish and compact. Up-to the-minute features. Send text, photos, sound. Email your mates.

FREE *mobile – if you apply within two weeks of this advert.*

- 500 texts
- Video messaging

More talk time too – 300 minutes!

- Call any UK network
- Call from abroad (selected countries)
- Call any landline

*Pick the plan that fits **your** needs.*

- Simple payment plans – free for the first month
- Extra deals on payment plans – see web for details
- Or pay as you go

Can you afford to miss this offer?

(No nerds need apply)

It's so easy –

Apply direct to <u>www.reallydeally.com/mobi/hip</u> for purchase and more details

Must complete 12-month term. Prices may increase within the term. Phones subject to availability. First choice may not always be guaranteed.

Calling all texters – layout

Different fonts and size for impact.

Calling all texters

Opening statement says what the advert is about.

Choose from a truly mind-boggling range of the very best mobiles. Stylish and compact. Up-to the-minute features. Send text, photos, sound. Email your mates.

FREE *mobile – if you apply within two weeks of this advert.*

- 500 texts
- Video messaging

Bullet points for easy reading.

More talk time too – 300 minutes!

- Call any UK network
- Call from abroad (selected countries)
- Call any landline

Picture suggests you could be like this if you buy the phone.

*Pick the plan that fits **your** needs.*

- Simple payment plans – free for the first month
- Extra deals on payment plans – see web for details
- Or pay as you go

Bold for impact.

Can you afford to miss this offer?

(No nerds need apply)

It's so easy –

Apply direct to <u>www.reallydeally.com/mobi/hip</u> for purchase and more details

Small print harder to read.

Must complete 12-month term. Prices may increase within the term. Phones subject to availability. First choice may not always be guaranteed.

What is it saying?

Adverts use words in different ways to sell goods.

Adjectives

Look at 'Calling all texters – advert'. It has strong adjectives.

1. Underline 'mind-boggling' in blue.
2. Find two more adjectives and underline them.
3. Why do you think strong adjectives are used?

Invented words

Some words are made up. This catches the reader's eye.

4. Find an example of a word like this.

Short sentences

The advert also has short sentences.

5. Underline three in red.
   Why do you think short sentences are used?

Affecting the reader

Adverts often make the reader feel they need the goods.

6. The following work on the reader in different ways. How?

- Can you afford to miss this offer?
- *Pick the plan that fits **your** needs.*
- **It's so easy**
- *(No nerds need apply)*

Our views

Group members: _____

Advert: *Calling all texters*

We discussed: *Would teenagers buy the phones or not and why?*

We agreed that:

1. _____

2. _____

3. _____

4. _____

We disagreed that:

1. _____

2. _____

3. _____

4. _____

We agreed that these points were important:

1. _____

2. _____

3. _____

4. _____

English Reading for meaning

Teacher's notes

Instructions

Objectives

- Read instructions and carry them out
- Learn the conventions used in instructions
- Understand that instructions may require visual information as well as written
- Understand the imperative

Prior knowledge

Students need to have basic IT skills and be able to follow simple instructions in a text.

English Framework links

Yr7 Sentence level 13d); Yr7 Reading 6

Scottish attainment targets

English Language – Reading
Strand – Reading for information
Level C
Strand – Knowledge about language
Level D

Background

Reading instructions brings together several skills. Students often need to pick up visual cues from diagrams or pictures, as well as grammatical cues, such as the imperative, which is often used in instructions. They also need to pick up spatial cues related to the layout of information on the page, for example in the use of bullet points or headings. These features make understanding instructions easier, but their absence, particularly the lack of diagrams, can make the task much more difficult.

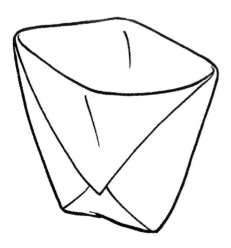

Starter activity

Explain to students that the imperative is a command and introduce 'imperative' as a **keyword**. Discuss examples and situations in which we use it (for example, 'Shut the door!' when we want something done quickly). You may wish to use the Activity sheet, 'Work it out!' here. Students should understand that the second-person singular remains a silent 'you' when the imperative is used and should recognise that instructions often use the imperative for conciseness.

Resource sheets and Activity sheets

Students will need a square piece of blank paper, either coloured or white. The task on the Resource sheet, 'Paper art', is an example of origami, the Japanese art of paper-folding. Students should read the instructions and make the object (which they should discover is a cup). You can give students a time limit, depending on their skill level, and then ask them to compare their results with a partner.

Once completed, go through the second Resource sheet, 'Look more closely', – the same instructions with annotations. The features are labelled but how they are useful is not given. Students should discuss this in a small group, addressing the questions in the Activity sheet, 'Thinking and talking', and report back to you, or another group. (They should grasp that all features aid clarity, sequencing and conciseness, however they express these points.) Point out that we 'read' the page in the broadest sense by picking up a range of useful cues. (See Background.)

The Activity sheet, 'Paper puzzle', can be used as the focus of further discussion. Students are not told that the instructions show how to build a sailing boat, a relatively simple task. However, the instructions are hard to follow despite being written clearly, because written instructions alone are not enough. Diagrams are needed and, ideally, a practical demonstration. Note how students cope and draw attention to the limitations of written information in such instructions.

Plenary

Ask students to perform some simple ICT tasks (such as 'cut and paste' or inserting symbols) and draw their attention to the way in which these practical skills differ from reading instructions. Then ask them to think of situations in which demonstration is not available and they must rely on reading (for example, assembling furniture, following recipes).

Paper art

☞ Read the instructions. Look at the diagrams. Make the object!

Equipment needed

A square piece of paper, coloured or white.

Instructions

- Fold paper in half along A to B as shown (see 1).
- Fold so that point A meets C (see 2).
- Fold so that point B meets D (see 3).
- Separate flaps E and F.
- Fold back flap E (see 4).
- Turn paper over and fold back F (see 5).
- Open paper out.

1.

2.

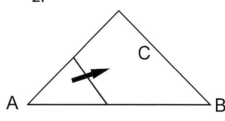

3.

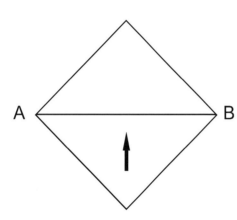

4.

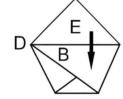

5.

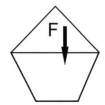

Look more closely

Bullet points

Sub-heading and list

Imperative
(a command, e.g.
'Fold', 'Turn', 'Open')

Short
sentences

Numbered diagrams

Equipment needed

A square piece of paper, coloured or white.

Instructions

- <u>Fold</u> paper in half along A to B as shown (see 1).
- Fold so that point A meets C (see 2).
- Fold so that point B meets D (see 3).
- Separate flaps E and F.
- Fold back flap E (see 4).
- <u>Turn</u> paper over and fold back F (see 5).
- <u>Open</u> paper out.

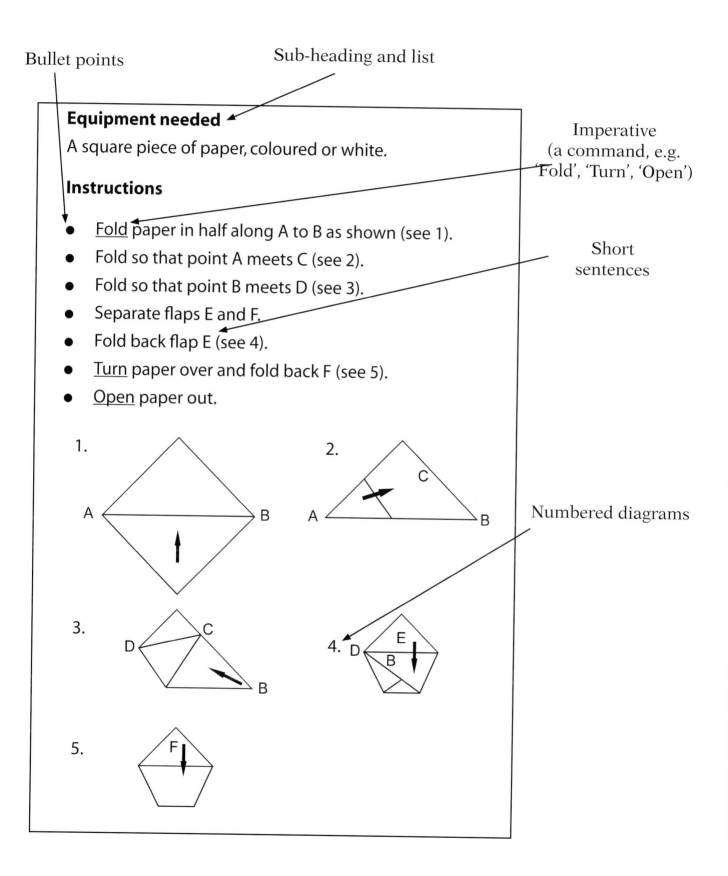

1.   A   B

2.   C   A   B

3.   C   D   B

4.   D   E   B

5.   F

Thinking and talking

☞   Read and answer these questions in a group.
      You will need the Resource sheet, 'Look more closely'.

1.   What do the instructions ask you to do?

2.   How well could you follow them?

3.   Decide why these are useful:

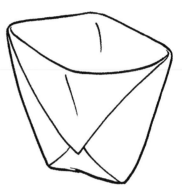

- bullet points
- sub-headings
- short sentences
- diagrams.

4.   Why do you think commands are used?

5.   The diagrams have lots of labels: A, B, C and so on. Why?

6.   Why are the diagrams numbered?

7.   Now read this:

Equipment

To make this object you will need a piece of square paper. It is best if it is coloured paper, but white will do if you have nothing else.

How is this different from the instructions on 'Look more closely'?
Why is this less useful? Think of two reasons.

8.   Sum up what good instructions should have.

Work it out!

A command is like an order.

Sometimes it is an angry command: *Shut that door!*

Sometimes it is a gentle one: *Remember to buy the milk.*

Sometimes it saves time. Most instructions are like these: *Fold the paper. Cut along the lines.*

| **Remember** |
| The word we use for command is 'imperative'. |

When we use imperatives we are really saying: 'You shut the door!',
or 'You remember to buy the milk'. But we drop the 'You'.
Read the instructions below.

You weigh 110g of plain flour and you put it in a bowl. You add a pinch of salt.

You take two eggs and you break them in the flour and you mix until smooth.

You add 275ml of milk and water. You melt 50g of butter in a frying pan and you

pour the mixture in. You cook until brown and eat with honey and lemon.

1. Cross out each second person: 'You'.
2. Underline each imperative in blue.
3. Underline in red eight short sentences you would use for instructions.
   (You will need to drop some words.)
4. Work out what the recipe is for.

☞ Did you notice that the sentences numbered 1 to 4 use imperatives?

Paper puzzle

☞ Read these instructions.

---

1. Take a square piece of paper.

2. Place it in a diamond shape.

3. Fold it down the middle.

4. Take the left-hand side. Fold it down the middle. Bring it into the middle of the paper.

5. Do the same on the right-hand side.

6. Fold the smaller triangle up to meet the larger one.

7. Fold again about 3cm from the base.

8. Press flat.

☞ Work with a partner.

1. Using a piece of paper, work out what to do.

2. What have you made? _____

3. What problems did you have?

   _____

   _____

4. Why do you think the instructions are hard to follow?

   _____

   _____

5. What could you do to improve them? Think of three things.

   _____

   _____

Teacher's notes

Explanation

Objectives

- Learn the typical features of explanation texts
- Learn to scan
- Locate relevant keywords to complete a flow diagram
- Understand the function of different connectives and locate them
- Make predictions

Prior knowledge

Students should have experience of explanations in subjects such as Science, History and Geography and understand simple cause and effect.

English Framework links

Yr7 Sentence level 13c); Reading 4, 7; Yr8 Reading 3, 5

Scottish attainment targets

English Language – Reading
Strand – Reading to reflect on the writer's ideas and craft
Level E

Background

Reports suggest that the melting of sea ice in the Arctic may be irreversible as a result of global warming. Both the Arctic Climate Impact Assessment, which involves more than 300 scientists, and the September 2005 report from the Arctic Council have findings that show this. It is generally accepted that before the end of the century the effect on the world will be profound, ranging from threats to indigenous communities and wildlife in the region to a rise in sea level. Ocean currents may also be affected, which in turn will affect the global climate.

Please note that the term 'connective' is used to mean linking words, including conjunctions. For further information on this, see Teacher's notes, 'Argument'.

Starter activity

Discuss the **keyword** 'cycle' with students, asking them to refer to any life cycles they have covered in Science, for example the life cycle of the frog/butterfly. Give them two minutes to think about different meanings of the word 'cycle'. Also ensure that they understand the **keyword** 'text'.

Resource sheets and Activity sheets

First, ask students to read the Resource sheet, 'Melting ice (1)', but discuss general points only, such as *What is happening to the ice? Where is this happening?*, and refer to the diagram. Then take students through the Activity sheet, 'Scanning', and show them the technique. Discuss their answers.

In the Activity sheet, 'The cycle', students should use scanning techniques to identify the explanation for the acceleration in the melting of the ice sheet. They need to grasp that it is a cycle before they complete the flow diagram, which should be along these lines: *1. More ice melts – 2. Means more open water – 3. Water absorbs heat from the sun – 4. More water means more heat*. Although it is relatively simple, you may need to guide some students through the cycle.

The Resource sheet, 'Melting ice (2)', highlights some typical features of explanatory texts. Go through the labels carefully with students. (Some examples of further connectives are: 'when', 'because', 'so', 'In this way'.)

Ask the students to complete the questions in the Activity sheet 'Finding information'. In the last question, they need to make predictions.

Plenary

Ask students to read out their answers from question 5 in 'Finding information' and discuss their examples. You may wish to add that many capital cities are near the coast or on flood plains. Discuss, for example, how the Maldives would disappear and the difficulties the Netherlands would experience. Refer to a globe or atlas.

Melting ice (1)

Arctic sea ice is no longer as thick as it was. Nor is it as large. So says the Arctic Council in its report of 2005. Climate change is the cause. The Earth is getting warmer.

Normally in the summer, some ice melts in the Arctic. In the winter it freezes again. But now less ice is freezing.

When sunlight falls on the Arctic ice, the white mass reflects it back into space. As more of the ice melts, so there is more open water. The water absorbs heat from the sun. More water means more heat, which means more ice melts and so on. In this way, the process speeds up.

In the future, the Arctic may have no ice during the summer. This is likely to happen between 2060 and 2100.

The Inuit people live in the area. They say that the ice is already thinner and that there are more storms. The polar bear is finding it harder to hunt for food because there is less floating ice. This means it does not have enough fat stored on its body for the winter months.

If the ice on Greenland begins to melt there will be more water in the sea and the sea level will rise. This will affect the whole planet.

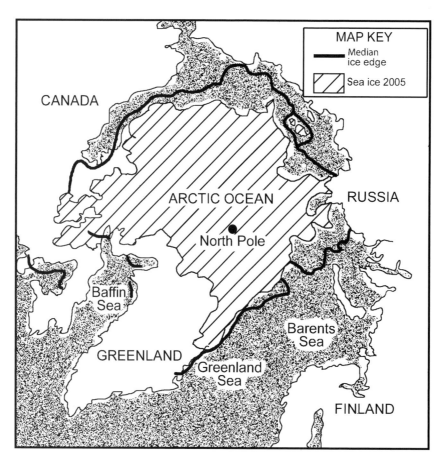

English Reading for meaning

Activity sheet – Explanation

Scanning

When you scan a text you skip words to find what you want. For example:

I read the first two sentences quickly, skipping over the words.

The Innuit people live in the area. They say that the ice is already thinner and that there are more storms. The polar bear is finding it harder to hunt for food because there is less floating ice.

I want to find out about polar bears.
So I search for the words.

☞ Scan these paragraphs to answer the questions below.

Arctic sea ice is no longer as thick as it was. Nor is it as large. So says the Arctic Council in their report of 2005. Climate change is the cause. The Earth is getting warmer.

Normally in the summer, some ice melts in the Arctic. In the winter it freezes again. But now less ice is freezing.

1. When was the report from the Arctic Council?
_____

2. What happens to the Arctic in summer?
_____

3. What is happening to the Arctic sea ice?
_____

4. What is the cause of the change to the Arctic sea ice?
_____

Activity sheet – Explanation

The cycle

☞ You will need 'Melting ice (1)'.

1. Scan the text. Find the paragraph that tells you what happens when the ice melts. Look for the words 'As more of the ice melts'.

2. Read the text again, but this time carefully.

3. Underline the main words that explain what happens.

4. Write in the boxes to show the cycle.

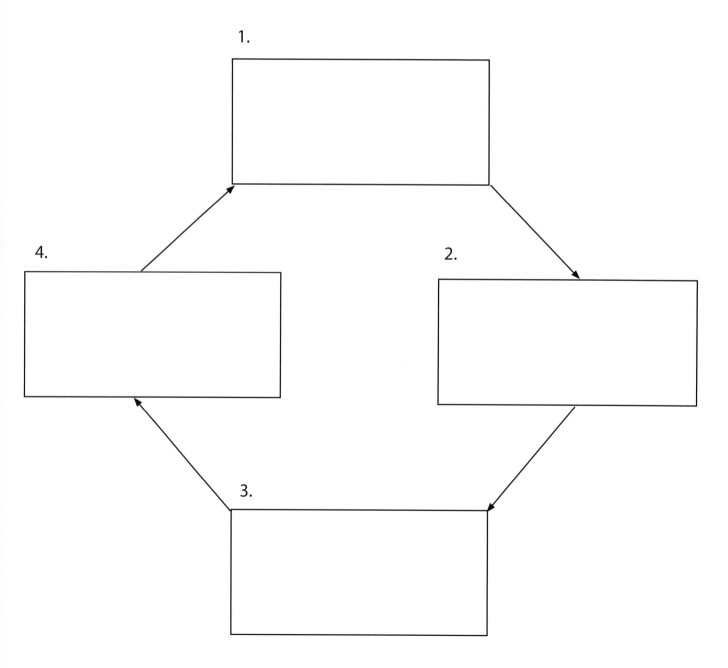

English Reading for meaning

Melting ice (2)

Present tense

Connective of cause and effect links what happens and why.

Opening paragraph on the topic

Arctic sea ice <u>is</u> no longer as thick as it was. Nor is it as large. So says the Arctic Council in its report of 2005. Climate change is the cause. The Earth is getting warmer.

Normally in the summer, some ice melts in the Arctic. In the winter it freezes again. But now less ice is freezing.

When sunlight falls on the Arctic ice, the white mass reflects it back into space. <u>As</u> more of the ice melts, <u>so</u> there is more open water. The water absorbs heat from the sun. More water means more heat, which means more ice melts and so on. In this way, the process speeds up.

In the future, the Arctic may have no ice during the summer. This is likely to happen between 2060 and 2100.

The Inuit people live in the area. They say that the ice is already thinner and that there are more storms. The polar bear is finding it harder to hunt for food because there is less floating ice. This means it does not have enough fat stored on its body for the winter months.

If the ice on Greenland begins to melt there will be more water in the sea and the sea level will rise. This will affect the whole planet.

Connective of time shows the order of things.

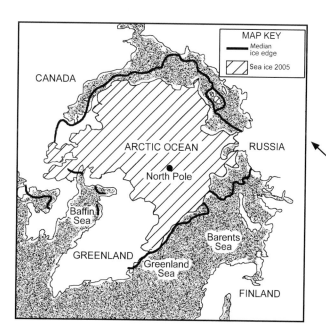

MAP KEY
Median ice edge
Sea ice 2005

CANADA

ARCTIC OCEAN   RUSSIA

North Pole

Baffin Sea

Barents Sea

GREENLAND

Greenland Sea

FINLAND

Diagram makes information clearer.

Finding information

☞ You will need 'Melting ice (2)'.

1. Scan the text to find another example of a connective of time.
Underline it in blue.

2. Scan the text to find two more examples of connectives of cause and effect.
Underline them in red.

3. Find two other explanations in the text.
Ring them in red. To help you,
scan the text for these words:

   ● Polar bears
   ● Greenland.

   Tell a partner what the explanations are.

4. The last paragraph says some very important things. Underline the keywords.

5. How do you think the planet could be affected? Think of examples.

   Write three sentences in the box below.

1. _____

   _____

2. _____

   _____

3. _____

   _____

Teacher's notes

Recount

Objectives

- Understand what biography is and that it is a recount
- Learn that recounts have a chronology
- Recognise that connectives of sequence (and sometimes others) are used in recounts
- Learn that recounts are mainly written in the past tense
- Learn to scan for information

Prior knowledge

Students need to know that events are usually sequenced in order and should be familiar with non-fiction texts that are recounts.

English Framework links

Yr7 Sentence level 13b); Yr7 Reading 2, 7; Yr8 Reading 5

Scottish attainment targets

English Language – Reading
Strand – Awareness of genre
Level E

Background

Martin Luther King Junior was, as a young man, influenced by Gandhi's non-violent approach to civil disobedience. Segregation laws were still heavily in force in the southern states in the post-war period and black people continued to suffer injustice across all states, north and south. Such injustice led to the growth of the civil rights movement in the 1950s, culminating in widespread resistance across the USA in the 1960s by people from all backgrounds. King travelled through Europe as well as the States, attracting vast audiences with his oratory. His most famous speech, 'I have a dream…', was given in 1963 in Washington in front of the Lincoln Memorial, to an audience of 250,000.

Please note that the term 'connective' is used to mean linking words including conjunctions. For further information on this, see Teacher's notes in the unit, 'Argument'.

Starter activity

Explain to students or remind them of the **keyword** 'biography'. Distinguish it from 'autobiography'. Emphasise the chronological nature of both. Also explain or remind students what 'scanning a text' means. (See also Activity sheet, 'Scanning', in the unit 'Explanation'.)

Resource sheet and Activity sheets

Read the Resource sheet, 'Martin Luther King Junior', with the students. Clarify vocabulary such as 'pastor' and 'civil rights'. Ask students some questions about the text, to note what they have inferred: *What did he care about? What kind of a man was he? What is a protest movement and why did this one grow?*

The Activity sheet, 'Time span', is concerned with chronology. Students should locate specific dates by scanning the text. They also need to follow events in sequence and make deductions by referring to dates.

The Activity sheet, 'My life', looks at autobiography. Students need to understand that it is written in the first person, 'I'. They should also be able to distinguish between biography and autobiography. Explain that biographies and autobiographies are recounts, as are history books or sports reports. Discuss why they are called this, referring to the annotated Activity sheet, 'Recounting events'. Help students to answer the questions as necessary.

In the Resource sheet, 'Getting the order right', students need to identify the time connectives and the dates to put sentences in order. They can work in pairs or check their answers against a partner's.

Plenary

Ask students to recall some of the similarities and differences between biographies and autobiographies. Ensure they grasp that both are recounts and that all describe a series of events. Students could also use the Internet, with your guidance, to explore the life of Martin Luther King Junior further and those who influenced him, such as Gandhi.

Martin Luther King Junior

Have you heard of Martin Luther King Junior? He was an African American who became an American hero. He was born in Atlanta, Georgia, in the southern states of America in 1929. At that time, black and white people were kept apart. They didn't live in the same areas. They didn't go to the same schools or colleges.

In the 1940s Martin Luther King Junior became a pastor. He had a powerful voice and gave people a sense of pride. Martin knew the laws were unjust so he set about trying to change things in a peaceful way.

Martin Luther King Junior

Around this time a protest movement began to grow. One event sparked huge support. It was 1955. In Alabama, black people had to give up their seats to white people on the buses. Rosa Parks, a black woman, refused to. She was arrested. So no black people used the buses. This went on for a whole year, until the Court ruled that Rosa Parks was in the right.

The movement spread. It became the civil rights movement of the Sixties. Black and

Rosa Parks

white people marched across America and some went to prison for their beliefs. In 1964 the government passed strong civil rights laws. The movement had made a real difference.

But Martin Luther King Junior's life was in danger. Four years later he was shot in Memphis, Tennessee. Despite his death, his values remained. Today, people still hold to his belief in peaceful protest.

Notes

Time span

The text in the Resource sheet, 'Martin Luther King Junior', tells us about his life. So it is a biography. It starts with his birth. Then it moves through his life. It is told in time order.

Martin Luther King Junior

1. Underline in blue the dates listed.

2. What is the first date? _____

3. The last date, when Martin Luther King Junior died, is not given. Choose the right paragraph for the answer, then work it out. _____

4. What time span do the events cover?

   _____

5. Scan the right paragraphs to answer these questions. (Make notes in the box on the Resource sheet.)

   - About how old was Martin Luther King Junior when he became a pastor? (**paragraph 2**)
   - Why were the 1950s important for Martin Luther King Junior? (**paragraph 3**)
   - When do you think he was at his greatest, in the 1950s or the 1960s? Why? (**paragraphs 3 and 4**)
   - How old was he when he died? (**paragraph 5**)

6. Now fill in the Fact File.

Fact File

Name: _____   Birth: _____

Where born: _____   Death: _____

Other important dates, places and events:

_____

_____

_____

My life

Sometimes we write about our own lives. This is called an autobiography. For example:

There is one event I always remember. It was the first time I climbed to the top of a mountain. It was not a very big mountain, but I was not very big either. In fact I was ten. When I reached the top I gasped. Not because I was tired. The whole landscape was spread out beneath me. I felt as if I was in another world. I have never forgotten the view – and I still love mountains.

An autobiography is always written in the first person, 'I'.

1. Why is an autobiography always written in the first person, 'I'?

2. Why is biography never written in the first person, 'I'?

3. Make a Fact File of your life.

   ● Write down important dates.
   ● Make notes on some special events.

My Life Fact File

English Reading for meaning

Recounting events

A biography is also a recount. It tells (or recounts) a series of events.

Time connective to link one event with another.

Mainly uses verbs in the past tense.

Third person

Have you <u>heard</u> of Martin Luther King Junior? <u>He</u> was an African American who became an American hero. He was born in Atlanta, Georgia, in the southern states of America in 1929. At that time, black and white people were kept apart. They didn't live in the same areas. They didn't go to the same schools or colleges.

<u>In the 1940s</u> Martin Luther King Junior became a pastor. He had a powerful voice and gave people a sense of pride. Martin knew the laws were unjust so he set about trying to change things in a peaceful way.

Martin Luther King Junior

Around this time a protest movement began to grow. One event sparked huge support. It was 1955. In Alabama, black people had to give up their seats to white people on the buses. Rosa Parks, a black woman, refused to. She was arrested. So no black people used the buses. This went on for a whole year, until the Court ruled that Rosa Parks was in the right.

The movement spread. It became the civil rights movement of the Sixties. Black and white people marched across America and some went to prison for their beliefs. In 1964 the government passed strong civil rights laws. The movement had made a real difference.

But Martin Luther King Junior's life was in danger. Four years later he was shot in Memphis, Tennessee. Despite his death, his values remained. Today, people still <u>hold</u> to his belief in peaceful protest.

May use other tenses, for example present tense if talking about the present.

☞ Now:
1. Find two more verbs in the past tense.
2. Find two more examples of the third person.
3. Find two more connectives of time.

English Reading for meaning 33

Getting the order right

The sentences in the box are about Martin Luther King Junior.
They are not in the correct order.

Martin Luther King Junior

1. Underline in blue all the time connectives.

2. Use the connectives and dates to put the sentences in order. Number them in time order.

3. There is some new information here. Choose the most important and add it to your Fact File on Martin Luther King Junior (see the Activity sheet, 'Time span').

☐ Martin Luther King Junior first started out as a pastor. He was 18 years old.

☐ He married Coretta in 1953.

☐ He received the Nobel Peace Prize in 1964.

☐ Two years later, the Kings travelled abroad again. This time they went to India.

☐ The Kings went to Africa in 1957.

☐ By the 1960s he was a great speaker. He gave his greatest speech in Washington DC in 1963.

☐ Three years before his death he went on a long march. This was to support voting rights for black people.

☐ When he was in his twenties he went to college in Boston.

English Reading for meaning

Teacher's notes

Reviews

Objectives

- Understand what a review is and note its features
- Recall details from memory
- Locate specific information
- Use context to understand a text
- Understand what informal language is

Prior knowledge

Students should be familiar with the blurb on the back of books and be aware that reviews are written about books, films, music and other media.

English Framework Links

Yr7 Sentence level 14; Reading 2, 4, 6, 8; Yr8 Reading 6

Scottish attainment targets

English Language – Reading
Strand – Reading to reflect on the writer's ideas and craft
Level D

Background

Students need to grasp that a review is more than an account of a film, book or other media. They do not have to grapple here with what criticism is. However, they do need to understand that an opinion is being expressed and that this is based on the reviewer's judgement and is not simply a question of personal preference.

Starter activity

Ask students to comment on the latest films they have seen and whether or not they liked them. They should be encouraged to express their own opinions fully but should also be asked to give reasons for their judgements. Encourage them to refer to different parts of the film to substantiate what they say.

Resource sheets and Activity sheets

Read the review on the Resource sheet, 'Goal! (1)', with students. Once read, carry out the exercise on the Activity sheet, 'Brainstorming', to establish that they can recall the essential points of the plot and the main characters. Students are asked to think of relevant questions. They can work on their own or agree questions as a group.

Next, take students through the annotated Resource sheet, 'Goal! (2)', along with the Activity sheet, 'Locating details'. The questions on the Activity sheet encourage students to work out some of the labels on 'Goal! (2)'. They will need to scan the text. (Refer to the unit, 'Explanation', and the Activity sheet, 'Scanning', for support if needed.)

Before students complete the final Activity sheet, 'What does it mean?', remind them of the informal style of the review. Section 1 deals with this. Students are likely to know some of the colloquialisms, but should also use context to work out or check meanings.

Plenary

Students should check their answers to 'Locating details' in pairs, but ask them to report back on the answers to 'What does it mean?'. To conclude, recap on the different reading strategies: scanning, using context and close reading.

Goal! (1)

2005
118 mins
Cert: 12A

Directed by: Danny Cannon
Screenplay: Ian La Frenais and Dick Clement

Kuno Becker, Marcel Lures, Stephen Dillane,
Alessandro Nivola, Anna Friel

This movie gets the star treatment. It's big-budget all right. Even Beckham gets a look in.

It tells the story of Santiago (<u>Kuno Becker</u>), a young Mexican. He lives with his father and grandmother in the USA. They've no money and he has to do two jobs. But football is his big love. When he gets spotted by the Newcastle scout, Glen Foy (Stephen Dillane), things look up. Helped by his gran he sets off for the UK and a new life. It doesn't always run smoothly, of course. How could it? But our hero does make out.

In the second half the love-interest (Anna Friel) has rather a boring part to play, though she does her best with it. This is a feel-good movie and <u>it all gets rather too sugary</u>. No doubt it has to appeal to the US market.

But the footie's exciting. There are some brilliant shots (in the net and from the camera). Becker is good. We can't help but like him and we do get a real sense of what football means to people. So if you're a football fanatic, this is the movie for you.

Activity sheet – Reviews

Brainstorming

☞ What can a remember about the review of *Goal!*?

1. Think of useful questions to ask a partner. Write them on the spidergram.
Then ask your partner to answer them.
It has been started for you.

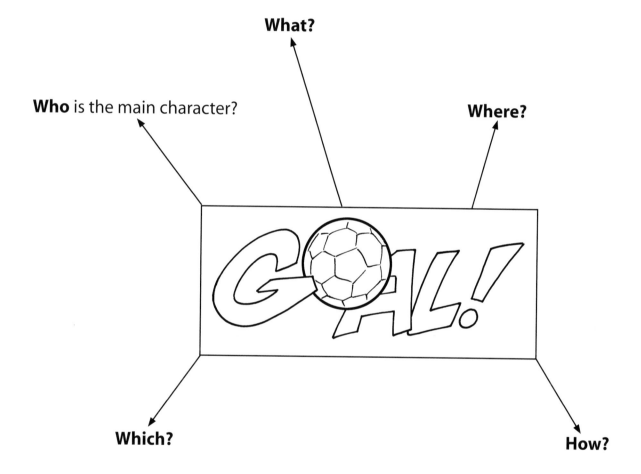

What?

Who is the main character?

Where?

Which?

How?

2. Test your partner on what he or she remembers about the review of *'Goal!'*.

Resource sheet – Reviews

Goal! (2)

2005
118 mins
Cert: 12A

Certificate

Film credits

Directed by: Danny Cannon
Screenplay: Ian La Frenais and Dick Clement

The cast

Kuno Becker, Marcel Iures, Stephen Dillane, Alessandro Nivola, Anna Friel

The main character

The story

This movie gets the star treatment. It's big-budget all right. Even Beckham gets a look in.

It tells the story of Santiago (<u>Kuno Becker</u>), a young Mexican. He lives with his father and grandmother in the USA. They've no money and he has to do two jobs. But football is his big love. When he gets spotted by the Newcastle scout, Glen Foy (Stephen Dillane), things look up. Helped by his gran he sets off for the UK and a new life. It doesn't always run smoothly, of course. How could it? But our hero does make out.

In the second half the love-interest (Anna Friel) has rather a boring part to play, though she does her best with it. This is a feel-good movie and <u>it all gets rather too sugary</u>. No doubt it has to appeal to the US market.

But the footie's exciting. There are some brilliant shots (in the net and from the camera). Becker is good. We can't help but like him and we do get a real sense of what football means to people. So if you're a football fanatic, this is the movie for you.

An example of the reviewer's opinion.

English Reading for meaning

Activity sheet – Reviews

Locating details

You will need the Resource sheet, 'Goal! (2)'.

1. Look at the details before the review to help you to answer these questions.

   - When was the film made? _____
   - How long is it? _____
   - Who is the director? _____
   - What does the director do? _____
     _____
   - What is the screenplay? _____
     _____
   - What does 'Film credits' mean'? _____
     _____
   - What does '12A' mean? _____
     _____
   - What is the cast? _____
     _____
   - Who is a member of the cast? _____
     _____

2. Find two more actors mentioned in the review. Who do they play?
   _____
   - Who do you think is the most famous star in the film? Why do you think this star is in it? _____
     _____

3. Write down in which paragraphs you can find the following:
   - The introduction _____
   - The reviewer's main comments _____
   - Who would like the film _____

4. What does the reviewer think are the strengths and weaknesses of the film? Find the words used.

   Strengths: _____
   _____
   Weaknesses: _____
   _____

What does it mean?

You will need the Resource sheet, 'Goal! (1).' Work with a partner.

1. Find these lines in the review of 'Goal!' Read the sentences before and after each one.

   - 'It's big-budget, all right.'
   - 'But our hero does make out.'
   - '…the love interest'
   - This is a feel-good movie…'
   - '…it all gets rather too sugary.'
   - 'But the footie's exciting.'
   - '(in the net and from the camera)'

2. Work out what each line means. Explain to a partner.

3. The reviewer says, 'We can guess what will happen.'
   Think of three things that could happen to the main character. Find clues in the review that tell you. Write notes in the box.

What could happen	Clues
1.	1.
2.	2.
3.	3.

Teacher's notes

Argument

Objectives

- Understand that an argument presents a particular viewpoint
- Understand that reason backs up points in an argument
- Understand that we can link ideas in or across sentences
- Express a point of view and give reasons to support it

Prior knowledge

Students should be able to recognise contrasting points of view in an argument.

English Framework links

Yr7 Word level 20, Reading 2,
Speaking and listening 11, 13; Yr8 Reading 10,
Speaking and listening 10; Yr9 Word Level 8,
Speaking and listening 9

Scottish attainment targets

English Language – Reading
Strand - Reading to reflect on the writer's ideas and craft
Level D
English Language – Talking
Strand – Talking in groups
Level D

Background

Arguments in a text often require higher-order skills and sound reading experience. However, if arguments are laid out in a way that separates and signals different points clearly, those students who experience difficulty have a chance to weigh up the issues. Students can then progress to reading argument texts. Connectives act as signposts and link in a variety of ways, such as across sentences and also paragraphs. Conjunctions (for example, 'and', 'but') are a type of connective. They usually link within a sentence, for example by linking clauses or sub-clauses. However, some conjunctions, such as 'so', also link across sentences and paragraphs. In order to avoid confusion, the term 'connective' or 'linking word' is used to cover both connectives and conjunctions.

Starter activity

Ask the children to explain the function of linking words. Discuss those of cause and effect, for example 'because', 'so' and 'therefore', in preparation for the Activity sheet, 'Connectives'. Introduce the **keyword** connective, if you wish.

Resource sheets and Activity sheets

The two Resource sheets, 'The Frenton bypass (1)' and '(2)', present reasons for and against a proposed bypass to resolve the traffic problems in the fictitious village of Frenton. The reasons are presented as comments from the villagers and are clearly set out. Students should be able to work systematically through the comments to grasp the points. Ask them to take it in turns to read and discuss the location of the bypass and other features on the map.

Students should then work in pairs to complete the Activity sheet, 'Making quick notes'. They are shown how to do this and as far as possible should work without help. Each pair should appoint a recorder and report back. Mark the Activity sheet with the students.

Next, turn to the Activity sheet, 'Connectives', and explain the connectives of cause and effect. The object here is for students to realise how these linking words help us to express and link ideas. Students can then turn to the Activity sheet, 'Talking it through', and work in pairs or groups to discuss the points for and against the bypass and make their own decision as to which view to support, or alternatively to think of other solutions, for example limiting traffic flow (through calming methods, pedestrian areas, public transport improvements and so on) without having to build the bypass.

Plenary

Ask students to report back with their comments. Discuss these and ensure students can distinguish between a viewpoint and the reasons that support it. Then point to the connectives that help us to express these reasons (for example, 'because'). Finally, ask the larger group to select the best reasons for or against the bypass.

Resource sheet – Argument

The Frenton bypass (1)

The main road runs through the village of Frenton, so it has a big traffic problem. A bypass is planned. Some people are pleased. Others are not.

1.

"I'm not very happy about the bypass, because it means I'll lose farmland."

2.

"I live on the main road so pollution is awful. I'm all for the bypass."

3.

"Heavy traffic has caused cracks in the walls of our house. We need a bypass so that they don't get worse."

4.

"I can't park anywhere along the main road. So a bypass will cut down the traffic."

5.

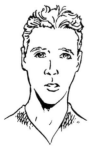

"I'm against the bypass because it will just mean more cars."

6.

"I own a shop. Therefore I'll lose business if the bypass is built."

The Frenton bypass (2)

7.

"There are too many crashes. Drivers get impatient and try to overtake. So we need the bypass to stop accidents."

8.

"We'll fight the bypass because this area is rich in wildlife. It has one of the few woodlands left."

9.

"Our house will be knocked down because it's in the way of the bypass!"

10.

"Heavy traffic runs past my school. The children are therefore at risk when they cross the road."

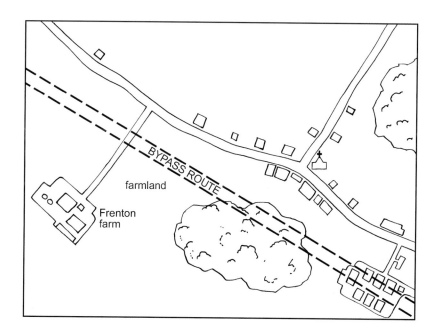

Activity sheet – Argument

Making quick notes

☞ Work with a partner. You will need
'The Frenton bypass (1)' and '(2)'.

1. Decide who is for and who is against the bypass.
2. Write the numbers in the correct boxes.
3. Then write the reasons why. Just write one or two words.
   The first has been done for you.

The Frenton bypass			
For	**Reason**	**Against**	**Reason**
		1	*will lose land*

Connectives

Some words help us to link one idea with another. We call them connectives.

He is going swimming <u>because</u> he enjoys it.

Connective of cause and effect. It links what he is going to do with why he is going to do it.

Here are some other connectives of cause and effect:

so   therefore

☞   Read the comments 1 to 10 in 'The Frenton bypass (1)' and '(2)'.

Underline the connectives of cause and effect.

● Fill in the table below with the connectives.

Connectives

1.
2.
3.
4.
5.
6.
7.
8.
9.
10.

● Read the comments again with a partner. Discuss how the connectives link ideas.

Talking it through

☞   Work with a partner or in a group. You will need your completed
copy of 'Making quick notes'. Choose someone to record points.

1.   Talk about the reasons for and against the Frenton bypass.
Which reasons do you think are important and which are
unimportant?

   ●   For example, look at comment 1. If you think the farmer
should not lose his land, you agree with that reason.
Use the connectives 'because' and 'so' to help you discuss the reasons.

   ●   List the reasons you agree with.

Reasons we agree with:

2.   Talk about three other ways in which traffic could be reduced in Frenton.
List them.

   ●   _____

   ●   _____

   ●   _____

3.   Finally, decide if:

   – you are **for** the bypass

   – you are **against** the bypass

   – one of **your ideas** is better.

   ●   Choose someone to report back.

Teacher's notes

Narrative

Objectives

- Understand that literal information is information we can be sure of
- Understand that inference means picking up clues to grasp meaning
- Predict what might happen

Prior knowledge

Students need to be familiar with a range of stories, whether they have read them or not, and have some knowledge of narrative structure (that is, beginning/middle/end). They need to be able to use a time line.

English Framework links

Yr7 Reading 2, 6; Yr8 Reading 5, 7; Yr9 Word level 7

Scottish attainment targets

English Language – Reading
Strand – Reading to reflect on the writer's ideas and craft
Level C

Background

Narratives can be described as the interplay between events and character and the degree to which one influences the other. At a simple level, a character may be swept along by events, unable to affect them. Or a character may be responsible for events, for example in the case of a villain. Usually, however, the relationship is more complex. The choices a character makes will affect events and events shape character.

Starter activity

Find out what the students' understanding is of narrative. Do they have any grasp of the typical structure (beginning/middle/end)? If so, you may wish to introduce the **keywords**: introduction, complication, climax, resolution, and discuss their meanings. Explain or reinforce other keywords such as: character and plot (or storyline) and encourage students to use them.

Resource sheets and Activity sheets

Read the Resource sheet, 'Charlie', to the students or ask them to share the reading, clarifying any expressions, such as 'Chickens have come home to roost'. Then ensure they have grasped certain key points before moving on, for example: *Who is the main character? Who are the other characters? Who is telling the story? What part of the story is this? (Introduction). Sum up what is happening.*

Then move to 'Charlie again!', the annotated Resource sheet, and take students through the points. They need to understand the difference between literal information and inference and how we can pick up clues in a text. Also point out that some sentences are isolated (the first, for example), giving additional emphasis to their meanings. Students should then work in pairs to underline examples of literal information in the text, to build information on the character and to complete the Activity sheet, 'What do we know?'.

The next Activity sheet, 'What can you guess?', is harder and it may be necessary to work directly with students. Additional help is given on the sheet. (Students should deduce that Charlie is a daydreamer, careless, mischievous and unable to see where events might lead, while Ellie is loyal, unafraid, thoughtful and quick-witted.)

Students should now have a full picture of the main characters and be able to predict possible outcomes. They should work in pairs to discuss possibilities, choose the best and complete the time line on 'What happens next?'. Please note the 'How' questions and ensure that the time line follows the conventional plot: introduction, complication, climax, resolution.

Plenary

Ask students to discuss their predictions. They should also consider the feasibility of their predictions, which will partly depend on the nature of the characters. Students should also ask themselves: *Is Charlie/Ellie likely to behave like this?*

Charlie

Charlie was always in trouble.

Not bad trouble, you understand, just trouble. He forgot his PE kit. Or he forgot his books. Or he missed the bus. That sort of thing. It didn't seem to bother him much. Most of the time he sailed through in a dream.

Except for once.

It started off in the usual way – a little bit of trouble. Then somewhere along the line it got out of hand. And Charlie was taken by surprise.

'Chickens have come home to roost', said his grandma when she found out that Charlie was up to his neck in it.

'I don't want to hear about it,' said his dad and turned over the television channel.

'That boy will wear me out,' moaned his mum.

There was only one person who seemed to care about Charlie. It was his sister Ellie. She always spoke up for him.

And the funny thing was, they were as different as chalk and cheese. Charlie was a small 12-year-old. He had blond hair and a wicked grin, and always looked happy. Ellie was tall with dark hair and a serious smile. She was shy and quiet. But it was Ellie who came to the rescue when disaster struck.

It all started when Charlie went on the school trip to Harwell Zoo.

English Reading for meaning

Charlie again!

We can be certain of this:
– **literal** information.

Charlie was always in trouble.

Not bad trouble, you understand, just trouble. He forgot his PE kit. Or he forgot his books. Or he missed the bus. That sort of thing. It didn't seem to bother him much. Most of the time he sailed through in a dream.

We can guess or **infer** that the story will be about this.

Except for once.

It started off in the usual way – a little bit of trouble. Then somewhere along the line it got out of hand. And Charlie was taken by surprise.

'Chickens have come home to roost', said his grandma when she found out that Charlie was up to his neck in it.

'I don't want to hear about it,' said his dad and turned over the television channel.

We can guess or infer that Charlie's dad:
– is cross with Charlie
– doesn't seem to care about Charlie.

'That boy will wear me out,' moaned his mum.

There was only one person who seemed to care about Charlie. It was his sister Ellie. She always spoke up for him.

And the funny thing was, they were as different as chalk and cheese. Charlie was a small 12-year-old. He had blond hair and a wicked grin, and always looked happy. Ellie was tall with dark hair and a serious smile. She was shy and quiet. But it was Ellie who came to the rescue when disaster struck.

It all started when Charlie went on the school trip to Harwell Zoo.

We can be certain of this: literal information.

Activity sheet – Narrative

What do we know?

1. You will need the Resource sheet, 'Charlie'. Underline in blue information about Charlie. This should be information that you are sure of.

    Find out about:
    – what he is like
    – what he looks like.

2. Add words about Charlie to the spidergram below.

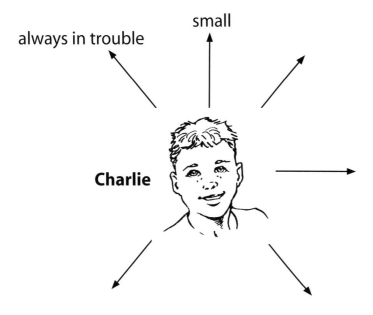

3. Now do the same about Ellie.

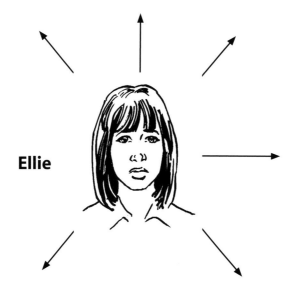

English Reading for meaning

Activity sheet – Narrative

What can you guess?

☞ Work with a partner.

1. You will need the Resource sheet, 'Charlie'. Underline in red these words and read them in the passage.

- 'He forgot his PE kit.'
- '…he sailed through in a dream.'
- '…Charlie was taken by surprise.'
- '…a wicked grin…'

2. Talk about what these words tell you about Charlie's character.
    Think of your own words to describe him.

- Add your words to the box.

Charlie	

3. Now do the same about Ellie, but find words in the passage on your own to describe her. Think about what Ellie is like compared to Charlie. Add your own words in the box as well.

Ellie	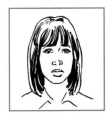

What happens next?

Time line

☞ Work with a partner

1. What do you think will happen to Charlie?
   Think of two ideas. Write them in the boxes.

> **Idea 1**

> **Idea 2**

2. Talk about these questions for both ideas.
   Make notes in each box.

   - How will it start and where?
   - How will it get worse?
   - How will it be serious?
   - How will Ellie be involved?
   - How will it end?

3. Choose the best idea and note what will happen
   on the time line.

Teacher's notes

Playscripts

Objectives

- Understand how to read a playscript, noting its conventions
- Understand character in order to perform a part
- Choose a part and act it
- Discuss and work within a group

Prior knowledge

Students need to be able to work in a group and be confident enough to read aloud within the group. The readability level of the text is seven years. Students with a higher reading age should be able to read the text with some expression.

English Framework links

Yr7 Reading 6, Drama 16, 19; Yr8 Reading 4, Drama 16; Yr9 Reading 4, Drama 14

Scottish attainment targets

English Language – Reading
Strand – Awareness of genre
Level C
Strand – Knowledge about language
Level D

Background

Playscripts are best acted out so that students can gain a better understanding of the action and the characters. Reading playscripts also furthers reading skill and comprehension, since the focus is on reading with expression. A good understanding of the conventions of playscripts is useful so that students avoid reading the stage directions aloud (a common mistake). This is usually overcome with practice. Students also need to grasp that plays are based on some kind of conflict between characters, that a climax is reached and there is an ending, in which the conflict may or may not be resolved happily.

Starter activity

Discuss the importance of gesture and body language with students when acting a part. Point out that we can convey meaning with a gesture without speaking. Give students the following to try: *How to tell someone to be quiet without being heard; How to show annoyance; How to show fear; How to show pride.*

Resource sheet and Activity sheets

Read the play extract on the Resource sheet, 'Zelda', with students, clarifying any unusual words such as 'pussyfooting'. Ensure they understand what is happening and have a basic grasp of the plot: *Zelda is an independent, volatile teenager who knows her own mind and chooses to dress in an unconventional fashion. Her parents, a conventional couple, are baffled by their daughter and devise various ploys to keep the peace.*

Give students some examples of how to read with expression, encouraging them to bring the characters to life (for example, Zelda hardly ever allows her mother to finish a sentence, so demonstrate interruptions). If necessary, go through the Activity sheet, 'Playscript', so that students can navigate the script.

Discuss the Activity sheet, 'What are they like?', guiding students through the questions. They should then split into groups of three and discuss the questions in the Activity sheet, 'Preparing for the part'. Once they have a sound grasp of the characters, their differences and similarities, students should choose parts and practise them before performing the play to other groups.

Plenary

Call the group or groups together and encourage them to discuss the strengths and weaknesses of their performances. They can work in pairs to complete a peer assessment.

Resource sheet – Playscripts

Zelda

Zelda's mum is half-asleep on the sofa. The newspaper is on her lap. Zelda enters.
Her mum turns to her and suddenly sits up.

ZELDA: What now?

MUM: I didn't say a word.

ZELDA: But you're thinking, it aren't you? I can tell by the look on your face.
Go on, admit it Mum.

MUM: (*sighs*) Now look here Zelda…

ZELDA: I know exactly what's going through your head.

MUM: There's no need…

ZELDA: You're thinking: 'You're not going out
looking like that are you?'

MUM: But Zelda…

ZELDA: Look, let's be honest, Mum.
That's what you're thinking. Right?

MUM: Well, I just feel…

ZELDA: Say it. Go on, say it. I don't mind.

MUM: It's not that I think you look…

ZELDA: Odd? Over-the-top? Way out?

MUM: Really, Zelda, I'm trying…

ZELDA: What words would you use, Mum?

Zelda's dad enters. He turns to Zelda.

DAD: And where's my lovely daughter off to?

English Reading for meaning

Zelda (continued)

ZELDA: Not you too. Don't lay this rubbish on me, Dad.
I know what you really think and it doesn't matter to me. OK?

DAD: I just said 'Where's my lovely daughter off to?' What's wrong with that?

ZELDA: (*sighs*) Because you don't think it's true. But like I said to Mum, I don't mind.

DAD: (*turns to Zelda's mum*) Now she can read my thoughts!

ZELDA: What I can't stand is this pussyfooting around.

DAD: (*confused*) But what have I done?

ZELDA: Look, I've had enough of this. I'm off. Enjoy the evening. I will.

MUM: Zelda, I just wanted to…

ZELDA: Bye!

Zelda leaves. The front door bangs.

DAD: What did I say?

MUM: Nothing. It's Zelda.

DAD: You said be nice to her, didn't you? And I was. Wasn't I?

MUM: Yes. You were fine. She's been upstairs all day. Dyeing her hair, I think.

DAD: Dyeing her hair? Again? I can't keep up with her.

MUM: Yes, I know. Why can't she be normal?

DAD: Normal? Zelda's never been normal.

MUM: That's not a very nice thing to say about your own daughter!

DAD: What's so good about 'normal' anyway? We just have to accept her.

And she always sees through you in any case.

From *Do it in Style* by Mary Green

Activity sheet – Playscripts

Playscript

☞ You will need the Resource sheet, 'Zelda'. This is how the playscript is laid out.

Stage directions set the scene. They show what props are needed. They also tell the actor what to do. Stage directions should not be read aloud by the actor.

Zelda

Zelda's mum is half-asleep on the sofa. The newspaper is on her lap. Zelda enters. Her mum turns to her and suddenly sits up.

ZELDA: What now?

MUM: I didn't say a word.

ZELDA: But you're thinking it, aren't you? I can tell by the look on your face Go on, admit it Mum.

This shows who is speaking. The name is followed by a colon :

These stage directions mean sound effects are needed.

Zelda leaves. The front door bangs.

DAD: What did I say?

MUM: Nothing. It's Zelda.

DAD: You said be nice to her, didn't you? And I was. Wasn't I?

The words spoken. Remember speech marks are not used in a playscript.

1. Find other examples of these features in the playscript.
2. Practise reading the script aloud. Follow the stage directions.

English Reading for meaning

What are they like?

☞ Work with a partner. Read this example first.

We can tell what **characters** are like from the words they speak.

> ZELDA: What now?
>
> MUM: I didn't say a word.

- Mum is trying to avoid an argument with Zelda. It tells us she likes a quiet life.

1. What do the words in the box below mean? What do they tell us about Zelda?

> ZELDA: What I can't stand is this pussyfooting around.

2. What do the words in the box below tell you about Dad and also Mum? Remember that Zelda has gone out at this point.

> DAD: You said be nice to her, didn't you? And I was. Wasn't I?

3. We can also get clues from the stage directions. For example, when Zelda walks into the living room we are told:

> *Her mum turns to her and suddenly sits up.*

- Why do you think her mum sat up suddenly?
- What does it tell you about how her mum feels?

Preparing for the part

Before you can act a part, you need to know the character.

☞ Work with a group and choose a character each.

Talk about what each one is like.

Think about the questions below.

Make short notes in the boxes.

Zelda

What kind of look and style do you think Zelda likes?

What does she think of her parents?

Do her parents affect what she does? What does this tell you about Zelda?

Mum

What does she think of Zelda?

How does she get on with her husband?

Dad

What does he think of Zelda? How is this different from his wife's view?

How does he get on with his wife?

Teacher's notes

Poetry

Objectives

- Enjoy reading poetry
- Read between the lines
- Understand how language creates effects
- Read aloud with expression and understanding

Prior knowledge

Students should feel sufficiently confident to read aloud.

English Framework links

Yr7 Reading 7, 8, 12, Speaking and Listening 3; Yr8 Word Level 11, Reading 5, Speaking and Listening 2; Yr9 Word Level 7

Scottish attainment targets

English Language – Reading
Strand – Reading aloud
Level C

Background

Charles Causley (1917–2003) was born in Launceston, Cornwall, where he was based for most of his life, although he did travel a great deal. He began writing seriously in 1944. He had an instinctive feel for verse. Much of his poetry for children is fresh, magical and closely observed. There are many references to Cornwall, its history and its culture. In 1986 he received the CBE and in 1987 The Queen's Medal for Poetry. He remains one of the foremost children's poets.

'Miller's End' is a short narrative poem, a ghost story, reminiscent of a ballad. It cleverly retains its secret until the last verse, having led the reader in quite the opposite direction.

Starter activity

Remind students of or explain some of the **keywords** used in poetry: image, verse, rhythm, rhyme (distinguish between rhythm and rhyme, which are often confused). Also explain what a traditional ballad is – a four-line narrative verse with regular rhythm and rhyme.

Resource sheet and Activity sheets

Read the poem to the students, noting whether they grasp the surprise ending and who is really the ghost. If they have difficulty, take them through the poem using the Activity sheet, 'What really happens?'. Before they begin, note that the speaker talks in the first-person plural, 'we'. Students can think of this as the family or children who have 'moved to Miller's End'. Once students have grasped the twist in the tale, direct them to the language. Ask them to underline the third and fourth lines and describe what they conjure up (such as mystery and the supernatural) and what senses they appeal to (such as sight, touch and even sound).

Next, refer to the Activity sheet, 'Looking at language', which students should complete in discussion with you. Ask them to think of a picture that comes to mind for each image and then what sense or senses the image appeals to. Also discuss the difference in the way the poet conjures up images of Miss Wickerby and Billy, the garden boy. The latter is portrayed as alive: 'his face was bright'. So not only are we misled by the image of Miss Wickerby, but also by the image of Billy.

Read the poem again to students and explain that reading with expression aids understanding. Students can use the final Activity sheet, 'Out loud', to help them to prepare a performance of the poem, working in pairs or groups of three. Draw attention to the final verse, which is repeated here. It needs to be read carefully to be understood. Also go through any words or names that might prove tricky, such as 'Wickerby'. Where students have difficulty reading aloud or lack confidence, encourage them to read a line or a verse in a small group.

Plenary

Ask students to assess their own performances. They could carry out a peer assessment, noting the following: voice projection, expression, body language and stance, and teamwork.

'Miller's End'

When we moved to Miller's End,
    Every afternoon at four
A thin shadow of a shade
    Quavered through the garden-door.

Dressed in black from top to toe
    And a veil about her head
To us all it seemed as though
    She came walking from the dead.

With a basket on her arm
    Through the hedge-gap she would pass,
Never a mark that we could spy
    On the flagstones or the grass.

When we told the garden-boy
    How we saw the phantom glide,
With a grin his face was bright
    As the pool he stood beside.

'That's no ghost-walk,' Billy said.
    'Nor a ghost you fear to stop –
Only old Miss Wickerby
    On a short cut to the shop.'

So next day we lay in wait,
    Passed a civil time of day,
Said how pleased we were she came
    Daily down our garden-way.

Suddenly her cheek it paled,
    Turned, as quick, from ice to flame.
'Tell me,' said Miss Wickerby,
    'Who spoke of me, and my name?'

'Bill the garden-boy.'
    She sighed,
Said, 'Of course, you could not know
    How he drowned – that very pool –
A frozen winter – long ago.'

Charles Causley

English Reading for meaning

What really happens?

☞ Discuss what happens in the poem. Use these questions to help you.
They follow the events in the poem.

What happens each afternoon at Miller's End?
At what time?

What does Billy say?

What does the speaker do next day?

How does Miss Wickerby respond?

What does she say?

Why are her words a shock?

Looking at language

Language	Images come to mind/ senses appealed to
'thin shadow of a shade/quavered'	**picture of a ghost sense of sight**
'Dressed in black from top to toe'	
'as though she came walking from the dead.'	
'Never a mark… On the flagstones or the grass.'	
'How we saw the phantom glide,'	
'With a grin his face was bright'	
'So next day we lay in wait,'	
'Suddenly her cheek it paled, Turned, as quick, from ice to flame.'	
'A frozen winter – long ago.'	

Miss Wickerby	Billy

English Reading for meaning

Out loud

The last verse in 'Miller's End' needs to be read carefully. Try it like this.

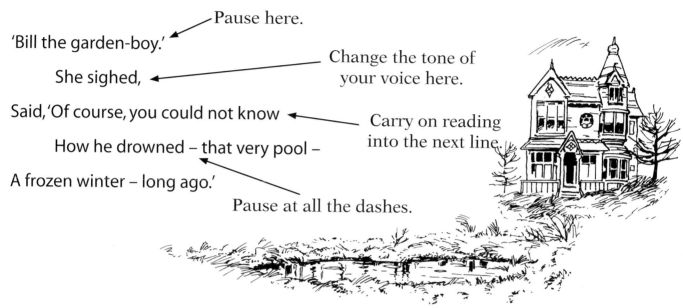

Pause here.

'Bill the garden-boy.'

She sighed,

Change the tone of your voice here.

Said, 'Of course, you could not know

Carry on reading into the next line.

How he drowned – that very pool –

A frozen winter – long ago.'

Pause at all the dashes.

☞ Read the poem with a partner or in a small group. Plan what you will do. Some ideas are given.

Who will perform what verses?   **Could read a verse each.**   **Different people could read Billy and Miss Wickerby.**
Where will you perform? How will you stand?
Where will you need to alter your voice most of all?
What is the hardest part to read?

Assessment sheet

Tick the boxes to show what you know or can do.

	know/ yes	not sure/ sometimes	don't know/ no
1. I listen to the teacher.			
2. I can work well with a partner.			
3. I can work well in a group.			
4.			
5.			
6.			
7.			
8.			
9.			
10.			

I know best/I can do best:

....

....

I need to: **(Write no more than three targets.)**

....

....

....